Toponym Resolution in Text:
Annotation, Evaluation and Applications
of Spatial Grounding of Place Names

Jochen L. Leidner

DISSERTATION.COM

Boca Raton

Toponym Resolution in Text:
Annotation, Evaluation and Applications of Spatial Grounding of Place Names

Dissertation.com
Boca Raton, Florida
USA • 2007

ISBN: 1-58112- 384-1
13-ISBN: 978-1-58112-384-5

Toponym Resolution in Text

Annotation, Evaluation and Applications of Spatial Grounding of Place Names

Jochen Lothar Leidner

Doctor of Philosophy

Institute for Communicating and Collaborative Systems

School of Informatics

University of Edinburgh

2007

Abstract

Background. In the area of Geographic Information Systems (GIS), a shared discipline between informatics and geography, the term *geo-parsing* is used to describe the process of identifying names in text, which in computational linguistics is known as named entity recognition and classification (NERC). The term *geo-coding* is used for the task of mapping from implicitly geo-referenced datasets (such as structured address records) to explicitly geo-referenced representations (e.g., using latitude and longitude). However, present-day GIS systems provide no automatic geo-coding functionality for *unstructured text*.

In Information Extraction (IE), processing of named entities in text has traditionally been seen as a two-step process comprising a flat text span recognition sub-task and an atomic classification sub-task; relating the text span to a model of the world has been ignored by evaluations such as MUC or ACE (Chinchor (1998); U.S. NIST (2003)).

However, spatial and temporal expressions refer to events in space-time, and the grounding of events is a precondition for accurate reasoning. Thus, automatic grounding can improve many applications such as automatic map drawing (e.g. for choosing a focus) and question answering (e.g. , for questions like *How far is London from Edinburgh?*, given a story in which both occur and can be resolved). Whereas temporal grounding has received considerable attention in the recent past (Mani and Wilson (2000); Setzer (2001)), robust spatial grounding has long been neglected.

Concentrating on geographic names for populated places, I define the task of automatic *Toponym Resolution* (TR) as computing the mapping from occurrences of names for places as found in a text to a representation of the extensional semantics of the location referred to (its referent), such as a geographic latitude/longitude footprint.

The task of mapping from names to locations is hard due to insufficient and noisy databases, and a large degree of ambiguity: common words need to be distinguished from proper names (geo/non-geo ambiguity), and the mapping between names and locations is ambiguous (*London* can refer to the capital of the UK or to London, Ontario, Canada, or to about forty other Londons on earth). In addition, names of places and the boundaries referred to change over time, and databases are incomplete.

Objective. I investigate how referentially ambiguous spatial named entities can be grounded, or resolved, with respect to an extensional coordinate model robustly on open-domain news text.

I begin by comparing the few algorithms proposed in the literature, and, comparing semi-formal, reconstructed descriptions of them, I factor out a shared repertoire of linguistic heuristics (e.g. rules, patterns) and extra-linguistic knowledge sources (e.g. population sizes). I then investigate how to combine these sources of evidence to obtain a superior method. I also investigate the noise effect introduced by the named entity tagging step that toponym resolution relies on in a sequential system pipeline architecture.

Scope. In this thesis, I investigate a present-day snapshot of terrestrial geography as represented in the gazetteer defined and, accordingly, a collection of present-day news text. I limit the investigation to populated places; geo-coding of artifact names (e.g. airports or bridges), compositional geographic descriptions (e.g. *40 miles SW of London*, *near Berlin*), for instance, is not attempted. Historic change is a major factor affecting gazetteer construction and ultimately toponym resolution. However, this is beyond the scope of this thesis.

Method. While a small number of previous attempts have been made to solve the toponym resolution problem, these were either not evaluated, or evaluation was done by manual inspection of system output instead of curating a reusable reference corpus.

Since the relevant literature is scattered across several disciplines (GIS, digital libraries, information retrieval, natural language processing) and descriptions of algorithms are mostly given in informal prose, I attempt to systematically describe them and aim at a *reconstruction in a uniform, semi-formal pseudo-code notation* for easier re-implementation. A systematic comparison leads to an *inventory of heuristics and other sources of evidence*.

In order to carry out a comparative evaluation procedure, an evaluation resource is required. Unfortunately, to date no gold standard has been curated in the research community. To this end, a reference gazetteer and an associated novel reference corpus with human-labeled referent annotation are created.

These are subsequently used to benchmark a selection of the reconstructed algorithms and a novel re-combination of the heuristics catalogued in the inventory.

I then compare the performance of the same TR algorithms under three different conditions, namely applying it to the (i) output of human named entity annotation, (ii) automatic annotation using an existing Maximum Entropy sequence tagging model, and (iii) a naïve toponym lookup procedure in a gazetteer.

Evaluation. The algorithms implemented in this thesis are evaluated in an intrinsic or *component evaluation*. To this end, we define a task-specific matching criterion to be used with traditional Precision (P) and Recall (R) evaluation metrics. This matching criterion is lenient with respect to numerical gazetteer imprecision in situations where one toponym instance is marked up with different gazetteer entries in the gold standard and the test set, respectively, but where these refer to the *same* candidate referent, caused by multiple near-duplicate entries in the reference gazetteer.

Main Contributions. The major contributions of this thesis are as follows:

- A *new reference corpus* in which instances of location named entities have been manually annotated with spatial grounding information for populated places, and an associated *reference gazetteer*, from which the assigned candidate referents are chosen. This reference gazetteer provides numerical latitude/longitude coordinates (such as $51°\,32'$ North,

$0°\,5'$ West) as well as hierarchical path descriptions (such as `London > UK`) with respect to a world wide-coverage, geographic taxonomy constructed by combining several large, but noisy gazetteers. This corpus contains news stories and comprises two sub-corpora, a subset of the REUTERS RCV1 news corpus used for the CoNLL shared task (Tjong Kim Sang and De Meulder (2003)), and a subset of the Fourth Message Understanding Contest (MUC-4; Chinchor (1995)), both available pre-annotated with gold-standard. This corpus will be made available as a reference evaluation resource;

- a new *method and implemented system to resolve toponyms* that is capable of robustly processing unseen text (open-domain online newswire text) and grounding toponym instances in an extensional model using longitude and latitude coordinates and hierarchical path descriptions, using internal (textual) and external (gazetteer) evidence;

- an *empirical analysis of the relative utility of various heuristic biases and other sources of evidence* with respect to the toponym resolution task when analysing free news genre text;

- a *comparison between a replicated method* as described in the literature, which functions as a baseline, *and a novel algorithm based on minimality heuristics*; and

- several exemplary *prototypical applications* to show how the resulting toponym resolution methods can be used to create visual surrogates for news stories, a geographic exploration tool for news browsing, geographically-aware document retrieval and to answer spatial questions (*How far...?*) in an open-domain question answering system. These applications only have demonstrative character, as a thorough quantitative, task-based (extrinsic) evaluation of the utility of automatic toponym resolution is beyond the scope of this thesis and left for future work.

To my family.

Declaration

I declare that this thesis was composed by myself, that the work contained herein is my own except where explicitly stated otherwise in the text, and that this work has not been submitted for any other degree or professional qualification except as specified.

(Jochen Lothar Leidner)

Table of Contents

List of Tables

List of Figures

Acknowledgements

First and foremost, I would like to express my gratitude to Claire Grover and Bonnie Webber, who have been great advisers. While my wide-ranging interests and activities have probably stretched their patience at times, they were always supportive, extremely helpful and ready to provide feedback and guidance. I am well aware that getting written comments on an email-ed paper draft within just a few hours is not something that many other PhD students can benefit from. Their experience, knowledge and kindness will serve as a role model for me beyond this thesis project. Thanks!

Steve Clark has been a supportive third adviser until his departure to Oxford and (no longer formally, but no less supportive) beyond. Bruce Gittings in the Department of Geography was always happy to chat about all matters geographical. Also many thanks to Ewan Klein and Dave Robertson for being such helpful internal examiners. Thanks to Richard Tobin and John Tait for valuable discussions on evaluation methodology, and to Mark Sanderson and Jon Oberlander, who form my thesis committee, for reading this thesis.

Edinburgh is a wonderfully vibrant and magically productive place, and the Potteresque maze of Buccleuch Place is home to some of the most brilliant researchers in natural language processing. Many people have wondered why this is so, and one possible explanation could be the phenomenon locally known as the Blind Poet (not a Potter novel—yet). Unlike in many other places, research in Edinburgh is always seen as something fun, and fun things are more fun if they are shared, so the boundaries of work and play are blurred.

Kisuh Ahn, Beatrix Alex, Amittai Axelrod, Markus Becker, Johan Bos, Jean Carletta, Heriberto Cuayahuitl, Johannes Flieger, Ben Hachey, Harry Halpin, Pei-yun Hsueh, Amy Isard, Frank Keller, Yuval Krymolowski, Mirella Lapata, Colin Matheson, Johanna Moore, Malvina Nissim, Jon Oberlander, Miles Osborne, David Reitter, Gail Sinclair, Andrew Smith, Mark Steedman, David Talbot, Tim Willis and many, many others provided feedback in numerous discussions, were fun to hang out with in the pub and on parties, but often both, even at the same time.

Ewan Klein, Harry Halpin and Sebastian Riedel were fascinating discussion partners in the GridNLP group; hopefully, some of the things we brainstormed will become standard.

Many thanks also to the system group for maintaining the DICE computing evnironment and to the administration staff for being so well-organised and proactive.

I am grateful for having such great friends during my PhD, in Edinburgh and elsewhere. Thanks to (in alphabetical order) Andrew, Annette, Anita, Andreas, Daniel, Carsten, Chia-Leong, Claudine, Christine (two of them), David, Dörthe, Francesca, Hannele, Jeanette, Maciej, Matthias, Michael, Vera, Priscilla, Rana, Rob, Sibylle, Tiphaine, and Yves, for your friendship, for keeping me sane, and for reminding me there is more to Edinburgh, the world and to life than academia.

Colin Bannard, Chris Callison-Burch, Nicole Kim, Manolis Mavrikis, Mark McConwell, Rafael

Morales, Victor Tron and Verena Rieser were not only pleasant office mates to have, they also ensured wide topic diversity of our daily office chat. Thanks to my flatmates Alice, Gabrielle, Georgios, and Manolis, for accepting a German bloke into their predominantly French and Greek flats, respectively, and for being great pals. Special thanks to Vera for her dear companionship, for many cups of peppermint tea together, for advice on *R*, and for discussions on statistics.

With Kisuh Ahn, Tiphaine Dalmas, Johan Bos, James Curran and Steve Clark (also known as the two 'C's in *C&C*) I have shared the unique experience of building the *QED* open-domain question answering system and 'doing TREC' together, which involved all things true geeks need to function, such as overnight hacking sessions or pizza-and-DVD self-rewards, plus some less common features such as Settler boardgame sessions, Scottish dancing (online and offline), and accordeon-accompanied evaluation runs.

Dietrich Klakow very kindly hosted me in his speech signal processing lab (LSV) at Saarland University, first as part of an International Graduate College 8-month exchange between Edinburgh and Saarbücken, and then gave me a research job that allowed me to continue to work on this thesis after my DAAD scholarship. Not only that, Dietrich was very supportive and the source for interesting conversations, always helpful and happy to provide feedback on any issue. In Saarbrücken, Andreas Beschorner was my amicable (and sometimes composing) office mate, and many items containing chocolate in one form or another were jointly disposed off while writing papers, debugging code, or marking student exercises. Many thanks also to Barbara Rauch, Irene Cramer and Andreas Merkel for many pleasant dinners, discussions, and ubiquitous joint walks to the campus supermarket to obtain ice cream to fight the summer heat, and to the rest of the LSV group for having me around.

Another round of thanks to my academic co-authors during my PhD period: Kisuh Ahn, Beatrice Alex, Colin Bannard, Johan Bos, Chris Callison-Burch, Steve Clark, James Curran, Irene Cramer, Tiphaine Dalmas, Claire Grover, Dietrich Klakow, Ewan Klein, Yuval Krymolowski, Harry Halpin, Stephen Potter, Sebastian Riedel, Sally Scrutchin, Matthew Smillie, Mark Steedman, Richard Tobin and Bonnie Webber; it was (and is) fun to work with you. Travelling to (or hanging out at) conferences with András, Chris, James, Johan, Markus, Miles, Olga, Steve and Tiphaine was always lots of fun (and often full of adventures).

The NLP, IR and GIS communities were a pleasant environment for study and research. Jean Carletta, Paul Clough, Fred Gey, Alex Hauptmann, Chris Jones, András Kornai, Marcus Kracht, Ray Larson, Douglas Oard, Andreas 'Olli' Olligschläger, John Prange, Ross Purves, Douglas E. Ross, Mark Sanderson, David A. Smith, Ralf Steinberger, John Tait, Erik Tjong Kim Sang, Yannick Versley, Richard Waldinger and countless others provided valuable input in numerous discussions in emails and on conferences spanning the very globe that is dealt with in this thesis.

The author is also grateful to the U.S. National Geospatial Intelligence Agency (NGA), the U.S. Geographic Survey (USGS) and the U.S. Central Intelligence Agency (CIA) for providing the gazetteer datasets, without which this research project would not be possible in its present form (especially regarding its scale). The Freedom of Information Act that made the data release possible is one of the greatest pieces of legislation since the Geneva Convention on Human Rights (if only the latter was as consistently applied as the former). I also thank my annotators Annette, Claudine, Darren, Ian and Vasilis.

A very practical 'toponym resolver', Fred Bull, from Aberdeen, Scotland, travelled 95,438 miles to visit most *other* Aberdeens on our globe from Jamaica to Hong Kong. Thanks to Fred for inviting me to his book launch party where he shared his experiences when meeting members of the global family of 'Aberdonians worldwide' (Bull (2004)). Unlike this thesis, which is bound to concentrate on a narrow technical topic, his book emphasises that places are founded by people, many of whom share a common history.

This research was funded by the German Academic Exchange Service (DAAD) under the three-year scholarship D/02/01831 and by Linguit GmbH under grant UK-2002/2. Financial support by the School of Informatics, University of Edinburgh, and a Socrates scholarship by the European Union are also gratefully acknowledged. The contribution of MetaCarta Inc. to the funding for annotating the TR-MUC4 corpus is likewise gratefully acknowledged. The author is further grateful to ACM SIGIR for a generous travel stipend as well as a useful stack of books accompanying an ACM SIGIR Doctoral Consortium Award.

Last but not least, I'm grateful for the endless love and support of my mother and grandparents; I dedicate this thesis to them.

Chapter 1

Introduction

Then I found out that there was a place called Black
in every state in the country, and actually in almost
every country in the world.
– Jonathan Safran Foer (2005),
Extremely Loud & Incredibly Close, p. 42

[Parts of this chapter have been published as Leidner et al. (2003) and Leidner (2004a).]

Space and time are two fundamental dimensions of human perception that we use to orga-
nize our experiences. Consequently, documents, as textual artefacts of human experience (real
or fictitious), make frequent use of expressions of space and time as points of reference.

With the availability of large amounts of textual data on computer networks and the parallel availability of increasingly powerful computing devices, information systems for spatial
and textual processing have been developed. To date, the automatic processing of text is investigated by the discipline of Natural Language Processing (NLP, comprising sub-fields such as
automatic information extraction and automatic question answering), whereas the processing
of spatial information is investigated by the discipline of geographic information systems. The
existing split into research disciplines is perhaps understandable, given the different nature of
textual and spatial data at the surface level, and the heritage of the disciplines, rooted in linguistics and geography, respectively (Figure 1.1). However, as a negative consequence of this
organizational divide, the full power of the data remains under-utilised: conventional information systems are unable to relate a text document reporting on a riot in Somalia with sensor
data (such as satellite imagery) covering exactly the spot where the riot took place.

It is the aim of this thesis to contribute to a wider effort to *'bridge text and space'*, which I
call for, and the objective of which should be to overcome the technical and organisational divides that prohibit the co-computation of textual and spatial relationships, mutually supporting

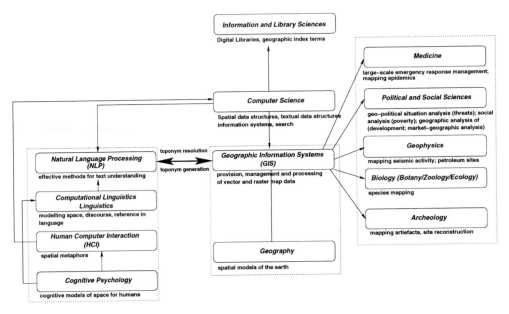

Figure 1.1: Disciplines concerned with geographic space.

each other, in order to take textual and spatial information processing to the next level.[1]

Textual and spatial information systems have matured in recent years, though by and large separately, and there have even been attempts to combine the two. However, the methods to link between the textual domain and the geographic domain are still premature, and, worse, the degree of their shortcoming has not been measured.

Toponym resolution, the mapping from place names to geographic referents in a spatial model (as defined more formally below) is one instance of the set of potential methods to link between text and space, and this thesis focuses on the evaluation aspect of the task. In the next section, the importance of the task will be motivated by listing several applications in which it could function as an enabling technology or that it could improve, and then we look at motivating the importance of evaluation of the task, which is the main contribution of this thesis.

---

[1]Of course, the time dimension also needs to be integrated likewise, but in this thesis, the focus is on space. See Mani et al. (2005) for a recent collection of many classical papers describing the treatment of time-related phenomena in language.

1.1 Motivation

Computers can perform powerful operations on numerical and symbolic models automatically. For example, assume a **spatial model** such as a set of polygons defined by sets of points is given. Then for two particular polygons (e.g. representing the US and Mexico, respectively), we can easily determine if they are neighbours (i.e., whether they share more than one point). However, given a text document about the two countries, a computer can no longer answer the question of country neighbourhood on purely geometric grounds without further ado. Instead, a different route has to be taken: explicit mention of phrases like 'the USA, Mexico's northern neighbour' or similar need to be present in the data to enable an information-seeking human searcher to retrieve evidence for the neighbourhood of the two countries based on a textual query. If we can bridge the gap between text and space by recognising place names (toponyms), resolving them to unique representations of the location intended by the author of the text, then we could use again the aforementioned methods for geometric computation based on the model rather than having to rely on the presence or absence of certain phrases or keywords. Now, assuming we have a method available, what use could it be put to? Resolving mentions of toponyms, i.e. proper nouns and location designators in text, has several potential application areas (some of which will be followed up in Chapter 7):

- **Spatial search**: Successful toponym resolution is expected to help increase precision in information retrieval applications by enabling the system to search by location (e.g. find all documents that relate to *Cambridge* in the USA (Cambridge, MA, not Cambridge, Cambridgeshire, England, UK) rather than just the explicit string `Cambridge`, whould could refer to several Cambridges). Geographic information retrieval is especially interesting as current Web search engines do not to date support a notion of geographic space, and a purely keyword-based attempt to constrain a search spatially cannot discriminate between the various toponym referents. Where there is doubt, toponym resolution will finally provide us with the right Cambridge, Edinburgh, Sheffield, Sana'a or Berlin.[2]

- **Map generation**: toponym resolution is a pre-condition for effective visualisation using dynamically generated maps – for instance, in a multimedia document surrogate that contains textual, video and map elements, we want to ensure that the map is centered around the places mentioned.

- Geographical **browsing/navigation**: 'click-able' maps or other forms of spatial navigation rely on a system's ability to project the objects to be organised into a space that is

---

[2]Ambiguity of place names is not restricted to the infamous examples of Paris, France versus Paris, TX, USA or the many Springfields in the USA. There are four Cambridges in the UK alone, in addition to Cambridge, MA, USA and many others (and at least 54 overall); to date, there exist at least 15 Edinburghs, 26 Sheffields, 5 Sana'as and 70 Berlins. Some place names inspired by saints (e.g. Santa Ana) have well over thousand potential locations on earth that they could be referring to.

intuitive to grasp for the human user. Spatial notions are deeply entrenched in the human cognitive apparatus, hence space is a very intuitive dimension for the browsing and navigation of digital libraries, e.g. using active (i.e., click-able) maps for exploration of document collections.

- Better **event detection/tracking and clustering** (Allan (2002)): if events are predications that hold in a space over a period of time, the reliable spatial grounding of an event should provide us with a solid basis for identifying events, helping not only to detect identical events, but also to order them in space, track them (i.e. what happened afterwards in the same location?), cluster them (e.g. using Euclidean distance in 3-dimensional geographic space as similarity metric), and merge two partial event descriptions (most types of events take place in a single location, and for partially instantiated templates in event extraction to be merge-able, they thus need to be spatially compatible (see for instance Li et al. (2002)).

- **Location-Based Services (LBS)** As mobile computing devices and wireless networking are becoming pervasive, the importance of Location Based Services (LBS) is increasingly recognised. The Global Positioning System (GPS) is already incorporated in many Personal Digital Assistants (PDAs) to determine the user's location (Nivala and Sarjakoski (2003)). Toponym resolution is the bridge that allows the user at position $P = (X,Y)$ to interact with services on the Web that are relevant to his or her position (including location-specific searches ('*where's the next hotel/bakery round here?*').

- Improving **information fusion**: information fusion methods have recently been applied to the comparison of answer extracts in open-domain question answering (Dalmas and Webber (2004)). Toponym resolution can serve a dual purpose in this context: First, as a knowledge source for (contextually resolved) geographical relationships (such as containment between *London* and *UK*), and secondly, to provide map surrogates for multi-modal question-based summarisation.

- Improving **question answering** (Yang et al. (2003); Leidner et al. (2004)) by grounding events: toponym resolution provides a basis for geographical reasoning. Firstly, questions of a spatial nature (*Where is X? What is the distance between X and Y?*) can be answered more systematically (rather than having to rely on accidental explicit text spans mentioning the answer).[3] So at least the following types of questions should benefit directly from accurate toponym resolution:[4]

---

[3]Of course, every non-extractive approach is beyond the evaluation procedure of the current TREC Q&A track task definition (Voorhees (2004)).

[4]These examples are artificial, not from a corpus.

1. *What is **X**?*

   Q: *What is Kangiqsualujjuaq?*

   A: *Kangiqsualujjuaq is a place approximately 1500 kilometers north of Montreal, Canada.* (For some place names, many humans cannot tell that they refer to places.)

2. *Where is **X**?*

   Q: *Where is Cannes located?*

   A: [should yield a surrogate based on textual descriptions generated from the gazetteer relations:

   X is-type *Y*, *X* part-of *Z* and the coordinates, plus a map as generated above, with additional images, e.g. from satellites or picture search engines as available.]

3. *What **X** is **Y** part of?*

   Q: *What is 'Bad Bergzabern' part of?*

   A: *Bad Bergzabern is part of the Federal Republic of Germany.*

   Q: *Is Andorra la Vella part of Spain?*

   A: *No, Andorra la Vella belongs to Andorra.*

4. *How far is **X** from **Y**?*

   Q: *How far is Cambridge from London?*

   A: *The distance between London, England, United Kingdom and Cambridge, England, United Kingdom is 79 km (49 miles or 43 nautical miles).*

Secondly, the fact that space-time provides a frame of reference to ground events can be used to discard candidate answer text spans that are outside the spatial presuppositions of the questions using inference. Consider the information need represented by

Name fire incidents in Canada.

A system could internally compute a candidate list of events:

(1.1) (a) ⟨1935; *Waterton Lake's last major fire*⟩

     (b) ⟨1908; *Westman Hardware, London, burned to the ground*⟩

     (c) ⟨1666; *Great Fire in London*⟩

     (d) ⟨1849; *Arsonist set fire to Canadian Free Press offices*⟩

Now *Waterton Lake* is indeed a place in Canada, so we are unable to discard (a) as a potentially valid response. Likewise, *London* in (b) is a place in Ontario, Canada, and if we can resolve the toponym correctly based on the document context, we are able to retain the candidate. But the *London* mentioned in (c), which refers to London, England, can be discarded if we can ground the toponym referents correctly, which improves our overall likelihood of returning only correct responses. Finally, *Canadian Free Press*, in the absence of evidence indicating otherwise, is likely (but by no means exclusively so) to have offices in Canada, so (d) can remain on the list of candidates.

These example applications shall suffice to motivate the importance of automatic toponym resolution as a task in general for the time being (we will return to the question of impact in Chapter 7. However, while other tasks in NLP have undergone careful evaluation studies, the same does not hold for toponym resolution. Woodruff and Plaunt (1994), trying to relate their early work to Hill (1990), write:

> The text corpus and the techniques used in this study do not seem easily du-plicable. However, although benchmarking is a daunting task, evaluation is ex-tremely significant. Consequently, *future work should include the development of a benchmark. The most meaningful evaluation would probably be a comparison of manually-assigned coordinate indexes of documents to those generated by [their system, JLL] GIPSY.*[5]

Unfortunately, despite some system building efforts, the lack of evaluation studies was not addressed during the next decade, as will become more clear in the literature review in Chapter 3.

Arguably, progress in a research field is limited if the quality of the methods developed is not systematically assessed. In NLP, if two alternative methods *A* and *B* are proposed, we need to be able to compare them with respect to metrics that correlate with human judgments. If *B* correlates better with human performance than *A* we may discard *A* in favour of *B* in system development. Furthermore, we may favour *B* over *A* when trying to incrementally improve the state of the art. In the absence of evaluation, progress cannot be measured, and consequently research efforts may be wasted.

This thesis aims to measure how referentially ambiguous spatial named entities can be resolved with respect to an extensional coordinate model robustly on news text. To this end, a gold standard is devised that allows large-scale experimental evaluation. Using this resource, past and new methods are compared on the same dataset for the first time to determine which sources of evidence help best in the toponym resolution task.

1.2 Problem Statement

After introducing and motivating toponym resolution, we can now formulate it as a computa-tional task in order to state what goals this thesis aims to address.

For a given document, we want to achieve two fundamental processing steps automati-cally:

---

[5]Emphasis added, JLL.

- **Toponym recognition** identifies a text span (i.e., character start and end positions) that constitutes a toponym and then classifying as such (marking up the text span as of type toponym as opposed to person name, product name etc).

  Since toponym recognition is a special case of general named entity recognition and classification (NERC)—we are simply only interested in one entity class LOCATION—it can be performed using an existing named entity recogniser. To perform toponym recognition, state-of-the-art systems first segment a document D_i into a sequence of tokens *TOKENS*. Typically, the NERC task is then cast as a sequence labeling task: a decision (rule-based, statistical, or hybrid) chooses the most likely label for each token, for example from a label set (B-LOC, I-LOC, O):[6]

Edinburgh	is	the	vibrant	cultural	capital	of	Scotland	,	perhaps	its
I-LOC	O	O	O	O	O	O	I-LOC	O	O	O

role	is	comparable	to	the	role	New	York	plays	in	the	US	.
O	O	O	O	O	O	I-LOC	I-LOC	O	O	O	I-LOC	O

- **Toponym resolution** then looks up a set of candidate referents (potential locations) and computes a projection function, which effectively picks the correct candidate referent, discarding alternative candidates that refer to the 'wrong', i.e. unintended location. In order to allow a computational treatment, we have to operationalise the notion of intended or 'true' referent, and we simply pass that responsibility on to the human annotator: the true referent in a gold-standard corpus is the one identified by a single human subject or the majority vote if multiple human judgments for the same decision are available.

More formally, the task can be describes as follows. We start with a corpus $\mathcal{D}$ comprising a set of documents $\mathcal{D} = \{D_1, \ldots, D_{|\mathcal{D}|}\}$ as input. Each document D_i comprises a sequence of tokens $TOKENS = (TOKEN[1] \ldots TOKEN[|TOKENS|])$. We further need a *gazetteer* $\mathcal{G}$, i.e. an inventory that lists all candidate referents $\mathcal{R} = \{R_1 \ldots R_{|\mathcal{R}|}\}$. A gazetteer entry $G(T_i)$ for a toponym T_i is a tuple containing a feature type[7] and set of referents $\mathcal{R} \subset \mathcal{G}$ for T_i. Here, referents are represented by the centroid of the location's latitude and longitude, respectively. A *toponym resolver* is a function $F_{\mathcal{G}}(\cdot, \cdot)$ that maps from a document $D_i \in \mathcal{D}$ in which the toponyms are not resolved yet, to a document with the same content in which the toponyms are resolved, i.e. where for each toponym (or for *some* toponyms, in the case of a *partial* toponym resolver) a referent from the set of candidate referents has been chosen. Referents can be represented in various ways, including polygons or simply pairs of latitude and longitude of the centroid of

---

[6]I-LOC can be read as 'inside text span that is referring to a location', O as 'outside of a text span referring to a location', and B-LOC is needed only to unambiguously separate adjacent entities of the same type. This scheme is the so-called BIO2 tagset (Tjong Kim Sang and De Meulder (2003)), which will be discussed later in more detail.

[7]For this thesis, the focus is on *populated places*, but in general, other types such as rivers, mountains, or artifacts (e.g. airports) are also of interest.

$\mathcal{D}$	set of documents (corpus)
D_i	a particular document
TOKENS	sequence of tokens that constitute a document
TOKEN[*i*]	a particular token
$\mathcal{T}$	set of toponyms
T_i	a particular toponym (e.g. *London*)
$\mathcal{R}$	set of referents
R_i	a particular referent (e.g. London, England, UK)
$\mathcal{G}$	a gazetteer (toponym/location inventory)
$G(x)$	a gazetteer entry
$\langle \cdot ; \cdot \rangle$	point on earth in decimal latitude/longitude representation (e.g. $\langle 51.5; -0.11 \rangle$)
$T_i \rightsquigarrow R_j$	T_i is resolved to R_j

Table 1.1: Synopsis of the symbols used.

the location. We write $T_i \rightsquigarrow R_j$ if and only if toponym T_i refers to the location represented by R_j.[8] For example:

(a)   The 1666 <u>London</u> fire was one of the country's
      most tragic accidents in history.
      $\rightsquigarrow$ London > England > United Kingdom
      (lat./long.: $\langle 51.52; -0.10 \rangle$)

(b)   The recent fire in <u>London</u> alarmed policy
      makers from Montreal to Inuvik.
      $\rightsquigarrow$ London > Ontario > Canada
      (lat./long.: $\langle 42.97; -81.24 \rangle$)

Table 1.1 summarises the notation used in this thesis. After defining (one instance of) the toponym resolution task above, we can now relate it to existing terminology in the domain of language and space.

- **Grounding.** In linguistic pragmatics, grounding is the general concept of relating a linguistic entity to (a model of) the world (Figure 1.2). For Lakoff, for example, the ultimate basis for the human cognitive ability of language comprehension is that language is grounded in experience (Lakoff (1993)). According to Lakoff, humans have built in physical properties that influence the way *homo sapiens* uses language, including the

---

[8]Read '$\rightsquigarrow$' as 'resolves to'.

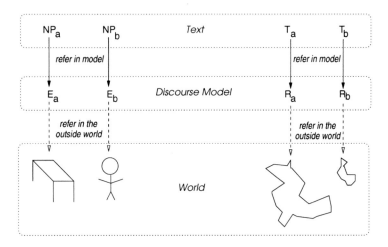

Figure 1.2: Discourse model.

universal perception of fundamental spatial dichotomies such as UP–DOWN.

- **Geo-coding.** A term from Geographic Information Systems (GIS), geo-coding in the general sense is any kind of method or process to connect data with a spatial model representation, or, in GIS terms, to transform *implicitly geo-coded* data into *explicitly geo-coded* data. In a narrower, more technical sense it is used as a synonym for *address geo-coding*. Therefore, toponym resolution is a special case of geo-coding (used in the general sense), in which the data annotated are names of places. At the same time, because it works on textual ('unstructured') data, it is also an alternative to address geo-coding, which operates on structured records only.

- **Address geo-coding.** State-of-the-art industrial GIS systems provide a functionality that analyses postal address records and maps them to a spatial representation. These records are structured in the sense that either they are dedicated text fields in a database that contain (only) postal addresses in the conventional form used by a particular country's postal services,[9] or the input address comes already pre-segmented into its constituent fields, so that the task is to simply look up the address parts in the country's address index. In the former case, simple rules (smaller in power than even regular expressions) define the allowed sequence of building blocks like house numbers, street name etc.

The relationship between these notions is summarised in Figure 1.3.

---

[9]The country needs to be specified by the human user prior to starting the geo-coding process.

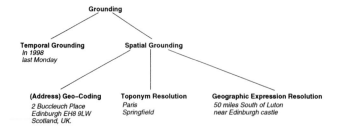

Figure 1.3: Types of grounding in language processing.

The advantage of address geo-coding is its simplicity and high precision. Its main disadvantages are very low 'recall': firstly, most data is unstructured—i.e., available in free text form (including the World Wide Web) with no special markup for postal addresses—and secondly, postal addresses are but a fraction of implicitly geo-coded material: in addition there are also mentions of plain toponyms, phone numbers, Internet domains etc.

- **Place-name disambiguation.** A precondition for resolving place names is that they are disambiguated: unless we are certain that a particular 'London' refers to the capital of the UK (i.e., it is classified as London$_3$ instead of London$_{42}$), we cannot ground it in an extensional coordinate model by assigning latitude/longitude to it. However, it is conceivable that a given system performs only the disambiguation step/sub-task without the grounding part. Systems that do not have a built-in gazetteer database fall into this category.

- **Place-name normalisation.** Sometimes used as a synonym for place-name disambiguation, the term is also occasionally used to map from a toponym referring to a location to a canonical form referring to the same location (e.g. relating the various surface forms *US*, *U.S.A.* and *United States of America*).

- **Toponym generation.** Figure 1.4 shows that *toponym generation* is the dual task of toponym resolution, namely the creation (or selection) of a textual name for a geographic location specified, given its model extension. For example, toponym generation is necessary to automatically create captions for photographs taken with a camera equipped with a *Geographic Positioning System* (*GPS*) receiver, and can generate meta-data or a caption saying London for a photo taken at GPS coordinates $\langle 51.5; -0.11 \rangle$, thus facilitating textual search by location (Naaman et al. (2006)).[10]

---

[10]In this thesis, geographic coordinates are by default given as decimal latitude and longitude.

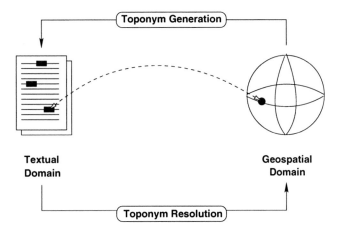

Figure 1.4: The dual role of toponym resolution and toponym generation in connecting text and geographic space.

Now that the task of toponym resolution has been introduced and the terminology has been clarified, we can turn to the main objective of this thesis and research questions addressed.

1.2.1 Research Questions

The central argument of this thesis is the following. As will we see in Chapter 3, a number of toponym resolution methods have been proposed in the last decade, but the development was not supported by efforts to relate new work to previous work, mainly due to the absence of evaluation data.

I claim that development of such data is vital to get an understanding of the task and the utility of the various types of input that the methods rely on, which in turn is essential to build systems in a principled way:

> **Central Thesis Objective**
> The relative utility of heuristics and evidence sources for
> toponym resolution needs to be measured in a principled way.

This is a normative statement, i.e. a call to follow the methodology proposed in the next section. Unlike a scientific hypothesis that may be supported or refuted, it is unlikely to receive opposition in principle; rather, the question is how such a methodology could look like and how it could be instantiated for the toponym resolution task. The following research questions can be derived from the objective above:

1. Can we find an order of relative utility of heuristics and other sources of evidence used in the past to resolve toponyms? (The question of *utility*.)

2. How can we construct toponym resolution systems in a principled way?
   This question leads to a number of corollary questions:

   (a) How referentially ambiguous are toponyms? (The question of *type ambiguity*.)

   (b) How well can humans resolve toponyms in a corpus? (The question of *agreement*.)

   (c) What degree of ambiguity is actually present in (news) documents? (The question of *token ambiguity*.)

   (d) Do previously proposed methods scale to world-wide geographic scope? (The question of *geographic scalability*.)

   (e) How does the performance of previously suggested methods compare? (The question of *component evaluation*.)

   (f) Are toponym resolution methods robust with respect to systematic errors introduced by toponym recognition (i.e. named entity tagging) systems? (The question of *system evaluation*.)

The remainder of this thesis aims to shed some light on these questions and intends to define a standard benchmark that further evaluation efforts can build on.

1.3 Methodology

In order to achieve a better understanding of the factors contributing to performance in toponym resolution, the following systematic methodology is proposed (and pursued in subsequent chapters):

1. **Analysis.** Analyse the existing research literature:

   - Construct pseudo-code in a unified notation for existing methods, which are mostly described in prose.

   - Extract a systematic inventory of heuristics and other evidence sources and relate them in a taxonomy.

2. **Curation.** Create a re-usable evaluation dataset:

   - Devise a markup language based on open standards.

   - Construct a reference gazetteer database to look up candidate referents from.

   - Implement an annotation tool that accesses the gazetteer and that supports the markup language.

- Select and annotate/supervise the annotation of benchmark corpora.

- Validate the setting by determining human inter-annotator agreement.

3. **Implementation.** Develop a software platform for experimentation.

   - Design and implement a basic infrastructure comprising Application Programming Interfaces (API) for corpus handling, access to corpora and geographic knowledge.

   - Reimplement the heuristic inventory.

   - Implement some complete toponym resolution systems.

4. **Evaluation.**

   - Choose and/or develop evaluation metrics for TR.

   - Evaluate empirically:
     - the relative utility of heuristics
     - the performance of complete, replicated systems.

To sum up, we shall employ an experimental engineering methodology to gain knowledge in a data-driven (i.e., empirical) fashion.

1.4 Scope

Textual corpora and geographic resources vary along many different dimensions, such as the language of the documents investigated or the type of spatial representation used. The following list gives the main design criteria followed in this thesis and attempts to delineate the scope of the present investigation.

1. **Toponyms.** We confine ourself to study simple toponyms (place names) as opposed to more complex (compositional) spatial expressions such as spatial phrases or postal addresses. For practical reasons, we adopt a notion of toponyms as place names referring to human-populated places including cities, countries, and continents.

2. **Open-domain text.** We would like toponym resolution methods to process text of unconstrained vocabulary size and unlimited topic areas, so our evaluation resource must not be artificially constrained along these dimensions.

3. **Contemporary English.** We only consider English-language online text. The focus of this study is on toponym resolution given the present state of the language (a synchronic study), i.e. no attempt has been made to trace place-name changes over time, often reflecting political change (e.g. *Chemnitz ≻ Karl-Marx-Stadt ≻ Chemnitz*). The texts used for system development and those used for evaluation are contemporary.

4. **News prose genre.** Ideally, our evaluation collection would be a balanced corpus sampled from various genres and text types. However, resource constraints have limited this project to one category, and news (journalistic prose) was the obvious genre due to its practical relevance and easy availability of articles in large quantities. The documents comprising the corpus used in this thesis are from online sources, but only documents are used that contain news prose (as opposed to, for instance, arbitrary HTML pages).

5. **Global geography.** While it is legitimate to restrict a method or system to a particular geographic area, we consider global, i.e. earth-wide, geographic scope rather than favoring a particular continent or region.

6. **Present-day geography.** We work with present-day earth geography.[11] Geographic boundaries change often due to administrative changes. The difference between (3.) and this criterion is that here not the name, but rather what is denoted by it, is subject to change.

7. **Earth geometry.** This study concentrates on geographic space on earth. No planets, moon, stars, or fictional toponyms are considered. Only macroscopic-scale objects are considered, e.g. geography of cities and countries rather than spatial relationships in the anatomy of cells.

8. **Free sources.** By using only freely available information sources we ensure that the resulting dataset can benefit wider academic/industrial audiences. Where this principle has to be compromised, there needs at least to be a methodology for replicating non-free material based on free sources.

The first criterion (1) relates to the problem studied, the next three criteria (2-4) state linguistic choices, another three criteria (5-7) are geographic in nature, and the final criterion (8) is a methodological choice that ensures that results can be replicated, one of the prerequisites for scientific progress.

Note that generalising statements in this thesis are to be seen in the context of the scope outlined above. This is not to say the methods evaluated and developed in this thesis are restricted to the choices given above; however, different results are likely to be expected when the set of assumptions is changed.

1.5 Contributions

I have coined the technical term *toponym resolution*[12] to describe the mapping from a place name in a prose text to an extensional representation of a location in a spatial model that

---

[11]More precisely, with a February 2003 snapshot of the resources described below.

[12]To the best of my knowledge, it was first used in Leidner (2004a).

the place name refers to. Before, the terms 'place-name disambiguation', 'geo-coding' and 'grounding' were often used, sometimes interchangeably, in a confusing way. Starting from the above analysis of how all these different notions are related, the main contributions of this thesis are the following:

- First, I provide a taxonomic analysis of previously proposed methods with respect to the heuristics and evidence sources they employed, and show that there is no consensus as to what contributing factors are most important in solving the task. The reason for this is the absence of evaluation data, a fact which has been recognised in the literature for a decade, but not solved.

- Second, I provide a new mark-up language, associated annotation guidelines, and an implemented annotation tool based on these. I also compile a reference gazetteer from free sources. Using these resources, I curate the first evaluation dataset for the toponym resolution task, comprising two sub-corpora with news text, one with global, and another with more local focus. I demonstrate the feasibility of the annotation task by determining human inter-annotator agreement for the setting.

- Third, I develop TextGIS®, a software platform for experimentation with toponym resolution algorithms. By offering a C++ API and several command line tools, it supports convenient integration of toponym recognition, gazetteer lookup, toponym resolution, evaluation, and visualisation. Based on the aforementioned software platform, I provide a re-implementation of a list of previously proposed heuristics, and carry out a replication study of a complete system documented in the literature as a baseline for experimentation.

- Fourth, I propose a new algorithm for TR based on the notion of *minimality heuristics* (Gardent and Webber (2001)) for the task, based on a novel '*geometric minimality heuristic*': assume the set of referent assignments that minimise the convex hull of the candidate referents. The algorithm uses the new heuristic together with the 'one referent per discourse' heuristic commonly used in Word Sense Disambiguation.

- Fifth, I present the first empirical comparison of individual heuristics and complete systems using the dataset and aforementioned software platform. The two available corpora allow the study of degradation effects comparing TR on global versus local news (component evaluation) on the one hand, and the comparison between oracle toponym recognition output versus output from a realistic state-of-the-art maximum entropy sequence tagger on the other hand (system evaluation).

- Sixth, I experiment with machine learning methods for TR to investigate how a principled approach that integrates heuristics, reinterpreted as features (instead of relying on human ad-hoc weights, rules, and thresholds) could outperform the state of the art. This is a difficult undertaking because unlike in other NLP tasks, the number of potential labels (classes) exceeds typical NLP sequence tagging tasks by several order of magnitudes.

- Seventh, I present several application case studies to show the relevance of the toponym resolution task, and, by implication, of its evaluation. The applications include

  - story visualisation: the generation of a polygon representing the 'spatial aboutness' of a narrative (where the action happens), as a visual spatial summary;

  - spatial browsing: using a three-dimensional real-time rendering engine with a global earth model, news stories can be explored in a fascinating new way if we resolve their toponyms and populate the virtual globe with automatically generated 'place-marks' representing each story's content;[13]

  - answering spatial questions: given a discourse model for a text that includes resolved toponyms, spatial questions about it can be answered accurately in a knowledge-based fashion, advancing the state of the art (where answers have to be explicit in the text to be extracted as strings) significantly;

  - geographic information retrieval: I introduce geo-filtering predicates, a technique intended to improve document retrieval performance by taking into account geographic relevance in addition to topic relevance.

1.6 Thesis Plan

The remaining chapters of this thesis are organised as follows.

Due to the interdisciplinary nature of this thesis, Chapter 2 gives some background about natural language processing, information retrieval, digital libraries and geographical information systems, to set the stage for the subsequent exposition.

Chapter 3 surveys some early work in toponym resolution and discusses its shortcomings, most notably the absence of comparable and realistic evaluation. In addition, an inventory of heuristics and knowledge sources used in past work are extracted and organised in a systematic taxonomy.

---

[13]At the time of writing, a similar application was independently built by Pouliquen et al. (2006). So while I cannot claim to be the first to publish this particular application, the fact that a 10-strong team at the EU's Joint Research Centre (JRC) have built the same application arguably supports my case for the importance of toponym resolution, and hence its systematic evaluation in a standard setting.

Chapter 4 describes the curation of a reference gazetteer and reference corpora for the toponym resolution task, and characterises the resulting datasets.

In Chapter 5, three methods for TR are presented: a replicated system from the literature, a new algorithm based on geometric minimality, and a machine learning method.

Chapter 6 describes the evaluation metrics used and discusses the evaluation results when applying the aforementioned heuristics and methods to the new benchmark corpora.

Chapter 7 outlines some applications for toponym resolution. As we will see, toponym resolution can be used to support the generation of visual summaries, spatial browsing of news, information retrieval and question answering.

Finally, Chapter 8 summarises and concludes with some suggestions for future work.

Chapter 2

Background

This stuff [Geographic Information Systems, JLL] saves lives.
– Alan Leidner,[a]
NYC head of GIS during 9/11

---

[a]Not related to the author of this thesis.

This thesis is interdisciplinary in the sense that it uses concepts drawn from geography, informatics and linguistics. To make its contents accessible to different audiences, this chapter describes some central notions from the various areas. The reader may thus want to skip sections covering his or her own area of expertise.

In Section 2.1, the reader is made familiar with some basic geographic ideas, and is alerted towards the existence of multiple geographic referencing systems. Geographic information systems and spatial databases are the topic of Section 2.2. Section 2.3 defines the notion of a gazetteer and describes some relevant gazetteer datasets. Turning from spatial processing to language processing, Section 2.4 discusses technologies for textual information access, namely digital libraries and information retrieval, as well as support technologies from natural language processing, including information extraction, question answering, and word sense disambiguation. Section 2.5, finally, tries to link together the spatial and linguistic threads by discussing the linguistics of space.

2.1 One Space, Many Geographies

Since this thesis concerns the relationship between language and geographic space, it ought to be noted first that the physical space on earth populated by humans can be structured and referenced in many alternative ways, or using various 'geographies'. For example, singling out an island or a group of islands such as the British Isles is an example of using a *physical geography* as a means of reference. In contrast, when we speak of the United Kingdom of Great Britain and Northern Island (or UK for short), we are using a political boundary as a means of delineation to refer to a *geo-political entity* (*GPE*). Other possible geographies that may be used as frames of reference include: delineation by ballot area, by postcode, by church parish, by common phone prefix, by national grid reference, and so forth. In this thesis, countries and continents do play a minor role (geo-political and physical, respectively), but the focus is on human-populated places (such as cities or villages), so the main underlying frame of reference is the geography of human settlements.

When trying to combine various datasets, a standard problem is the integration of geographically referenced datasets that use different reference systems. *GeoXwalk*[1] (pronounced 'geo-crosswalk') is a project and system carried out at the EDINA Data Library at the University of Edinburgh aiming at supporting the translation between alternative geographies (Medyckyj-Scott et al. (2001); Densham and Reid (2003)).

Independent of the particular system of boundaries used, a *geographic coordinate system* has to be used to define the positions of the boundaries. A point can be defined by $P = \langle \phi, \lambda \rangle$, where ϕ is the *latitude*, i.e. the angle between a point and the equator (in degrees ranging -90...+90), and *longitude* λ, the angle east or west of an internationally agreed zero point near the Royal Observatory, Greenwich (England, UK), ranging from -180...+180 degrees.[2]

2.2 Geographic Information Systems (GIS) and Spatial Databases

A *Geographic Information System* (*GIS*) is software for the storage, retrieval, processing and rendering of spatial data. The main functions of GIS are:

- data storage and processing: import of spatial datasets, format conversion, compact storage, efficient access;

- manual data exploration (e.g. Adrienko and Adrienko (2005)[3]) facilities to discover new relationships in existing data: provision of an interactive interface that allows visualisation and navigation using mouse, pen, or keyboard, including zoom, and map overlay;

- automatic data analysis: ability to carry out numerical methods, e.g. built in or specified in a custom script language; and

- map generation: export in various graphics formats, and high-resolution plots.

---

[1] http://www.geoxwalk.ac.uk (accessed 2006-08-21).

[2] Note that latitude and longitude are always relative to a *geodetic reference system*, i.e. a mathematical model approximating the shape of the earth, such as the *World Geodetic System 1984* (*WGS84*). Evolving models are a result of increasing precision regarding the measurement of the irregular shape of the earth (Seeger, 1999, p. 428–430).

[3] Reviewed in Leidner (2006c).

ID	NAME	FUNCTION	SALARY
1	Doe John	Assistant Cleaner	$20,000
2	Miller Jack	Vice President Sales	$400,000
...	...	...	...

(a)

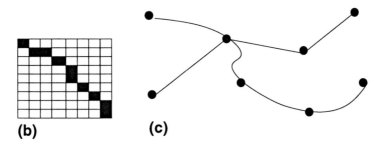

(b)　　　　**(c)**

Figure 2.1: Data representation: RDBMS versus GIS: (a) relational data, (b) raster data, and (c) vector data.

The first dedicated GIS systems were built in the 1960s, when computer systems were not yet powerful enough to provide the storage capacity for models of the whole earth, processing capacity to provide online (near real-time) analysis capabilities, or display of high-resolution graphics, all readily available today. Modern representatives of the genre like ESRI Inc.'s *ArcGIS*[4] or the freely available *GRASS*[5] (Neteler (2004)) on the other hand, are powerful tools for environmental analysis, climate study, market research, the exploration of socio-economical trends or military planning.

One of the main differences between GIS and the Relational Database Management Systems (RDBMS) ubiquitous in the business world, for instance, is their focus on efficient storage and processing of *spatial* data, typically supporting hybrid representations. Whereas RDMBs mainly deal with tables of textual and numerical data (such as names of employees in a company, or names and prices of products, see Figure 2.1(a)), GIS systems are tuned towards processing *spatial data*, which consists of *raster data*, sets of points given as coordinates on a grid (Figure 2.1(b))—also known as *bitmaps*—and *vector data*, objects defined by points on their boundaries (Figure 2.1(c)).

Spatial data structures. The *quad-tree* family of data structures is based on a recursive partitioning of space into four quadrants (Samet (1984, 1989)). Figure 2.2 shows an example

[4]http://www.esri.com (accessed 2006-08-21).
[5]http://grass.itc.it (accessed 2006-08-21).

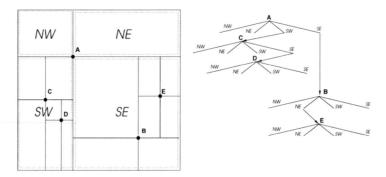

Figure 2.2: Quad-tree example.

of a *point quad-tree*. A first point *A* is inserted into the tree, dividing the 2-dimensional pane
into the four sectors NW (north west), NE (north east), SE (south east) and SW (south west)
indicated by the blue dotted rectangles. The insertion of the next point (*B*) leads to the division
of the SE quadrant, and so on. The name quad-tree indicates that the scheme is implemented
using 4-ary tree data structures. The obvious advantage compare to a *grid* data structure, a
2-dimensional array of cell blocks or linked lists, is that no memory is wasted for unoccupied
parts of the pane. A disadvantage is that to access a point, a traversal of the path becomes
necessary, the length of which is dependent on the number of data points stored in the same
region. Other data structures include *grid files* and *R-trees* (see Rigaux et al. (2002) for an
accessible introduction to spatial data structures).

   Underlying GIS systems is either a custom implementation of these data structures, or they
interoperate with standard *spatial databases* such as the commercial *Oracle Spatial Option* or
the free *Postgres GIS* (an add-on for the *PostgreSQL* RDBMS).

   Apart from differences between internal storage details between GIS and RDBMS, functionality also differs: GIS data can be loaded in different storage layers which can then be
rendered or combined based on processing. For example, one layer might contain a standard
background map (such as a map showing the national boundaries of Europe), whereas a second layer may show the degree of childhood poverty in the location concerned. Combining the
two, we obtain a *thematic map*. It is also possible to overlay map data with aerial photographs
(Figure 2.3) or satellite images.

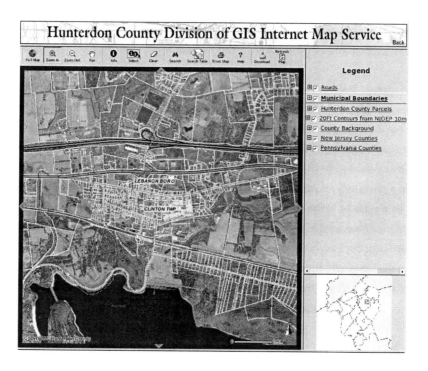

Figure 2.3: Internet GIS application showing parts of Hunterdon (New Jersey, USA).

Internet GIS. Recently the Internet has led to the increased availability of GIS systems online (Figure 2.3 is one example[6]), which may even resort to distributed data sources given from servers controlled by different organisations, a development that has become possible by agreeing on international standards for data exchange and service interoperability, codified by the International Organization for Standardization (ISO) task force TC211 and the Open Geospatial Consortium (OGC). The term *Internet GIS* has been described to refer to this development (Peng and Tsou (2003)). More recently, in the emerging field of *grid computing*, software tools for the computer-supported design and execution of experiments (so-called *workflow systems*) have emerged. In such a paradigm, each experiment would be formally specified by a graph of interconnected processing components, possibly distributed across computer networks or even organisations (see Grover et al. (2004) for an example of such a workflow 'pipeline').

Mapping. Perhaps the single most important result or 'product' of applying GIS software are *maps*. However, only 3-dimensional globes can truthfully represent areas, angles and lengths at the same time. Maps on paper or flat computer screens, due to their 2-dimensional nature, have to sacrifice some of these properties. A *map projection* is a transform of a point on the 3-dimensional globe (e.g. given in latitude/longitude) onto a flat pane. Figure 2.4 shows the earth in a *Mercator projection*,[7] which is a transform that maps the points on the 3-dimensional globe on a cylinder, which is then unwrapped onto a 2-dimensional plane. Since the earth's shape differs from a cylindric shape the most at the north and south pole, land area near the poles are most distorted in this approach. However, its angle-preserving nature makes the Mercator projection useful for navigation. Figure 2.4 was produced using *GMT*, the free *Generic Mapping Tools* (Wessel and Smith (2004)). Given a point on the globe with latitude ϕ and longitude λ, the Mercator projection is defined as

$$x = \lambda - \lambda_0 \tag{2.1}$$

$$y = ln[tan(\frac{1}{4}\pi + \frac{1}{2}\phi)] \tag{2.2}$$

$$= ln[\tan\phi + \sec\phi], \tag{2.3}$$

where λ_0 is the longitude of the map centre. There exists a wide range of dedicated software for mapping in addition to mapping functionality provided as part of GIS systems, including Internet services (such as *Google Maps*) or desktop applications Microsoft *MapPoint* (see Erle et al. (2005) for a introduction to practical mapping). A recent trend is toward making maps multi-modal and more interactive (Oviatt (1997)).

---

[6]Interestingly, in this example from New Jersey, we can already observe *geo-geo ambiguity*—ambiguity between two locations Lebanon, NJ, USA and the Middle Eastern country Lebanon—and *geo/non-geo ambiguity*—between the person name Clinton and the region Clinton, NJ, USA.

[7]After Gerhard Mercator (b. 1512, d. 1594), German mathematician and cartographer, who invented the conformal (angle-preserving) projection.

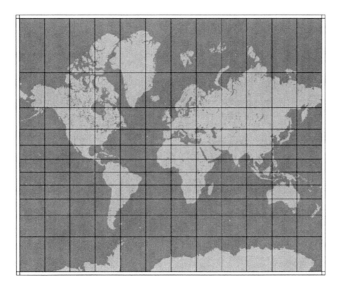

Figure 2.4: Mercator projection of the earth (created with GMT).

Distance computation. While on a two-dimensional plane, the distance between two points $P_1 = (a,b)$ and $P_2 = (c,d)$ is given by the formula

$$\Delta = \sqrt{(a-c)^2 + (b-d)^3},\tag{2.4}$$

which follows from the *Pythagorean Theorem*, on Earth things are not quite so simple due to its 3-dimensional, uneven curvature. Assume a spherical Earth with a radius of $R = 6,367\ km$ (3,957 miles) and two points in spherical coordinates $P_1 = (lon_1, lat_1)$ and $P_2 = (lon_2, lat_2)$, then the *Haversine Formula* (Sinnott (1984)) can be expected to give very good distance approximation:

$$d_{lon} = lon_2 - lon_1,\tag{2.5}$$

$$d_{lat} = lat_2 - lat_1,\tag{2.6}$$

$$a = (\sin(d_{lat}/2))^2 + \cos(lat_1) \times \cos(lat_2) \times (\sin(d_{lon}/2))^2,\tag{2.7}$$

$$\Delta = 2 \times R \times \arctan(\sqrt{(a)}, \sqrt{(1-a)}),\tag{2.8}$$

Geo-coding. *Geo-coding* (or *spatial resolution*) can be defined as converting *implicitly geo-referenced* data (i.e. data in which the references are represented as a name, an address, or in another *intensional* form) into *explicitly geo-referenced* data (i.e. data in which the references are represented in *extensional* form, for instance given as coordinates on an ellipsoid). For example, Crosier (2004) describes the *address geo-coding* process in *ArcGIS* (Figure 2.5). First,

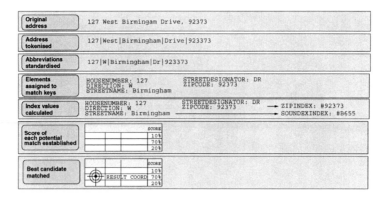

Figure 2.5: The geo-coding process, modified after (Crosier, 2004, p. 38).

the input string that contains a (here: US) street address is broken down into parts (tokens). Then, certain parts that can may occur in alternative forms (e.g. abbreviated) are converted to a canonical form for easier comparison. Then the elements of the address are recognised as belonging to certain classes (for instance, *127* fills the house number 'slot'). Then, index numbers are computed for fast access of candidate lists. Candidate location entries are sorted by degree of match, and the most highly ranking entry is chosen. Its coordinates represent the geo-coding result for the given street address.

Figure 2.6 shows a Web interface for *Eagle*, an US address geo-coder available on the Internet. At the top, the input screen is shown, where an address can be entered. At the bottom, the output of the Web application is given, including geographic coordinates of a *bounding box* that includes the address and a map. Note that using different input fields for address entry eliminates the need to tokenise into parts and assign the address parts to the address element type.

Unfortunately, geo-coding available in GIS systems today is only capable of processing structured address records, i.e. lists of pre-formatted addresses (in a given format, for instance one address per line). What is not supported by the state of the art is the automatic extraction of addresses or just toponyms from unstructured textual documents. Another caveat is that easily available geo-coders can only process US addresses, which represent only a tiny fraction of the world's address formats.

Geo-coding is a powerful mechanism that allows one to relate knowledge in unforeseen ways. Since addresses are addresses of *people* that live or work at the address, questions of privacy protection need to be raised. Curry (1999) discusses some of these concerns.

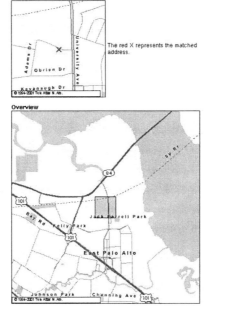

Figure 2.6: Example geo-coder: Eagle.

Applications of GIS and Geo-coding. GIS systems can be used for many purposes (see Longley et al. (2005) for an accessible introduction). For example, an environmentalist may study the correlation between types of trees in a forest and the kind of soil. A criminologist may want to establish the so-called crime 'hot-spots' in order to ask for more patrols to attend to them. A supermarket chain may want to open a new store in a city, and may need to identify the best location with respect to that part of its customer base which is not already being served by existing stores, friendly or competing. A real estate agent may want to manage a portfolio of properties using GIS.

Greene (2004) describes how Alan Leidner, the director of GIS for the New York City Department of Information Technology and Telecommunications (DoITT), and his colleagues had to re-create New York's GIS infrastructure from backups in the aftermath of the attacks on September 11, 2001, in order to support emergency response teams with accurate maps of buildings and underground geography. GIS as a support technology for emergency response can prove life-saving in emergencies involving earthquakes, explosions, fires, floods, epidemics, hurricanes, landslides, social unrest (including crime, war, or terrorist attacks), tornados, toxic spills, tsunamis, and volcanos.

Botanical uses for geo-referencing. Beaman and Conn (2003) report on a system able to partially ground records describing animal specimens part of large herbarium collections. It uses a gazetteer of over 330,000 Malesian toponyms extracted from the USGS GNIS gazetteer. Their system, *BioGeoMancer*, is designed as a Web service so that virtually no computing expertise is necessary on the client side. According to them, whereas "Georeferencing provides the means to link specimen data to the rapidly growing body of spatial environmental data for interdisciplinary research into complex phenomena," an estimated 70%-95% of the records in major specimen collection databases have not been geo-referenced yet. Human annotators in the *Mammal Networked Information System* (MaNIS) project, for whose support *BioGeoMancer* was developed, can resolve between 20 to 100 localities per hour. Using 3 collections with sample size $N \approx 10^4$ Beaman and Conn (2003) report 77%-87% to be accurately geo-referenced, with 12%-26% of records left that could not be grounded due to ambiguity despite the spatial restriction imposed (Malaysia only). No distinction between development set and test set is apparent from the exposition. *BioGeoMancer* is also able to produce limited maps of geographical distribution of species, ignoring ambiguous toponyms and relying on a gazetteer limited to Malaysia. Automatic toponym resolution can be expected to increase the percentage of resolved toponyms in such systems. Figure 2.7 mentions some of the spatial language in the collection used.

Location-Based Services. Recently there has been a surge in development of mobile devices, and a lot of usage scenarios have to take into account the geographic position of

Example textual locality	Challenge posed
Wakarusa, 24 mi WSW of Lawrence	Two or more locations descriptors that are not exactly the same place
Moccasin Creek on Hog Island	Topological nesting
Bupo [?Buso] River, *15 miles [24 km] E of Lae*	Complex interpretative description
16 km (by road) N of Murtoa	Linear feature measurement
On the road between Sydney and Bathurst	Linear ambiguity
Southeast Michigan	Vague localities
Yugoslavia	Political borders change over time
British North Borneo	Historical place names

Figure 2.7: Sample locality descriptions from herbarium specimen records from (Beaman and Conn, 2003, page 48).

the mobile user. Consequently, *Location-Based Services* (*LBS*) have emerged as a research field (Küpper (2005)). Typical examples include information systems that allow queries of the type '*where is the nearest X*' (pizza restaurant, petrol station, cinema, copy shop, hotel) or route planners. Address geo-coding and more general toponym resolution provide the basis for making content available that is relevant to a user in a given location.

2.3 Gazetteers

Inventories of toponyms pertaining to a geographic region with descriptions of its social statistics and physical features have been known as *gazetteers*. Essentially, a gazetteer in this sense of the word is a geographic encyclopedia which lists for each place name interesting facts about the location concerned (cf. Munro and Gittings (2006, to appear) for an example).

In contrast, a *short-form gazetteer* (often just called 'gazetteer' for short, sometimes known as an *authority list*) is a more compact collection of place names. Hill (2000) identifies the following three constituents of a short-form gazetteer entry:

- *toponym*: name (of a location), possibly including variants;

- geographical *feature type*: one out of a set of possible classes of place that the name refers to (which may include 'country', 'county', 'city', 'bridge', 'airport' etc.);

- *spatial footprint*: representation of the location (point as latitude/longitude, polygon etc.) referred to by the toponym.

Gazetteer Name	World Wide Web Location
Alexandria Gazetteer	`http://www.alexandria.ucsb.edu/gazetteer`
US CIA World Fact Book	`https://www.cia.gov/cia/publications/factbook/index.html`
Getty Thesaurus of Geographic Names	`http://shiva.pub.getty.edu/tgn_browser/`
US NGA GEOnet Names	`http://164.214.2.59/gns/html/index.html`
Ordnance Survey (OS) 1:50,000 Scale Gazetteer	`http://www.ordnancesurvey.co.uk/oswebsite/products/`
Seamless Administrative Boundaries of Europe (SABE)	`http://www.eurogeographics.org/eng/03_projects_sabe.asp`
United Nations (UNECE) UN-LOCODE	`http://www.unece.org/cefact/`
US Census Gazetteer	`http://www.census.gov/cgi-bin/gazetteer/`
US Geological Survey Geographic Names	`http://www-nmd.usgs.gov/www/gnis/`

Table 2.1: Some gazetteers available in digital form (accessed 2006-08-01).

It is this latter sense of gazetteer that is relevant for this thesis. Table 2.1 gives a synopsis of commonly used (short-form) gazetteers available in digital form.[8]

2.4   Textual Information Access and Natural Language Processing

2.4.1   Digital Libraries

A *digital library* (DL) is an information system that serves the same purpose as a traditional library, but one in which most (often all) of the resources are available in digital form and accessible over a computer network. Edward A. Fox (Witten and Bainbridge, 2003, p. xxii f.) defines the following '5S checklist' for digital libraries:

- Societies: serving the needs of societies, and being used by them;

- Scenarios: support a range of user tasks, including search (data and meta-data) and browsing (navigation for exploration);

- Spaces: resources and people around the globe are supported;

- Structures: data encoding, markup, and meta-data define how the data is represented and stored;

- Streams: processing and preservation of many different kinds of data streams and layers of data, from character strings to audio sequences and complete videos.

---

[8]'Available' here means the resource exists in the online medium. This does not necessarily imply free availability.

The *International Children's Digital Library* (*ICDL*),[9] created by the University of Maryland, is an exemplary digital library that aims to build a large international collection of online versions of books for children from many different cultures (Figure 2.8). It is a good example of meeting the above list of criteria.

Greenstone is a powerful generic system to build digital libraries easily and quickly. It offers the following features (among others) typical of a whole range of more idiosyncratic systems (Witten and Bainbridge, 2003, paraphrasis of a subset of their criteria on p. 26 f.):

- permits full-text and field search: powerful search and sorting capabilities are provided that allow searching multiple indices;

- offers flexible browsing facilities: users can explore lists of authors, titles, structures and so forth;

- makes use of meta-data: standards for meta-data are supported;

- multi-medial: text, images, audio, and video are all supported media types for documents;

- allows hierarchical browsing: hierarchical indices can be navigated interactively; and

- scalable: suitable for collections up to several Gigabytes.[10]

Witten and Bainbridge (2003) is a practical introduction into building digital libraries. However, it does not yet mention search by location.

The connection between digital libraries and the toponym resolution theme is the desire to be able to browse and search documents by geographic space, and the attempt to achieve this goal automatically using computational document analysis rather than by manual creation of spatial meta-data.

2.4.2 Information Retrieval

Whether in digital libraries, on computer file systems or across the World Wide Web (WWW), search is a primary function to cope with the amount of information available. *Information retrieval* (IR) is the discipline that investigates the effective and efficient indexing, storage and retrieval of information. Since the 1950s, the most prevalent form of automatic information retrieval has been *document retrieval*, a task that can be characterised as follows. At *index time*, a *document collection* is processed document by document. For each instance of term, the documents in which it occurs are stored in an *inverted index*. At *retrieval time*, a user encodes an *information need* in a *query*, which gets analysed by the *retrieval system*. Using a *ranking*

---

[9]http://www.childrenslibrary.org/ (accessed 2006-08-21).
[10]http://www.nzdl.org (accessed 2006-08-21).

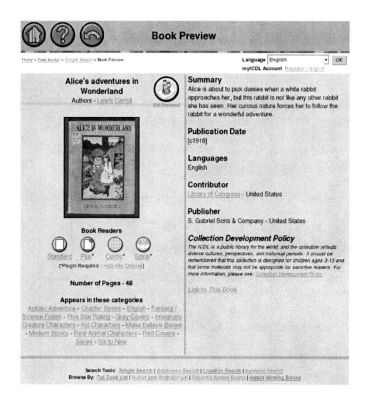

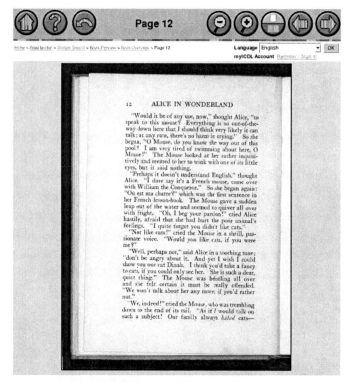

Figure 2.8: The International Children's Digital Library: Meta-data (top) and a sample page

function the system then orders the documents in order of decreasing relevance with respect to the query.

Evaluation. IR has a long record of principled evaluation. Kent et al. (1955) introduced two measures still widely used, Precision (P) and Recall (R), to measure the quality of a ranking function, given a system's output and a set of associated binary relevance judgments:

$$P = \frac{|retrieved\ documents \cap relevant\ documents|}{|retrieved\ documents|} \qquad (2.9)$$

$$R = \frac{|retrieved\ documents \cap relevant\ documents|}{|relevant\ documents|} \qquad (2.10)$$

Building on this work, van Rijsbergen (1979) defined *F-score*, a combined score based on *P* and *R*, providing a convenient single measure of system retrieval quality:

$$F_\beta = \frac{(\beta^2 + 1)PR}{\beta^2 P + R} \qquad (2.11)$$

In Chapter 6, we will define a variant of these measures for toponym resolution.

Geographic IR. A canonical IR system treats all terms equally. The emerging field of *geographic IR* (or *GIR* for short) differs in that the special role of (geographical) space is acknowledged and explicitly modelled as part of the retrieval process.

As Belew points out (Belew, 2000, pp. 238–241):

> In contrast to all the other abstract, disembodied dimensions along which information often barrages a user's screen, place information is special.
> [...]
> People already know what space means, how to interpret it, and how to work within it.

Belew observes further that users also immediately grasp the notion of 'drawing' a spatial query as a supplementary mode of input.

Figure 2.9 shows the geography-aware part of a typical geo-aware IR system (*spatial pipeline*). In this model, *Toponym recognition* and *toponym resolution* are essential processing steps to create meta-data for the documents that encodes the geo-spatial locations and relationships. Some implementations may use two separate indices, a topical index and a geographic index, due to the different nature of textual and geo-spatial data.

For further reading on IR in general, consult Belew (2000) and Baeza-Yates and Ribeiro-Neto (1999), two accessible and comprehensive textbook accounts of the field.

2.4.3 Information Extraction

Information Extraction (*IE*) is the task of identifying and classifying all instances of names and relations—from a given a set of predefined classes—in textual documents (Cowie and Lehnert

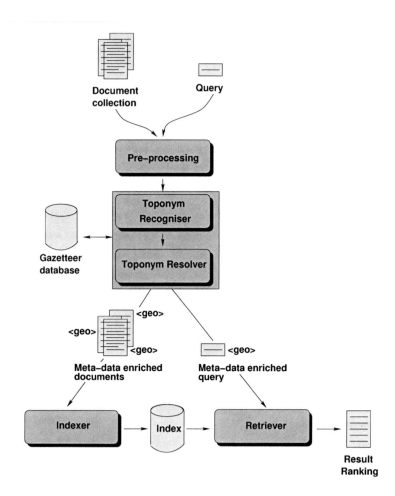

Figure 2.9: Spatial pipeline in a geography-aware retrieval system.

Evaluation	Year	Domain
MUCK-I	1987	Naval Tactical Operations
MUCK-II	1989	Naval Tactical Operations
MUC-3	1991	Latin American Terrorism
MUC-4	*1992*	*Latin American Terrorism* (see Chapter 4)
MUC-5	1993	Joint Ventures/Micro-Electronic Production
MUC-6	1995	Corporate Management Transitions
MUC-7	1998	Plane Crashes (training)
		Air Vehicle Launches (test)

Figure 2.10: Message Understanding Contest history.

(1996)). Whereas types of entities and relations are usually narrowly restricted to a particular application domain, no restrictions are imposed on the texts.

2.4.3.1 Historical Background

Perhaps the earliest effort in extracting information from text was the 'Linguistic String' project at New York University (Sager (1981)). DeJong (1982) developed *FRUMP*, an IE system based on the notion of 'sketchy scripts'. It was also one of the first NLP systems for which a large-scale evaluation was reported based on six days worth of unconstrained news stories. In the late 1980s, a US DARPA-funded series of evaluations with participants from multiple sites on a set of different domains was initiated (Figure 2.10). These Message Understanding Contests (MUCs) defined a shared task for researchers, provided a forum, but also data, gazetteers,[11] and evaluation software (Chinchor (1995, 1998)) for benchmarking the state of the art.

There are several tasks in MUC-style evaluations: the objective of the Named Entity (NE) task is to identify and classify text spans referring atomic entities; Figure 2.11 shows the classes of entities used in MUC-7. These include names of persons (*George W. Bush*), organisations (*UNICEF*), other proper names (*Fido*), locations (*Edinburgh*, *Chile*), temporal expressions (*5:30 GMT*, *seven o'clock*), monetary amounts (*£7.95*), and percent expressions (*17%*). In the Coreference (CO) task, identity, ie NEs referring to the same referent, are to be detected (*Tony Blair ~ Blair ~ he*). In the Template Element (TE) task, attributes of NEs (e.g. LOCATION of the *White House*) descriptive elements such as titles (*Capt.* Kirk) are collected.

---

[11]In information extraction, a 'gazetteer' is typically simply a list of example entities.

ENAMEX	TIMEX	NUMEX
PERSON	DATE	PERCENT
ORGANIZATION	TIME	MONEY
LOCATION		

Figure 2.11: MUC-7 named entity sub-types.

For the purpose of this thesis, toponyms are of course the most relevant class, so we give an example of the way they are marked up here:

```
...

The Prime Minister met leaders of the country in

<ENAMEX TYPE=LOCATION>London</ENAMEX> before heading off to

the summit in <ENAMEX TYPE=LOCATION>Italy</ENAMEX>

...
```

In the Template Relation (TR) task, systems have to build factoids (relations, facts, predications) from combinations of entities and relation types, such as EMPLOYEE_OF (e.g. Bush EMPLOYEE_OF US Government). Finally, the Scenario Template (ST) task then glues together the template relations to form complex relationships that are directly defined by the task: if joint ventures are chosen as a domain, then whenever a joint venture is announced, this can be seen as an instance of a two-place relation between two organisation between which a certain Template Relation holds.

2.4.3.2 Methods

Shallow Processing. How does the typical MUC-style IE system work? Initially, several approaches entered the competition. But a crucial development was SRI's move for MUC-4 from *TACITUS* (Hobbs (1986)), a 'deep' text understanding system based on syntactic analysis and abductive inference, to *FASTUS* (Hobbs (1992); Appelt et al. (1993)), a lightweight system based on cascaded Finite State Transducers (FST), a pattern-based approach that required much less built-in knowledge. In *FASTUS*, first a text segmentation step divides the document into regions and sentences; each word token is paired up with lexical attributes and part-of-speech. A part-of-speech (POS) tag is a label that marks the morpho-syntactic category in a particular context in which they occur. For instance, in the sentence *He can can the can*, the analysis

```
        He_PRP can_MD can_VB the_DT can_NN ._.
```

means that 'He' is a personal pronoun (PRP), the first 'can' is a modal auxiliary verb (MD), the second 'can' is a full verb (VB), 'the' is a determiner/article (DT), and the last 'can' is a common noun (NN). A program that can compute POS tags is called a *POS tagger.*

A simple keyword trigger condition then filters out all sentences that do not contain any pattern words and are thus not relevant. A *chunker* identifies base noun phrase (like *the former home secretary*) and verb groups (such as *has been forced to resign*). After this, a shallow *parser* constructs a set of parse tree fragments, which describe the sentences. A fragment combiner merges the parse tree fragments (with their associated logical form fragments) into larger sentence units. From these, a semantic interpretation module tries to derive a logical form of a sentence or fragment. A lexical disambiguation step is applied to predicates in the logical form. Thereafter, co-referential entity references are linked together. A fragment combiner subsequently produces logical form fragments. Finally, a template generator produces the format required by the MUC judgment software. The SRI team ranked second best with *FASTUS*, which was developed in a very short time, and the shallow techniques performed well while speeding up runtime from 36 hours (for 100 MUC-3 texts) to 12 minutes (for 100 MUC-4 texts). Soon this type of system served as the canonical architecture, and IE was established as a mainstream field within NLP research.

Supervised Machine Learning.   Rule-based approaches together with the domain specificity still required an unfortunate amount of skilled manual labour, which led to research on machine learning, i.e. automatic induction using generalisation from annotated examples (*supervised learning*) and automatic techniques for the acquisition of rules via *bootstrapping* from a few seed examples (Riloff and Jones (1999)). The most popular techniques employed include *Hidden Markov Models* (Zheng and Su (2002)) and *Maximum Entropy* (*MaxEnt*) classification (Borthwick et al. (1998); Curran and Clark (2003b)).

Hybrid NERC and DCA.   The most accurate system in the MUC-7 NE task, the University of Edinburgh Language Technology Group (LTG)'s *LT TTT* system, used a five-pass processing regime comprising a mixture of rules and MaxEnt classification (Mikheev et al. (1999); Grover et al. (2000)). First, so-called 'sure-fire rules' are applied, followed by a partial match phase, which creates all possible partial orders to find variants in organisation names, and applies maximum entropy classification to all the candidates, taking into account a wide range of capitalisation, local contextual, per-document, and other features. Then rules are relaxed and re-applied, followed by a second MaxEnt pass. In a final step titles are handled, since they often deserve special treatment due to unique capitalisation conventions. The system is an example of the *Document Centered Approach* (*DCA*), i.e. document-global evidence is used for local consideration in a later phase. This idea is also relevant for the processing of toponyms.

Evaluation/ Task	Named Entity	Co-reference	Template Element	Template Relation	Scenario Template
MUC-3					$R < 50\%$
					$P < 70\%$
MUC-4					$F < 56\%$
MUC-5					$F < 53\%$
MUC-6	$F < 97\%$	$R < 63\%$	$F < 80\%$		$F < 57\%$
		$P < 72\%$			
MUC-7	$F < 94\%$	$F < 62\%$	$F < 87\%$	$F < 76\%$	$F < 51\%$
MET-1	$F < 85\%$ (Chinese)				
	$F < 93\%$ (Japanese)				
MET-2	$F < 91\%$ (Chinese)				
	$F < 87\%$ (Japanese)				

Table 2.2: MUC/MET: achieved performance (modified after Chinchor 1998).

2.4.3.3 Evaluation

In MUC and most of the following experiments using its data, scoring was done using precision, recall and F-measure. Table 2.2 gives some indicators of the quality levels achieved.
More recently, the Conference on Natural Language Learning (CoNLL) has offered a 'shared
task', an open evaluation exercise in named entity tagging (Tjong Kim Sang and De Meulder
(2003)). The US DARPA 'ACE' programme U.S. NIST (2003) also contains a named entity
evaluation, which (unlike MUC and CoNLL) distinguishes between toponyms as physical features on the one hand, and geo-political entities (GPEs, such as country names) on the other
hand. Unfortunately, the ACE initiative is not very open regarding dissemination of research
results.

2.4.3.4 Challenges and Research Directions

The following list of problems are currently receiving a lot of interest in the IE community:

- how to extend IE from relatively few types of coarse-granular Named Entities to more
  NE types (e.g. Fleischman and Hovy (2002); Sekine et al. (2002));

- how to learn a hierarchical organisation of entity classes (*ontology*) automatically from
  un-annotated text (Mädche (2002));

- how to identify named entities, relations and events across documents (Bagga and Baldwin (1999); Masterson and Kushmerick (2003));

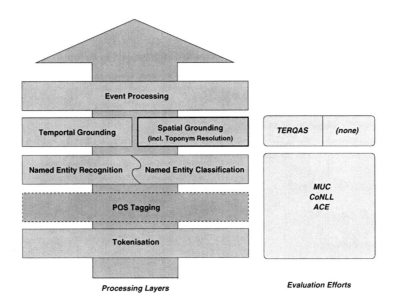

Figure 2.12: Toponym resolution as an additional NE processing layer.

- how to rapidly construct IE systems for minority languages in the face of extreme knowledge/resource bottlenecks. For example, in the US DARPA 'TIDES' Surprise Language Task (Oard et al. (2003)), a whole set of applications, including POS taggers, parsers, NE taggers, summarisers, machine translators etc. was to be built within 30 days for languages such as Cebuano and Hindi;

- how to ground unconstrained text in space and time; currently, most research is on temporal processing, especially in the TERQAS project within the US DARPA 'AQUAINT' programme (see Setzer (2001); Pustejovsky and Mani (2003) for the development of a recent temporal markup scheme, on which subsequent efforts will build). At the time of writing, work on spatial annotation has been begun by the same research group,[12] and it will be interesting to see how spatial and textual processing can improve the interpretation of events in the long run.

The last problem is of course central to this thesis. Toponym resolution can be seen as an extension to current NERC that adds a grounding layer to the processing (Figure 2.12). However, unlike NERC, TR does not have an established evaluation exercise yet. It is hoped that the benchmark for the task as defined in this thesis can contribute to the efforts to eventually bring together researchers to compare their systems.

---

[12]Personal communication, Inderjeet Mani (2006-05-15).

2.4.4   Question Answering

Automatic *question answering* (*Q&A*) is concerned with providing the user with results of a finer granularity than the document level used in document retrieval systems. Q&A systems take a query in question form as input, e.g.

- *Who is the president of Austria?*,

- *When was Leonardo da Vinci born?*, or

- *Where is Guadalupe?*

and return, if successful,

- *Heinz Fischer*,

- *April 15, 1452*, or

- *North of Mexico City (Mexico)*, respectively.

There is a technical distinction between Q&A systems that retrieve answers from structured databases (*database Q&A*) and those systems that extract answers from text collections. We will concentrate on the latter here. Another distinction can be made between domain-specific systems and open-domain systems. Since space is a universal physical property, we will look at systems without restrictions to a particular domain.

2.4.4.1   Historical Background

The accomplishment of having built the earliest textual question answering system can perhaps be attributed to A. V. Philips, who developed the system *The Oracle*[13] in LISP under the supervision of John McCarthy (Philips (1960)). The *BASEBALL* system (Green et al. (1961)) is an early prototype in the sports domain. Simmons presents a meta-algorithm (Algorithm 1), which still resembles in spirit the core of some current systems (Simmons (1973)).[14] Within the DARPA-funded TIPSTER programme, the Text Retrieval Conference (TREC) carried out annually by the US National Institute of Standards and Technology (NIST) established a 'question answering track', in which international research groups can evaluate their Q&A systems in a comparable setting (Voorhees and Tice (1999); Voorhees and Harman (2005)). Starting with TREC-8, participating sites were delivered a collection of text documents. The initial task was to find a set of strings (50 and 250 characters long, respectively) that best answer a list of questions, and to submit the five best answer candidates the system can determine. Questions were partially hand-crafted, partially taken from the *FAQ Finder* logfile (a retrieval

---

[13]Not to be confused with the RMDBMS vendor with a similar name.

[14]See Appendix A for notational conventions used for describing algorithms in this thesis.

system from 'Frequently Asked Questions' collections found on the Internet). A ranked score was then computed based on the correctness, which was defined by the matching of a set of regular expressions against answer strings describing the gold-standard answers as given in the collection and prepared by NIST. For subsequent TREC Q&A tracks, the precise answer had to be returned. The series of TREC evaluations spurred interest in question answering.

Algorithm 1 Simmons' Meta-Algorithm for Question Answering.

1: **Accumulate** the semantic representation for each sentence.

2: **Select** a relevant subset, where relevancy is measure by lexical concept overlap between question and answer.

3:

4: **for all** answer candidates **do**

5:     {**Match** question and answer}

6:     **if** question head verb matches head verb of answer candidate **then**

7:         proceed analogously for the other question words so as to map the question representation into the form of the answer candidate.

8:         match quantifiers, tense and negation

9:         determine whether the answer satisfies the question type

10:     **else**

11:         **if** not(recursion limit reached) **then**

12:             return current answer candidate

13:         **else**

14:             return without answer

15:         **end if**

16:     **end if**

17: **end for**

2.4.4.2 Methods

Figure 2.13 shows the architecture of the University of Edinburgh's *QED* (Leidner et al. (2004)), a state-of-the art Q&A system.[15] Like many other systems, it follows a standard model (Hirshman and Gaizauskas (2001)): firstly, the question is classified into one or more semantic classes according to a pre-defined taxonomy. Then questions are syntactically parsed. From the obtained representations, an IR query is constructed. A number of documents are retrieved, which are then segmented. The segments are ranked, and the top-ranked segments are parsed to construct a quasi-logical form that represents their meanings. Answer candidates are extracted, and questions are matched against each candidate, obtaining a score; a variety

---

[15]A version of *QED* obtained the tenth rank in the world in the TREC 2005 Q&A track.

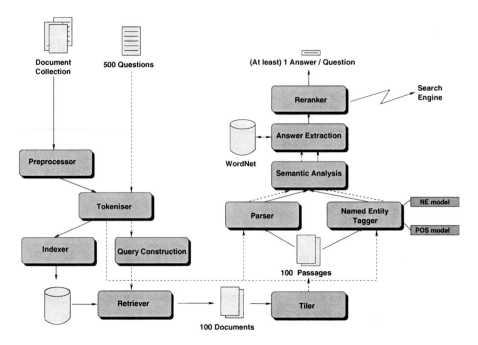

Figure 2.13: The *QED* Q&A system architecture (Leidner et al. (2004)).

of matching strategies is used. The result is a ranked list of answer candidates which can be
directly output, but is often re-ranked using heuristics, filters, or statistical machine learning.
NERC plays a key role in constraining the number of answer candidates by imposing an answer
type derived from the question class.

Q&A and Spatial Reasoning. *QUARK* (Waldinger et al. (2004)) is a deductive Q&A
system comprising a theorem prover that integrates several external knowledge sources, including the Alexandria Gazetteer, the CIA World Factbook, as well as procedural knowledge (Web
services) such as for coordinate conversion.[16] It can translate a natural language question into
a first-order logic query, for which the theorem prover tries to find a solution using the knowledge sources. The theorem prover uses both topological relationships and geographic distance,
but toponym resolution is *not* performed by the system, so a full (manual) qualification like
Springfield, IL, US is required from the user.[17]

Note that the setup of the TREC Q&A track is formulated as an *answer extraction* task.
Unfortunately this means that if more advanced (knowledge-based) methods that can *infer*

---

[16]There also exists a special version focusing on geographic reasoning called *GeoLogica* (Waldinger et al.
(2003)).

[17]Personal communication, Richard Waldinger (2006-08-27).

answers (like those in *QUARK*) lead to quality improvements in Q&A, then they cannot be assessed by a TREC-style evaluation, which expects all answers to be found explicitly in the documents.

2.4.4.3 Future Directions

In the USA, the ARDA AQUAINT programme, a US DARPA initiative, has produced a roadmap for Q&A research (Maybury, 2004, p. 13), which suggests, among other topics, the investigation of

- models for question processing (understanding, ambiguity, implicatures, reformulation);

- models of context and user (model interests, habits and intentions);

- Q&A against heterogeneous data sources;

- multilinguality;

- interactivity (dialogue models for Q&A);

- use of advanced reasoning; and

- temporal questions.

Interestingly, spatial questions are not part of this agenda, but we will return to them in Chapter 7.

2.4.5 Word Sense Disambiguation

Automatic Word Sense Disambiguation (WSD) is the task of classifying polysemous words according to an inventory of candidate senses (i.e., different possible meanings), given a particular context. For example, the word *bank* can denote different concepts in

(1) *He walked his dog along the <u>bank</u> of the Thames.* (river bank)

(2) *She deposited all her savings at the small <u>bank</u> branch nearby.* (monetary institution)
However, the boundaries between different senses are by no means clear. Lesk (1986)'s paper sub-titled 'how to tell a pine cone from an ice cream cone' exposes the problem: on first sight, an ice cream cone is part of some sweet type of food, whereas a pine cone is part of a plant. However, a critic might rightly argue that the word 'cone' itself merely describes a shape, and both types of cones indeed share aspects of shape.

One of the problems of WSD is low agreement on senses by humans. Véronis (2003) found that human taggers using dictionaries as a reference perform poorly on the WSD task. Comparing subjects, Cohen's Kappa (κ), a measure for inter-annotator agreement that factors out agreement by chance (Krippendorf (1980)), was found to be low ($\kappa = 0.49$), and Véronis rightly criticised that the question of human agreement had not been properly addressed:

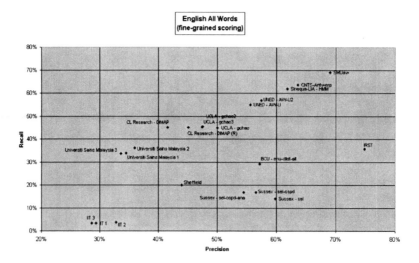

Figure 2.14: SENSEVAL3: the majority of systems performed between 40% and 70% precision and recall.

> [C]omputerisation of this task has yielded very modest results despite numerous efforts. [...] I find it extremely surprising, however, that an entire field of research can develop without a clear view of human performance in the area. (Véronis (2003))

I concur with this view, and unfortunately the same holds for toponym resolution. However, for TR this issue will be addressed in Chapter 4.

SENSEVAL. Since 1998, a series of open WSD evaluations has been carried out in order to benchmark the task under comparable conditions, namely the SENSEVAL exercise (Kilgarriff and Rosenzweig (2000)). SENSEVAL addressed the lack of inter-annotator agreement by defining a task setting in which agreement could be shown to be 88% or higher by choosing professional lexicographers as annotators, who would first be allowed to assign multiple senses to each word, and an arbitration phase in which a second-level annotator would settle cases of disagreement. At SENSEVAL-3, the third evaluation in the ongoing series, Snyder and Palmer (2004) report that human inter-annotator agreement was 72.5% and that already

> the best systems have hit a wall in the 65%-70% range. This is not surprising given the typical inter-annotator agreement of 70%-75% for this task. (Snyder and Palmer (2004))

Figure 2.14[18] shows that no single system performed at F=70% or higher, and that only three systems exceed an F-score of 60%. In Chapter 4, we will see how humans and algorithms can perform in the toponym resolution task in comparison.

Methods. Here, the main algorithms that have emerged in the field are briefly surveyed since WSD is similar to toponym resolution, and so it comes as no surprise that some heuristics from WSD have been applied to TR as well, as we shall see in the next chapter. In this section, I will closely follow the exposition in (Manning and Schütze, 1999, Chapter 7). Knowledge of elementary probability theory is assumed (DeGroot and Schervish (2001)). Below, w denotes an ambiguous word, s_k a sense of w, c_i the i-th context word of w in a corpus and v_j words used as contextual features for disambiguation.

2.4.5.1 Bayesian WSD

Algorithm 2 Bayesian WSD, after (Manning and Schütze, 1999, p. 238).

1: **[Training.]**
2: **for** all senses s_k of w **do**
3:     **for** all words v_j in the vocabulary **do**
4:         $P(v_j|s_k) := \frac{C(v_j, s_k)}{C(v_j)}$
5:     **end for**
6: **end for**
7: **for** all senses s_k of w **do**
8:     $P(s_k) := \frac{C(s_k)}{C(w)}$
9: **end for**
10: **[Disambiguation.]**
11: **for** all senses s_k of w **do**
12:     $score(s_k) := \log P(s_k)$
13:     **for** all words v_j in the context window c **do**
14:         $score(s_k) := score(s_k) + \log P(v_j|s_k)$
15:     **end for**
16: **end for**
17: choose $s' := \arg\max_{s_k} score(s_k)$
18: return s'

The *Naïve Bayes Classifier* (*NBC*) for WSD is a decision procedure that takes into account a context vector of words around a certain word which is to be disambiguated and uses it as evidence to select a sense. The selection is carried out by applying *Bayes decision rule*, which maximises the probability of the correct class and can be proven to minimise the error of misclassification, but under the simplifying assumption of conditional independence (Duda et al., 2000, pp. 20–27). Since the independence assumption is violated in the case of natural

---

[18]http://www.senseval.org (cited 2006-08-29).

language sentences, where words of course *do* depend on one another, the actual performance depends on the *degree* of the violation of the assumption. However, in practice the Bayes classifier has shown to be a baseline that is often surprisingly hard to beat by more sophisticated methods. In a training phase, the sense probabilities (lines 7-9) and the conditional probabilities of the vocabulary words, given the senses (lines 2-5), are estimated by simple counting (*maximum likelihood estimation*).[19] This is usually done only once in an offline stage.[20] The disambiguation proper then iterates over the senses (lines 11-16) and computes the best word sense, i.e. the candidate that maximises (line 17) a score, defined as the product of the individual feature probabilities. Multiplication is allowed under the independence assumption, and in practice addition of the logarithms of the probabilities is used instead of multiplication so as to avoid rounding errors caused by floating point representation imprecision (line 13).

2.4.5.2 Dictionary-Based WSD

Lesk (1986) pioneered the use of dictionary definitions for WSD (Algorithm 3). He used a 10-word window c and counted word overlap (line 3) between the text window and each of the various senses in the dictionary (lines 2-4). D_k stands for the set of words comprising the dictionary definition of sense s_k, and E_{v_j} is the union set of all definitions of v_j. Then the sense/dictionary definition s' with the maximum overlap count is chosen (lines 5-6).

Algorithm 3 Dictionary-Based WSD.

1: Given a context c

2: **for** all senses s_k of w **do**

3:      $score(s_k) := overlap(D_k, \bigcup_{v_j \in c} E_{v_j})$

4: **end for**

5: $s' := \arg\max_{s_k} score(s_k)$

6: return s'

2.4.5.3 Yarowsky's Algorithm

The Yarowsky algorithm (Yarowsky (1995); Gale et al. (1993), Algorithm 4[21]) is shown at work in three snapshots of the various stages in Figure 2.15. It comprises three phases, an initialisation (lines 1-7), the application of the 'one sense per collocation' heuristic (lines 8-16) and the application of the 'one sense per discourse' heuristic (lines 17-21). In the beginning, a set of *seeds* are used to inform an otherwise unsupervised method (lines 2-4). For each sense s_k,

---

[19]To avoid the problem that a single probability of 0 results in a product of 0, redistribution of probability mass from seen to unseen events (*smoothing*) is usually applied.

[20]Except in applications where dynamic adaptivity is required, such as email spam classification.

[21]Cited after (Manning and Schütze, 1999, p. 252).

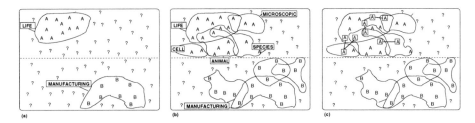

Figure 2.15: Yarowsky's algorithm at work: (a) initial state, (b) intermediate state, (c) final state (Yarowsky, 1995, p. 191-2).

two sets E_k and F_k and are maintained: E_k is the set of context windows of the ambiguous word w that are currently assigned to s_k and is initially empty (lines 5-7). F_k is a set of collocations from dictionary definitions that contain the collocates with the sense label corresponding to the headword in the collocation's definition. F_k is used to tag all training examples. For example, if *plant life* is a collocation in the dictionary definition of *plant*, then tag all occurrences of *plant* followed by *life* with the LIFE label (sense A in Figure 2.15(a)). Similarly, if *manufacturing plant* is a collocation in the dictionary definition of (one sense of) plant, then tag instances of of *plant* preceeded by *manufacturing* with a second sense label, MANUFACTURING (B in Figure 2.15(a)). This step will leave over 80% of *plant* occurrences untagged ('?' in the figure). In the main iteration (lines 9-16) of this *fixpoint algorithm*,[22] the seed training instances are used to train (lines 10-12) a *Decision List classifier* (Rivest (1987)), which is then used to find further collocations that reliably partition seed training data, ranked by log likelihood (line 14). This classifier is then applied to the whole set of samples (lines 13-15). The seed set is extended with those samples from the residual set whose likelihood exceeds a threshold α (line 14). Next, for all instances of words w that are still ambiguous, the majority interpretation is assigned to them (lines 18-21), which corresponds to the application of the 'one sense per discourse heuristic'. Applying this heuristic can bridge sub-clusters (i.e. connect existing and new collocations that may not otherwise share a context with collocations previously included in the training set), as depicted in Figure 2.15(b) by the instances in square boxes connecting various sense sub-clusters. Finally, once the bootstrapping process has converged (Figure 2.15(c)), the induced classifier can be applied to new, untagged data. While Yarowsky (1995) reports performance figure for his semi-supervised method that rival supervised methods (accuracy above the 90% band), a very serious drawback of these experiments is the simplification of the task: Yarowsky's experiments induce merely a binary classifier, i.e. the resulting decision procedure

---

[22]A fixpoint algorithm is an algorithm that contains a loop the body of which gets executed repeatedly until no changes to an object occur.

is only able to discriminate between exactly two senses for all words investigated, not all of them. To the best of my knowledge, to date the method has not yet been shown to scale up to more realistic task settings.

Algorithm 4 Yarowsky's algorithm.

1: **[Initialize.]**

2: **for** all senses s_k of w **do**

3:     $F_k := \{$ the set of collocations in s_k's dictionary definition $\}$

4: **end for**

5: **for** all senses s_k of w **do**

6:     $E_k := \emptyset$

7: **end for**

8: **[One-sense-per-collocation.]**

9: **while** at least one E_k changed in the last iteration **do**

10:    **for** all senses s_k of w **do**

11:        $E_k := \{c_i | \exists f_m : f_m \in e_i \wedge f_m \in F_k\}$

12:    **end for**

13:    **for** all senses s_k of w **do**

14:        $F_k := \{f_m | \forall n \neq k \wedge \frac{P(s_k|f_m)}{P(s_n|f_m)} > \alpha\}$

15:    **end for**

16: **end while**

17: **[One-sense-per-discourse.]**

18: **for** all documents d_m **do**

19:    determine the majority sense s_k of w in d_m

20:    assign all occurrences of w in d_m to s_k

21: **end for**

In theory, WSD could help with a large array of tasks, including machine translation (selecting the right word in the target language depends on the sense of the word in the source language), information retrieval (filtering out the ice cream cone when looking for pine cones) etc. However, as Sanderson (1994) shows in a simulation experiment, WSD methods would actually have to perform better than F=90% for WSD to improve IR, which is unfortunately beyond the state of the art. Furthermore, many tasks including IR carry out a certain level of WSD implicitly.

See Ide and Véronis (1998) for a broad survey of the methods used in WSD and the state of the art before the arrival of SENSEVAL, as well as Snyder and Palmer (2004) for a more recent performance overview in the context of the SENSEVAL-3 evaluation.

2.5 The Language of Geographic Space

Semantics of Names. In Leech's popular 'seven types of meaning' taxonomy (Leech, 1981, p. 126), the question of *reference* cuts across the two types CONCEPTUAL MEANING[23] and CONNOTATIVE MEANING[24] (*ibd.*, p. 12), and proper names (which include toponyms as a special case) are simply labels that have no CONCEPTUAL MEANING, because no componential analysis can be performed for them. This also holds for toponyms, but in fact many place names are at least meaningful etymologically speaking (e.g. *Edin·burgh* = burrough of Edina, the city's ancient Roman name; *Cam·bridge* = bridge over the river Cam), whether or not this etymology is apparent to the user of the language or not.

Toponyms. Names for places, whether they are cities or whole countries, exhibit their own idiosyncracies and thus deserve a special treatment. On the one hand, coordinates on the globe can be used to represent the *extensional semantics* of a place, and the availability of world-coverage gazetteers makes the creation of a candidate pool for reference resolution easier than the difficult demarcation of different word senses (like in the *cone* example), but on the hand places other undergo frequent change.

Toponym Variability and Change. Toponyms and the locations they refer to are not constant. Because places are territorial and therefore political entities, boundaries of locations change due to mergers, separatist movements and wars. For example, Germany has changed its size and shape during the 20th century several times. After reorganisation places are often renamed to reflect the new political situation. For example, as O'Brien points out (O'Brien, 2003, p. 342), *Tsaritisyn* was changed into *Stalingrad* (which in Tartar means 'town on the Yellow River'). The Eastern German city of *Chemnitz* was known in German Democratic Republic times as *Karl-Marx-Stadt*, a change that was reversed after four decades. Some cities now in Poland and mentioned in the MALACH corpus have been reported to have had their country affiliation changed more than five times within a few years around World War II.[25] The same location is often known by different names, including short forms, local variants, and of course different transliterations of *exonyms*, names from countries where a different language is the norm (*Praha* instead of the *endonym Prague*, from an English perspective).

Ambiguity and Vagueness. In a geospatial context, there are at least three types of *ambiguity*:

- *discord*: the lack of agreement due to territorial dispute between nations or disparate definitions of geographic terms by national geographic agencies (for instance, at the time of writing, there are territorial disputes over Palestine, Kashmir, the Himalaya etc).

---

[23]CONCEPTUAL MEANING: logical, cognitive or denotative content.
[24]CONNOTATIVE MEANING: What is communicated by virtue of what language refers to.
[25]Personal communication, Douglas Oard (2005-09-23).

- *non-specificity*: lack of preciseness as to which definition is being used. For example, as Longley and colleagues point out, 'A is north of B' does without further explication potentially invoke one of three notions of NORTH−OF:

    - A lies on the same line of longitude as B, but closer to the north pole then B, or

    - A lies somewhere to the north of a line running east to west through B, or

    - A lies in the sector between north-east and north-west, most likely even north-north-east and north-north-west of B, which corresponds to the common language usage (Longley et al., 1999, vol. 1, p. 198).

- *linguistic ambiguity*:

    - *morpho-syntactic ambiguity*. A token/word may constitute a toponym or it may not be a name at all but belong to another word-class: e.g. *He is driving to Democrat.* (toponym; referring to Democrat, NC, USA) versus *She's a democrat.* (common noun denoting a political orientation, i.e. non-toponym);

    - *feature type ambiguity*. The same toponym can refer to more than one type of feature: e.g. *Ireland* (the GPE, i.e. the short form for the Republic of Ireland) versus *Ireland* (the island); and

    - *referential ambiguity*. A name does not uniquely refer to a location: e.g. *London* (the city in England, UK) versus *London* (the city in Ontario, Canada). This is, of course, the phenomenon that is dealt with in this thesis.

Amitay et al. (2004) call the first type *geo/non-geo ambiguity* and the other two cases *geo/geo ambiguity*. Table 2.3 has some more examples of geo-geo and geo/non-geo ambiguity.

Ambiguity is different from *vagueness*, e.g. the intrinsic impossibility to assign precise boundaries to continuous phenomena in the physical world (where does a mountain end?), but unfortunately, quite often the two notions are not properly distinguished. Or, to give an example from the language side, the phrase 'near X' does not exactly specify spatial distance in metres, and is further relative to the size of the entities related by the expression (compare 'near the shed in the garden' versus 'near New York').

Metonymy. Language use is often non-literal. *Metonymy* is a figure of speech whereby a word is substituted by another in a way so as to denote a more complex concept by a simpler, but related one. An example in journalistic prose is 'Washington (said) ...', which refers to the US government (which at the time of writing happens to reside in Washington, DC, USA) rather than claiming the place itself to be able to speak. Whether metonymic toponyms in documents should be resolved or ignored depends on the application.

Type of Ambiguity	Candidate 1	Candidate 2
Geo/Geo Ambiguity	*Aberdeen, Scotland, UK*	*Aberdeen, Jamaica*
	Edinburgh, Scotland, UK	*Edinburgh, Trista Da Cunha, UK*
	Cambridge, England, UK	*Cambridge, South Africa*
	Boston, England, UK	*Boston, MA, USA*
Geo/Non-Geo Ambiguity	*In, Thailand*	*in* (preposition)
	Over, Germany	*over* (preposition)
	Of, Turkey	*of* (preposition)
	Dog, Korea	*dog* (noun) animal
	Ball, Syria	*ball* (noun) toy
	Orange, Lithuania	*orange* (adjective) colour

Table 2.3: Examples for geo/geo and geo/non-geo ambiguity.

There are different types of metonymic use of toponyms. Markert and Nissim (2002) provide an English corpus and associated study of metonymy. For toponyms the cases 'literal', 'place for event', 'place for people' and 'place for product' are distinguished. In an $N = 1000$ sample, 74% of all toponyms are literal, 16% are of type 'place for people', and only 0.3% are 'place for event'. 'place for product' is not found at all (the remainder constitute toponyms with mixed types). Table 2.4 contains some example cases of 'place for event' compiled from O'Brien (2003). To ensure functional communication, the hearer must share knowledge of the event with the speaker in order to be able to process the metonymy.

Formal Representations. If we want to be able to reason over the spatial aspects of what has been said, we need an appropriate representational device for space, especially its topological underpinnings. Furthermore, the meaning of linguistic expressions need to be formally analysed and encoded (Kracht (2004)) in order to be represented and processed by computers. For example Gapp and Maass (1994) implement a system capable of navigating in a 3-dimensional virtual space based on the user's verbal spatial route directions. Technically meaning is mostly modelled using a customised form of logic. Past work (e.g. Cohn et al. (1997); Randell et al. (1992)) has resulted in a family of definitions of an *interval logic* called *Region Connection Calculus* (*RCC*), which is suitable for representation and reasoning about space and topology. It uses spatial regions as individuals and is based on the single primitive, dyadic, reflexive[26] and symmetric[27] relation $C(x,y)$, read as 'x connects with y'. In its simplest

---

[26] Axiom: $\forall x : C(x,x)$.
[27] Axiom: $\forall x : \forall y : [C(x,y) \rightarrow C(y,x)]$.

Toponym	Location	Time	Event
Amritsar	India	1984	Sikh extremists take over Golden Temple in a move to strive for independence
Arnhem	Netherlands	1944	British troops under Gen. Montgomery fail to take the bridge of Arnem in a move losing nearly 80% of the UK forces involved
Bhopal	India	1984	Over 3,000 people die in chemical havoc resulting from an act of sabotage by a disgruntled chemical worker
Chernobyl	Ukraine	1986	Explosive and massive radioactive fallout result from ignorance of nuclear power plant management
Dachau	Germany	1933	First Nazi concentration camp opens
Dunblane	United Kindom	1996	Gunman kills teacher and her 15 pupils at school massacre
El Alamein	Egypt	1942	British Gen. Montgomery defeats German army under Gen. Rommel in a key battle
Fatima	Portugal	1916	Three children experiencing a religious vision
Gettysburg	USA	1863	Abraham Lincoln delivers his address
Guernica	Spain	1937	Nazi Condor Legion targets civilians in Basque carpet bombing
Hastings	United Kingdom	1066	The Norman William the Conqueror takes the British throne after winning key battle
Hiroshima	Japan	1945	USA drop first nuclear bomb, killing 280,000
Lockerbie	United Kingdom	1988	297 plane passengers die in bomb attack
Lourdes	France	1858	14-year-old Bernadette Soubirious reports repeated visions of Mary
Pearl Habor	USA	1941	Japanese surprise attack on Hawaii kills 2,400 and causes the US to enter WWII
Srbrenica	Bosnia and Herzegovina	1995	Dutch UN troops fail to prevent the genocide of several thousand Muslims by Bosnian Serbs
Stalingrad	Russia	1941	Hitler's army gets trapped and defeated by Stalin's army and the Russian winter
Trafalgar	Spain	1805	Admiral Nelson defeats the Spanish Armada in battle costing 7,770 lives
Versailles	France	1918	Key WWI peace treaty
Waco	USA	1993	US Bureau of Alcohol, Tobacco and Firearms' attempt to storm building occupied by 'Branch Davidian' sect results in nearly 100 casualties
Woodstock	USA	1969	450,000 gather for '3 days of peace and music'

Table 2.4: Examples of place-for-event metonymy.

form (RCCS8), 8 basic relations are defined, e.g. $DC(x,y) \equiv \neg C(x,y)$ (read: x disconnected from y), $P(x,y) \equiv \forall z : [C(z,x) \rightarrow C(z,y)]$ (read: x is a part of y), $O(x,y) \equiv \exists z : [P(z,x) \land P(y,z)]$ (read: x overlaps y), and so forth.

However, current implemented spatial reasoning systems do not yet scale up to global coverage; they are still 'micro worlds', a barrier which needs to be remedied if reasoning is to support and improve the handling of world wide GIS datasets, including the georeferenced text collections of the digital libaries of the future.

See Olivier and Gapp (1998) for a representative cross-section of recent work in computational handling of the spatial dimension. Jessen (1975) contains a comprehensive analysis of spatial expressions in English. Svorou (1994) is an account of space in a cognitive semantics framework. Last but not least, taking a wider perspective, Tuan (1977) deals with the spatial dimension and its effects on human experience, including themes like space and the human body, place and child development, space and architectural awareness, the role of places in mythology, attachment to homeland and human belonging.

2.6 Chapter Summary

In this chapter, the background has been laid for the rest of the thesis by introducing some basic notions ranging from geographic information systems over word sense disambiguation to digital libraries and natural language processing.

The fact that this thesis crosses the boundaries between GIS and NLP has some consequences for the presentation. Firstly, experts in either field will probably feel that the above presentation states the obvious. However, there are very few people who are equally acquainted with both the worlds of geographic information systems and the world of natural language processing, and I hope this fact justifies the presentational approach taken. And secondly, for reasons of lack of space, the descriptions of the various topics could barely scratch the surface. However, pointers to literature in each section will hopefully compensate for this. The subsequent chapters will gradually make it clear why the various background topics were covered and how they support or contribute to the argument of this thesis.

Chapter 3

Previous and Related Work

[Parts of of this chapter have been published in the technical report Leidner (2006e).]

3.1 Processing of Geographic References

In this chapter, I review previous work in toponym resolution (TR) and related work in the area of processing of geographic references. I will point out weaknesses in these early approaches, notably the absence of a rigid evaluation procedure (on a held-out test set), and I will collect types of sources of evidence that have been used to solve the task. I then relate them in a taxonomy, and this inventory will help later to quantify the contribution of individual knowledge sources and heuristics, and to recombine them in a novel, superior method.

In this thesis, I am interested in fine-grained processing on the level of the individual toponym. However, we start out by describing an early project, in which a geographic characterisation on the *document level* rather than on the level of the individual geographic reference was attempted. Woodruff and Plaunt (1994) are interested in improving *document* retrieval, where a per-*document geographic focus* is sufficient, whereas in this thesis evaluation *per toponym* (i.e., on a sub-document level) is presented. One interesting ultimate objective behind attempting spatial resolution per toponym instance is to enhance finer-grained (again, sub-document level) tasks such as open-domain answer retrieval.

Woodruff and Plaunt (1994): Geographic Focus for GIR. The *Sequoia 2000* digital library project and system for the Earth sciences (Larson et al. (1995); Larson (2003)) investigated storage, indexing, retrieval and browsing of geographic documents based on integrating the *POSTGRES* relational database management system with a full-text IR engine. In this context, Woodruff and Plaunt describe the *GIPSY* sub-system for automatic geo-referencing of text Woodruff and Plaunt (1994), whereby a *geographic focus* is computed per document in order to be able to carry out geographically constrained information retrieval of environmental science abstracts about California.

Algorithm 3.1 outlines the mechanism (see Appendix A for a description of the notation used). First, toponyms are identified in the text using the gazetteer (line 1), and associated sets of polygons representing the candidate referents are looked up (line 2). For each candidate shape (lines 4-15), the two-dimensional (i.e. 'flat') polygon representing one location (shown in Figure 3.1 (a) in the column on the left side of the arrows) is extended by a third (z-)dimension so as to become a *polytope* (Figure 3.1 (a), right-hand side column of the arrow). The polytopes representing all candidate referents are now dropped on an initially empty map (Algorithm 3.1, line 6; Figure 3.1 (a), line 1 and 2), and later instances of the same candidate referents or shapes fully contained therein lead to stacking (Algorithm 3.1, line 9; Figure 3.1 (a), line 3). Overlapping polytopes lead to a split into three non-overlapping sub-polytopes (Algorithm 3.1, line 11; Figure 3.1 (a), line 4).

By virtue of this stacking of shapes (lines 6, 9, and 12 in the algorithm) representing geographic entities that are candidate referents, the highest point in the map can be taken to be the most geographically relevant point for the document under consideration. Figure 3.1 (b) shows the resulting grid polygonal model created from a text paragraph on California with a peak indicating the geographic centroid of the whole document.

A thesaurus incorporating synonymy relations, kind-of relations (hyponymy, hypernymy), and part-of relations (i.e., *meronymy*, the relation between a part and the whole, and its converse, *holonymy*) from *WordNet*, and non-stopwords occurring as components of multi-token toponyms (which they call 'evidonyms') as well as several other, more domain-specific databases are used to detect feature types in the face of linguistic variability, and to detect referent sizes heuristically: 'small' (100 m) 'medium' (1 km) or 'large' (10 km), but no details are provided as to how this knowledge is incorporated.

Application to IR. The *expected relevance* R_E of a term-polygon pair $\langle T; P \rangle$ is computed using the formula

$$R_E(T,P) = w(T) \cdot F_T(T) \cdot F_P(T), \qquad (3.1)$$

where $F_T(T)$ is the number of times the term occurs in the thesaurus (reflecting the degree of ambiguity), $F_P(T)$ is the number of polygons associated with the term and $w(T)$ is a discrimination weight that is high for uncommon words as checked against existence in the *UNIX ispell* dictionary.

Algorithm 5 Finding the geographic focus in *GIPSY*.

1: **[Identify.]** Since toponyms can be multi-word units (containing spaces), a greedy longest match strategy is used to find those location names that occur in the gazetteer.

2: **[Locate.]** Lookup associated polygons of longitude/latitudes with each candidate referent.

3: **[Resolve.]**

4: **for** each polygon representing a candidate referent **do**

5:    **if** $\neg$(polygon intersects with base of existing polygon) **then**

6:       lay it on base map beginning at the bottom $(z = 0)$

7:    **else**

8:       **if** polygon completely contained within existing polygon **then**

9:          stack it on top

10:       **else**

11:          {intersects, but not wholly contained.}

           split polygon into three new ones (old polygon, new polygon, and intersecting part)

12:          stack the overlapping portion on top of the old polygon, and the non-intersecting portion at lower level

13:       **end if**

14:    **end if**

15: **end for**

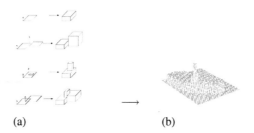

(a)   (b)

Figure 3.1: Geographic focus computation using polygon intersection (after Woodruff and Plaunt (1994)): the polygon model shows California (North is left).

Interestingly, Woodruff and Plaunt (1994) already apply heuristics for relative location expressions: the phrase *south of Lake Tahoe* is mapped to a spatial representation south of Lake Tahoe approximately covering the area of the lake. However, the authors report runtime problems due to the cost of the polygon manipulations and issues with noise. Whereas the latter problem could be remedied using a state-of-the-art NE tagger before gazetteer lookup, the performance problem of the polygon stacking approach is more serious: given that the presented method was only implemented for California, an earth-scale (global) application of it is unlikely to scale due to the algorithmic complexity of the polygon operations involved; Woodruff and Plaunt (1994) already report computational efficiency problems for full text processing compared to paragraph or abstract processing when only considering California.

The notable absence of an sharable, annotated corpus has been pointed out by Clough and Sanderson (2004), among others, and a solution will be presented in Chapter 4. However, there exists also one attempt to circumvent the lack of data for training and testing using a simulation experiment or *pseudo-disambiguation*, which is described next.

Smith and Mann (2003): Naïve Bayes Country-State Recovery.   In the absence of a gold standard toponym resolution evaluation corpus with news text, Smith and Mann (2003) investigate the pseudo-task of recovering deleted disambiguation cues such as '*Maine*' in '*Portland, Maine*' in un-annotated news text. But referential ambiguity can even occur within a single state or country, for instance there are 97 *Georgetowns* in the USA, which means some states must contain more than one, and this is not accounted for by their experimental setup. They use a Naïve Bayes classifier to classify mentions of locations with respect to the underlying U.S. state or (non-U.S.) country Smith and Mann (2003). Back-off models are built for states and countries in order to be able to assign labels for cases not seen in the training data. The advantage of such a pseudo-disambiguation task is that arbitrarily large amounts of training data can be automatically created simply by turning disambiguation cues into class labels.

Trained on a raw text representation (content words only) of two years of AP Newswire text and two months of Topic Detection and Tracking (TDT) data, and tested on one month of TDT data, Smith and Mann report 87.38% accuracy. Their definition of the task is a simplified version of the general toponym resolution task, as they do only provide the disambiguation cues as class labels, rather than provide actual coordinates as output.

They also investigate type ambiguity. Considering the toponym types in the *Getty Thesaurus of Geographic Names* (TGN)—rather than the tokens in a corpus—, they find that 57.1% of US place names are referentially ambiguous, compared to only 16.6% in Europe Smith and Mann (2003).

In a follow-up experiment, the same statistical classifier performs at 77.19% and 21.82% accuracy against a hand-labelled corpus of American biographies and Civil War texts, respectively, which was created using manual post-correction of the output labels of another system described below Smith and Crane (2001).

It remains to be investigated whether this big difference is due to place name changes or other factors. Smith and Mann (2003) suggest the construction of a reference corpus with more recent texts for future work.

So far, I have described work on systems for the English language. One research project on French needs to be singled out next because its focus is depth rather than breadth of processing, and because it uses complex spatial representations.

Bilhaut et al. (2003): Definite Clause Grammars. Bilhaut et al. (2003) present a linguistic analyser, which computes untyped feature structures describing the semantics of spatio-temporal descriptions from French text (Figure 3.2) using a hand-written DCG with 160 rules over POS tags and surface form strings Bilhaut et al. (2003). The system, which is implemented using *LinguaStream*, an NLP workbench that integrates PROLOG, the POS tagger *TreeTagger* and XML processing tools with a portable GUI. The objective is to support passage retrieval with a spatial search facility in natural language.

$$
\begin{bmatrix}
\text{quant} & \begin{bmatrix} \text{type} & \text{exhaustif} \end{bmatrix} \\[4pt]
\text{type} & \begin{bmatrix} \text{ty\_zone} & \text{département} \end{bmatrix} \\[4pt]
\text{zone} & \begin{bmatrix}
\text{egn} & \begin{bmatrix} \text{ty\_zone} & \text{pays} \\ \text{nom} & \text{France} \end{bmatrix} \\[6pt]
\text{loc} & \text{interne} \\[2pt]
\text{position} & \text{nord}
\end{bmatrix}
\end{bmatrix}
$$

Figure 3.2: Representation for 'Tous le départment du nord de la France' (after Bilhaut et al. (2003)).

The system is interesting in that using unification, compositional processing of expressions is attempted, a more difficult task than considering only toponyms. However, this generality comes at a price: the system is more language-dependent and less geographically scalable than most other systems described here. Not only is the system restricted to French text, its geographic scope is also restricted to the geography of France, i.e. it could not handle a French document about Algeria. No evaluation is reported.

After this brief survey of work in the processing of geographic references provided as background, we will now look at seven instances of previous work in toponym resolution proper in some more detail.

3.2 Previous Work in Toponym Resolution

After having surveyed the broader area of processing of geographic names, I now turn to the previous work in toponym resolution proper. I describe seven existing proposals; the first two systems described constitute early efforts from the area of digital libraries, and five very recent systems indicate the increasing attention that the topic is currently receiving in academia and industry.

After each individual system is described, I attempt to factor out a set of shared heuristics and knowledge sources, which facilitates comparison. These carved-out aspects will later be used in a systematic evaluation to determine the relative utility of the knowledge sources and heuristics.

3.2.1 Hauptmann and Olligschlaeger (1999): TR for Speech Data

In the context of the *Infomedia* digital video library project, Hauptmann and Olligschlaeger describe a location analysis system Hauptmann and Olligschlaeger (1999); Olligschlaeger and Hauptmann (1999); Wactlar et al. (2000) used to plot locations mentioned in automatically transcribed news broadcasts on an active (click-able) map. They report working with 1.5 Terabytes of video data containing about 40,000 news stories transcribed using two versions of the CMU *Sphinx* speech recognizer in separate phases for efficiency reasons. Hauptmann and Olligschlaeger use the *NYMBLE* NE tagger[1] for speech data and match each entity against a commercial global gazetteer of 80,000 places and their locations.[2]

Algorithm 6 describes how the toponyms are resolved using a cascade of decisions.[3] First, toponym occurrences that are ambiguous in one place of the document are resolved by propagating interpretations of other occurrences in the document based on the 'one referent per discourse' assumption (lines 3-6). For example, using this heuristic together with a set of unspecified patterns, *Cambridge* can be resolved to Cambridge, MA, USA, in case *Cambridge, MA* occurs elsewhere in the same discourse. Besides local patterns and the discourse heuristic, spatial knowledge is used in the form of a 'superordinate mention' heuristic (lines 8-16), which is applied on the state, country and continent levels. A mention of *Tennessee* in the same document where the resolution of *Memphis* is attempted, triggers the interpretation Memphis, TN, USA, based on the geographic knowledge in the form of *is-part-of* relations (lines 9-10). On the country level, *Paris* is taken to refer to Paris, France, if *France* is mentioned elsewhere (lines 12-13). And on the continent level, *Cambridge* is likely to refer to Cambridge, Cambridgeshire, England, UK, when mentioned together with *Europe* (lines 15-16). Hauptmann and Olligschlaeger (1999) do not mention how ties are dealt with, but taking the frequency of mention into account would be an obvious choice. If despite all these heuristics a toponym could not be resolved completely, it is either left unresolved (i.e., resulting in a partial algorithm) or the first candidate in the gazetteer is selected as a default (lines 18), where a complete algorithm is required.

In a small evaluation, 269 out of 357 (or 75%) were resolved correctly. Four sources of errors impact the correctness of the overall resolution system: (i) Out-of-Vocabulary words (OOV) and errors in the automatic speech transcription (5%); (ii) errors in the HMM-based NE tagger (35% false positives); (iii) errors due to the limitations of the gazetteers (18%); and (iv) errors due to the heuristic rules. 17% were missed, due to either an NE tagging error or by conservative behaviour of the heuristic. The system is reported to also use defaults based on

---

[1] A heavily customised derivative of an early version was used, which was modified to use trigrams instead of bigrams, among other things (personal communication, Dr. Andreas M. Olligschlaeger, 2004-10-20).

[2] http://www.esri.com/

[3] I am grateful to Dr. Alexander G. Hauptmann for sharing parts of the original source code of this system (personal communication, 2004-11-04). The description here is based on the published paper.

Algorithm 6 Toponym resolution (Hauptmann and Olligschlaeger).

1: **for** each toponym *t* **do**

2:      **if** more than one candidate referent **then**

3:          **['One referent per discourse.']**

4:          **if** other mentions in the document provide cues **then**

5:              propagate these interpretations to resolve *t*

6:              {e.g. 'Cambridge' and 'Cambridge, MA'.}

7:          **else**

8:              **[Superordinate mention.]**

9:              **if** other mentions favour a state **then**

10:                 {e.g. 'Memphis' and 'Tennessee'.}
                    resolve to candidate within that state

11:             **else**

12:                 **if** country level evidence provides cue **then**

13:                     {e.g. 'Paris' and 'France'.}
                        resolve to candidate within that country

14:                 **else**

15:                     **if** continent references provide cue **then**

16:                         {e.g. 'Cambridge' and 'Europe'.}
                            resolve to candidate within that continent

17:                     **else**

18:                         discard (ignore; do not resolve) toponym
                            {or pick first candidate (depending on application)}

19:                     **end if**

20:                 **end if**

21:             **end if**

22:         **end if**

23:     **else**

24:         pick single candidate referent

25:     **end if**

26: **end for**

---

number of mentions, population size, proximity to large cities and country, but it is not specified in the paper how these are used to score candidates. Unfortunately, the results reported are of limited value for comparisons over e.g. a corpus-based or Web-based system since the NE tagger was trained and run on all-uppercase data (speech recognizer output).

The resulting location information is stored in a relational database and used to enrich the meta-data of the video data to improve retrieval. Maps are used as visual summaries. A selected rectangular area of the map can be used as a *spatial query* to find all stories mentioning any place mentioned within it (*query-by-region*). Since unlike Woodruff and Plaunt (1994), Hauptmann and Olligschlaeger (1999)'s work performs not just referent assignments at the document level, but at the toponym occurrence level, their system is the earliest account of automatic toponym resolution that I have been able to discover. However, the small sample size and the setting, in which toponym resolution errors interact with speech recognition errors, severely limit the usefulness of the small evaluation. No re-usable gold standard was created.

3.2.2   Smith and Crane (2001): Centroid-based TR

Figure 3.3: Screen capture of the Web interface to the Perseus digital library.

In the context of the *Perseus* digital library project (Figure 3.2.2), a collection of historic texts with over one million references to places, Smith and Crane proposed a method for toponym resolution Smith and Crane (2001), which relies on a per-document centroid (Algorithm 7), very similar to the ideas of Woodruff and Plaunt (1994), but which also resolves individual toponyms rather than just determining a per-document geographic focus.

First a map M, an array of 360×180 representing the globe is populated with all referents for all mentioned toponyms t in a document (lines 1-7), weighted by frequency of mention $freq(t)$. Then the geometric centroid of all potential referents is computed, and all candidates with a greater distance than two standard deviations from it are discarded (lines 8-13). After this pruning step, the centroid is updated (lines 14-15). Then for each toponym instance in the document, a sliding window containing four (unambiguous or previously uniquely resolved) toponyms to the left and to the right is constructed (lines 16-18). For each referent, a score based on the spatial distance to other (resolved) toponyms in the context window, the distance to the document centroid, and its relative importance is computed (lines 20-21). Relative importance is determined using an order of feature types (country interpretations carry more weight than city interpretations), but the scoring formula is not given. Finally, the candidate with the highest score is selected (lines 24). However, Smith and Crane mention a necessary condition for this:

> 'Also at this stage, the system discards as probable false positives places that lack an explicit disambiguator, that receive a low importance score, and that are far away from the local and document centroids.' (Smith and Crane (2001), p. 133)

It is not clear whether such discarded toponyms are left unresolved or if not how they are processed. The system seems to have incorporated some knowledge that prohibits very unlikely—but by no means not impossible—interpretations:

> 'The system prunes some possibilities based on general world knowledge, so that Spain the country, and not the town in Tennessee, will be counted.' (Smith and Crane (2001), p. 133)

No details about the extent of manual elimination of such potential interpretations is mentioned. In a document on Roman poetry Smith and Crane (2001) are able to discard the spatial (mis-) interpretation of Ovid, Idaho, as a referent for the name *Ovid* using the distance to Italy by eliminating referents too far away from a centroid. They report F-measures between 0.81 and 0.96 but conclude:

> 'we characterise the document context or central "region of interest" of a document by the centroid of the most heavily referenced areas. There seems to be some lack of robustness in simply using the centroid, and we are experimenting with using a bounding rectangle or polygon to represent a document's region of interest.' (Smith and Crane (2001), p. 135)

Smith and Crane (2001) also do not report the curation of a re-usable evaluation corpus.

3.2.3 Li et al. (2003): A Hybrid Approach to TR

More recently, the Cymfony *InfoXtract* IE system (Srihari et al. (2000)) has been extended by a component to normalise spatial, temporal and measurement expressions (Li et al. (2003, 2002)). Toponym resolution is largely based on local pattern matching, discourse co-occurrence analysis and default referents. The basic mechanism is given in Algorithm 8. In the first step, candidate referents are looked up in the DARPA TIPSTER gazetteer (line 1), in which an optional rank number for an entry indicates how salient the referent represented by the entry is (default referent). In TIPSTER, salience indicators are either based on the order

---

Algorithm 7 Smith and Crane (2001): Centroid-Based Toponym Resolution.

1: **[Initialise.]**

2: Let M be a 2-dimensional, $1°$-resolution map $[\pm 180; \pm 90]$.

3: **for** all possible toponyms t in a document **do**

4:     **for** all possible referents t_r of t **do**

5:         Store $freq(t)$ in M at the coordinates for t_r.

6:     **end for**

7: **end for**

8: **[Centroid and pruning.]**

9: Compute the centroid c of the weighted map M.

10: Calculate standard deviation σ from c.

11: **for** each point associated with any t_r in M **do**

12:     Discard all points that are more than 2σ away from c.

13: **end for**

14: **[Centroid re-computation.]**

15: Re-compute centroid c.

16: **[Sliding window.]**

17: **for** each toponym instance t in the document **do**

18:     Construct a context window w with ± 4 unambiguous or uniquely resolved toponyms to the left and to the right of t.

19:     **for** each candidate referent t_r of t **do**

20:         **[Scoring.]**

21:         Compute candidate score s based on:

            – proximity to other toponyms in w,

            – proximity to c, and

            – its relative importance (e.g. $s(Spain) > s(Madrid)$).

22:     **end for**

23:     Pick un-discarded candidate t_r with highest s as referent.

24: **end for**

---

of magnitude of the population of the place or on human intuition about importance, but unfortunately these two sources of evidence are not formally distinguished. Figure 3.5 shows all TIPSTER entries for *Cambridge*: the UK university town interpretation (line 1) is given the highest rank ('3' is a smaller number and thus indicates a higher rank than '4', and also higher salience than entries without any rank number). However, the TIPSTER gazetteer is very small (246,907 entries as of version 4.0), and contains only default referent information for 32.78% of its entries.

Rules implemented as finite state transducers over surface strings and chunk labels are applied

---

Algorithm 8 Toponym Resolution in InfoXtract.

1: **[Gazetteer.]** Look up all location names in the TIPSTER gazetteer to associate candidate referents with each toponym.

2: **[Assume Country.]** If exactly one referent is a country, select this referent.

3: **[Local patterns.]** Invoke patterns that resolve some toponyms based on local context (e.g. *Oxford, UK*).

4: **[Assume Province or Capital.]** If exactly one referent is a province or capital, select this referent.

5: **['One referent per discourse.']** For each resolved toponym, *propagate* the selected referent to all other mentions of the toponym it is associated with.

6: **[Maximum-Weight Spanning Tree.]** The discourse sub-module is invoked and uses an *MST Algorithm* (see explanation in the text) to find candidate assignments for remaining referential ambiguities.

7: **[Default Referent.]**

8: **for** each toponym **do**

9:    **if** still ambiguous $\wedge$ decision score lower than threshold **then**

10:       choose default referent.

11:    **end if**

12: **end for**

---

after the lookup (line 3) to utilise local context for both toponym recognition and resolution Li et al. (2003), as in the following example:

    LOC + ',' + NP[head='city'] $\sim$ ... *Chicago, an old city* ...

Before and after the local pattern search, country, province and capital heuristics are applied (lines 2 and 4). Then, the 'one reference per discourse' heuristic is used to propagate referents from now unambiguous instances to not yet resolved ones (line 5). In order to find the set of the most likely referents for remaining toponyms, a graph algorithm is applied as follows. First, an undirected weighted graph $G = \langle V, E \rangle$, is constructed, where V is a set of vertexes representing the candidate toponym referents looked up in a text (Figure 3.4, (1)) and E

$type(r_i)$	$type(r_j)$	condition	weight $E(i,j)$
City	City	$inSameState(r_i, r_j)$	2
¬City	City	$inSameCountry(r_i, r_j)$	1
any	State	$inSameState(r_i, r_j)$	3
any	Country	$inCountryWithoutState(r_i, r_j)$	4

Table 3.1: Weight function in InfoXtract (after Li et al. (2003)).

is a function mapping pairs of vertexes to edge weights, $E : V \times V \to \mathbb{R}$. Table 3.1 specifies the vertex weight function based on the geographic feature types of the arguments and spatial relations. The predicate $inSameState(r_i, r_j)$ holds if and only if two referents r_i and r_j are located in the same state, $inSameCountry(r_i, r_j)$ holds if and only if two referents r_i and r_j are located in the same country, and $inCountryWithoutState(r_i, r_j)$ is defined as 'in country without state (e.g. in Europe)', which might indicate the predicate holds if and only if the second argument is a country that (unlike the USA) has no state subdivisions, but details are left open.

This graph is partial: all but the nodes of competing candidate referents are connected by edges with non-zero arc weights (Figure 3.4, (2)). Maximum Spanning Tree (MST) algorithms (Kruskal (1956); Prim (1957)) can then be used to find a sub-graph that contains every vertex of the original graph, has a tree shape, and simultaneously maximises the total weight of the nodes (Figure 3.4, (3)). Nodes on the resulting maximum-weight spanning tree are the most promising referents for their respective toponym (Figure 3.4, (4)).

Li et al. (2003) found Kruskal's algorithm used in their earlier work problematic due its time complexity; switching to Prim's algorithm yielded an increase in runtime performance. Further following Li et al. (2003), notions of frequency and textual proximity can be incorporated in the search by computing a vertex weight W_{r_i} for each candidate referent r_i by calculating

$$W(r_i) = \sum_{j=0}^{m} E(i,j) * freq(t_{r_j})/dist(t_{r_i}, t_{r_j}) \tag{3.2}$$

where $freq(t_{r_j})$ is the number of mentions of toponym t_{t_j} and $dist(t_{r_i}, t_{r_j})$ is the textual proximity between two toponym mentions t_{r_i} and t_{r_j}. The selected referent is then

$$r_i = \arg\max_{j}(W(r_j)) \tag{3.3}$$

In a final step (lines 7 ff.), the default referents from the gazetteer and from the Web are used in cases of a tie between referents or where the highest-scoring referent's weight does not exceed an unspecified threshold. Default referents are acquired from the Web Li et al. (2002) by imposing the *Yahoo* directory's geographical ontology—salient locations are mentioned

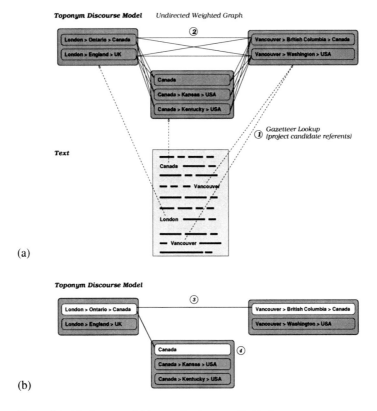

(a)

(b)

Figure 3.4: Maximum-weight spanning tree applied to toponym resolution.

there and are taken to be the defaults, whereas locations of minor importance are absent from the hierarchy–, thus biasing the system toward a U.S.-American view, which is helpful for the processing of news stories they test their system on.

A set of seven CNN news stories and four regional US travel guide texts are evaluated in Li et al. (2003), which total 261 ambiguous location tokens. Accuracy for the ambiguous toponyms only is reported to be 96%. Default senses alone achieve 89.9%, while pattern-based disambiguation only accounts for 12% accuracy. Their graph–based search method alone using Kruskal's algorithm, and without taking frequency and textual proximity into account as reported in their previous work Li et al. (2002), performs at 73.8% accuracy. Their new method based on Prim's algorithm alone, but with frequency and proximity in the weight function, performs at 86.6%. Without frequency and textual proximity, not even a combination of Kruskal search, patterns and default referents outperforms default referents alone; only when switching from Kruskal's to Prim's maximum spanning tree algorithm with frequency and textual proximity weighting are they able to beat the baseline (the TIPSTER default referents) by 6.1%. Still, in absolute terms this difference corresponds to just 16 differently tagged tokens, which could correspond to anything from just 1 to 16 different tagging decisions when considering toponym referent *types*). It is thus not clear how significant these results are. Due to the small size of the gazetteer used, the toponym resolution problem is significantly simplified compared to a scenario using a large-scale world-wide gazetteer. The evaluation sample size is very small, so differences in performance might not be significant (it is not reported whether statistical tests to this end have been carried out). Another, more methodological, issue of this study is that no split of the documents into development set and test set is reported. Unfortunately for the purpose of this thesis, Li et al. (2003)'s system is proprietary and thus not available for in-depth analysis or experimentation.

3.2.4 Rauch et al. (2003): Confidence-based TR.

Rauch et al. (2003) describe the commercial *MetaCarta Text Search* (*MTS*) system Frank (2004), which is based on *confidence*. Toponyms are recognised and resolved using both supportive and negative contexts Rauch et al. (2003). For every candidate referent to a toponym n to a location p, the confidence that n 'really' belongs to p is estimated. Features used as evidence or counter-evidence include the presence in a location gazetteer, presence of U.S. postal addresses, explicit coordinates[4], local linguistic context, matching of spatial patterns, population heuristics associated with potential referents, and relative reference cues.

Rauch et al. (2003) mention the use of an supervised learning regime to induce contexts that are positive or negative indicators of terms being toponyms, particular referents of them, and to estimate confidence in these indicative contexts. First, each toponym-location pair $\langle n; p \rangle$ is initialised with the average confidence assigned to an instance in the training corpus. Then,

> [f]or any context C, an adjustment is applied to the confidence which is a non-linear function of the probability of a geographic reference occurring in C in the tagged corpus. (Rauch et al. (2003), p. 53)

Unfortunately the training corpus mentioned is a proprietary resource, and no details about its size, composition or annotation scheme are revealed. Details of the iterative training procedure mentioned are also not given.

Application to IR.   Rauch et al. (2003) apply the results of their geographic document processing to ranking in information retrieval: for a query $m = \{m_i\}$ and a set of documents, they use a relevance ranking function R_{total} for each query-document pair, which is computed as the weighted sum of both a *geo-relevance* function R_g and a traditional (Robertson and

---

[4]Rare in non-military texts.

Cambridge (CITY 3) United Kingdom (COUNTRY)

Cambridge (CITY 4) Ontario (PROVINCE) Canada (COUNTRY)

Cambridge (CITY 4) Waikato (PROVINCE) New Zealand (COUNTRY)

Cambridge (CITY) Alabama (PROVINCE 1) United States (COUNTRY)

Cambridge (CITY) Idaho (PROVINCE 1) United States (COUNTRY)

Cambridge (CITY) Illinois (PROVINCE 1) United States (COUNTRY)

Cambridge (CITY) Iowa (PROVINCE 1) United States (COUNTRY)

Cambridge (CITY) Kansas (PROVINCE 1) United States (COUNTRY)

Cambridge (CITY) Kentucky (PROVINCE 1) United States (COUNTRY)

Cambridge (CITY) Maine (PROVINCE 1) United States (COUNTRY)

Cambridge (CITY) Maryland (PROVINCE 1) United States (COUNTRY)

Cambridge (CITY) Massachusetts (PROVINCE 1) United States (COUNTRY)

Cambridge (CITY) Minnesota (PROVINCE 1) United States (COUNTRY)

Cambridge (CITY) Missouri (PROVINCE 1) United States (COUNTRY)

Cambridge (CITY) Nebraska (PROVINCE 1) United States (COUNTRY)

Cambridge (CITY) New Jersey (PROVINCE 1) United States (COUNTRY)

Cambridge (CITY) New York (PROVINCE 1) United States (COUNTRY)

Cambridge (CITY) North Carolina (PROVINCE 1) United States (COUNTRY)

Cambridge (CITY) Ohio (PROVINCE 1) United States (COUNTRY)

Cambridge (CITY) Oklahoma (PROVINCE 1) United States (COUNTRY)

Cambridge (CITY) Pennsylvania (PROVINCE 1) United States (COUNTRY)

Cambridge (CITY) South Carolina (PROVINCE 1) United States (COUNTRY)

Cambridge (CITY) Tennessee (PROVINCE 1) United States (COUNTRY)

Cambridge (CITY) Texas (PROVINCE 1) United States (COUNTRY)

Cambridge (CITY) Vermont (PROVINCE 1) United States (COUNTRY)

Cambridge (CITY) Virginia (PROVINCE 1) United States (COUNTRY)

Cambridge (CITY) Wisconsin (PROVINCE 1) United States (COUNTRY)

Cambridge (PROVINCE 2) England (PROVINCE 1) United Kingdom (COUNTRY)

Figure 3.5: Entries for 'Cambridge' in the TIPSTER gazetteer.

Spärck Jones (1997)) term relevance function R_w:

$$R_{total} = (1 - W_w(|m|))R_g + W_w(|m|)R_w.\tag{3.4}$$

The weight $W_w(\cdot)$ allows one to modify the importance of the geographic aspect of a particular search, dependent on the query. This weight is computed so as to ensure that for longer queries, the geo-relevance is lower: if the user query has $|m|$ terms in total (geographic and non-geographic), then a weight of

$$W_w(|m|) = \frac{1}{2} + \frac{|m|-1}{|m|}(M - \frac{1}{2}),\tag{3.5}$$

is used, where M is a value between 0 and 1 that ensures the geographic influence remains within certain boundaries (but its value is not given). They define geographic relevance as

$$R_g = C_g \cdot E(P_n, B_n, F_n, S),\tag{3.6}$$

where C_g is the 'geo-confidence', a value that indicates the degree of confidence in a term being a geographic term (but again, no definition is given), E is an *emphasis function* which takes into account P_n, the position of a toponym in the text, B_n, the degree of *prominence* of a toponym in the document (higher if it is part of a title/header, or typeset in large font), F_n, the frequency of the toponym in the document, and S, the frequency of other toponyms in the document.

Definitions of the E-function and the confidence are unfortunately not revealed, and no evaluation is presented to assess the utility of the presented combined geographic/non-geographic ranking. Specifically, it remains unclear whether Rauch et al. (2003) utilise any resolution information for retrieval at all (and if so, how), or whether geographic terms and phrases a simply weighted differently (thus conflating e.g. all Londons rather than treating them as different terms).[5]

3.2.5 Pouliquen et al. (2004, 2006): Multilingual TR and Mapping.

Pouliquen et al. (2004) describe a multilingual mapping tool to visualise a collection of news reports Pouliquen et al. (2004). By statically restricting their application to Europe, they can afford to eliminate small places outside Europe from their gazetteer offline so as to reduce ambiguity, but sacrificing some recall. They use gazetteer lookup combined with a set of language-specific 'geo-stop lists', terms that are never taken to be toponyms by the system, because they coincide with words of a particular language (for instance, *Split, Croatia* versus English 'to split' when capitalised in sentence-initial position). For the resolution proper, they rely on 'one referent per discourse' and prefer locations with a larger population. Details of the algorithm are not given in the paper; however, on request the authors kindly provided me with an unpublished, more detailed description of a more recent version of the method to resolve all toponyms in a text (from which Algorithm 9 was reconstructed).

---

[5]We will come back to geographic relevance in Chapter 6.

Algorithm 9 TR in a Multilingual System (Pouliquen et al. 2004).

1: **for** each toponym t **do**

2:     Initialise all candidate referent scores $r_{t\,score}$ to 0.

3:     r_0 = referent of the unambiguous toponym which is textually closest to t.

4:     **[Check Disambiguators.]**

5:     **for** each disambiguator term $T^i_{r_t}$ for toponym t **do**

6:         **if** $T^i_{r_t}$ (which supports referent r_t) appears in context of t **then**

7:             { Increase the score for that interpretation }

8:             $r_{t\,score} = r_{t\,score} + C_1$

9:         **end if**

10:     **end for**

11:     **for** each interpretation r_t **do**

12:         **[Country heuristic.]**

13:         **if** context includes mention of country $c \wedge contained(r_t, c)$ **then**

14:             $r_{t\,score} = r_{t\,score} + C_2$

15:         **end if**

16:         **[Distance heuristic.]**

17:         $r_{t\,score} = r_{t\,score} + F(distance(r_t, r^*))$

18:     **end for**

19:     Select referent r_t with highest $r_{t\,score}$

20: **end for**

The method works as follows. All toponyms in a document are resolved independently in a loop (line 1). For each, a search for an unambiguous toponym t_0 in a textual context window of unspecified size is carried out (line 3). For each toponym, a set of disambiguator terms ('triggers') for t, i.e. terms which are indicative of particular referents, are searched in the context of the toponym (lines 5-6). Each hit modifies the score for that referent (line 8). Again, the context window size for this step and the constants are not specified. Scores for candidate referents are then modified based on whether or not the name of a country in which a particular candidate referent is located, is mentioned in the proximity (lines 13-14). Again, the context window size for this step and the additive constant used are not mentioned. Then a function F is used to modify candidate referent scores based on distance to the unambiguous toponym t_0 (line 17). F is not defined, but is likely to be bigger for smaller distances. Ultimately, the candidate referent with the highest score is selected (line 19).

In a subsequent version of the system (Pouliquen et al., 2006), the static focussing by 'thinning out' of the gazetteer is supplemented by a *dynamic focus* algorithm: in a first phase, the context of the document is set (e.g. by resorting to a human-made list of publication places for important European newspapers) and by using a process that the authors call *shallow geo-parsing*, i.e. by means of taking important unambiguous ('sure fire') toponyms and by finding the country that their referents are located in. This list of countries is then used in a second phase (called *deep geo-parsing*) to filter out all interpretations that are outside the countries on the list built in the first pass.

The gazetteer that the system used is based on the Global Discovery database, the Estonian multilingual KNAP database and a multilingual list used by the European Commission. Using their gazetteer, Pouliquen et al. (2006) measured an average F-score of 77% for toponym resolution across the 16 languages that their system supports (English: 84%), which compares very favourably to the 38% F-score that their previous system version achieved on the same data, a selection of four news topics from 2004 covered by 10 stories each (i.e., 40 stories in total for English). Their system has a very powerful GUI that also supports Social Network Analysis (SNA) for the key players reported in the news.

3.2.6 Amitay et al. (2004): Web-a-Where.

Amitay et al. (2004) report on *Web-a-Where*, a system based on IBM's *WebFountain* framework for large-scale textual data mining Gruhl et al. (2004); Tretau et al. (2003). *Web-a-Where* is able to resolve individual toponyms from Web pages to hierarchical path descriptions and assigns a ranked list of geographic foci to each page. The system relies on a gazetteer with 75,000 entries from different sources (including GNIS, the World Gazetteer[6], a UN-SD country/continent list, and ISO 3166-1 country abbreviations). They rely on a spatial taxonomy to represent

---

[6]http://www.world-gazetteer.com/

referents, and subsequently do *not* utilise any knowledge based on spatial coordinates.

The lack of a highly-reliable named entity tagger leads to errors in geographic text processing at the recognition stage. To avoid the confusion of toponyms with common words, the IBM system's gazetteer contains a flag that tags each entry as possible common word. These tags were derived from extracting non-capitalised words from a corpus (Algorithm 10) using manual post-editing to ensure that strings which could be either toponyms or common English words, but occur more often than a toponym interpretation warrants, are dealt with correctly. Based on these 'non-toponym stop lists', toponym recognition is reduced to gazetteer lookup, except for short entries, which are ignored at this step.

Algorithm 10 Spotting gazetteer entries as potential common words in *Web-a-Where*.

1: **for** each entry t in gazetteer **do**

2:     **if** in corpus, $count(t) > 100 \wedge count(uppercase(t)) < count(lowercase(t))$ **then**

3:         might be common English word

4:         flag t as potential non-toponym

5:     **end if**

6: **end for**

The toponym resolution step in *Web-a-Where* comprises a simple four-step cascade for each toponym, given in Algorithm 11, in which confidence scores are determined based on heuristics. First, local disambiguating patterns are matched (lines 4-10), and a confidence of 95% is assumed if as a result of the pattern matching exactly on referent remains (line 8). Where pattern-based disambiguation is only partial, nothing is done at this stage. The largest referent in terms of population is then given a confidence of 0.5 (lines 11-14). Then the 'one referent per discourse' heuristic is applied, i.e. referents for unambiguous toponym mentions are propagated to ambiguous ones (lines 15-22). A slightly higher confidence of 0.9 is assigned if a referent disambiguated by such a propagation coincides with a candidate referent picked using a largest population heuristic; otherwise, 0.8 is used. All these confidence values appear to have been derived from using manual experimentation. They then resolve remaining ambiguities by computing regions (as represented by prefixes in paths of the spatial ontology) in the confines of which toponym interpretations become unique (lines 23-32). For instance, *Berlin* (Europe/Germany/Berlin, NorthAmerica/USA/CT/Berlin, among others) and *Potsdam* (Europe/Germany/Potsdam) both share the path prefix Europe/Germany, which represents a spatial context with respect to which *Berlin* and *Potsdam* are unambiguously resolved (more about this geometric minimality heuristic in Chapter 5). Finally, the candidate referent with the highest confidence score is assigned (line 33).

Amitay et al. (2004) evaluate *Web-a-Where* on three collections of Web pages: an arbitrary collection of 200 HTML pages $> 3K$, a random 200-page sample from a 1,200,000 TREC corpus of U.S. government Web pages, and 200 randomly chosen Web pages from the *Open Directory Project*[7].

However, instead of curating a reusable, manually-annotated gold standard from these raw texts, they assess their system by applying it to the dataset and by letting a human judge decide *a posteriori* whether any given system tagging decision is correct or not. This limits the usefulness of the study also because human judgement of system output might be biased compared to the methodology proposed here, namely to first prepare a reference resource in which toponyms are annotated *a posteriori*, without letting annotator decisions be influenced by exposure to system output.

Amitay et al. (2004) also give a page-focus algorithm, which is reported to perform at 38% accuracy (precise match; 92% on country level).

3.2.7 Schilder et al. (2004): Cost Optimisation for German TR.

Schilder et al. (2004) describe the first toponym resolution experiment for German on unconstrained news text. To recognize toponyms, they run a standard POS tagger followed by applying a handcrafted *Definite Clause Grammar* (DCG) over the POS labels.

For the TR step proper, they prefer resolving toponyms to referents in which these are in the same country ('one *country* per discourse') and assume that singleton toponyms are very likely to refer to country capitals, if this is an option. Based on candidates from the UN-LOCODE gazetteer and hierarchical paths (such as CA_LOND for London, Ontario, Canada) rather than numerical coordinates, they assign cost constants to capital, country, region, and city interpretations, respectively, and use *Iterative Deepening Search* Korf (1985) to find the cost-minimal assignment to referents. A detailed description is not given.

They report 64% accuracy for the toponym resolution step when evaluating on 12 newspaper articles in German language. Unfortunately, the size of the gazetteer used in this study is very small, and it is not clear whether the method could scale up.

3.2.8 Clough (2005): TR in SPIRIT: Source Preference Order.

The SPIRIT system Clough et al. (2004), intended to run on large-scale Web collections was designed to take into account scalability concerns. In this context Clough (2005) describes a toponym resolution experiment covering some countries in Europe, namely the UK, France, Germany and Switzerland.

Clough (2005) reports that toponym recognition with a combination of gazetteer lookup and stop-lists exceeded the performance of the ANNIE named entity tagger part of the GATE system, which agrees with the findings by Mikheev et al. (1999) that for toponyms (unlike for other categories of named entities) large gazetteers are very valuable.

---

[7]http://www.dmoz.org/

Algorithm 11 Toponym Resolution in IBM *Web-a-Where* (Amitay et al. 2004).

1: **for** each toponym t **do**

2:    **for** each candidate referent t_{r_i} **do**

3:       Initialise confidence scores $c(t_{r_i}) = 0$.

4:       **[Local patterns.]**

5:       **if** disambiguating pattern matches **then**

6:          {e.g. 'Cambridge' and 'Cambridge, MA'}

7:          **if** disambiguation is unique (1 interpretation) **then**

8:             Set $c(t_{r_i}) = 0.95$ for this candidate referent

9:          **end if**

10:       **end if**

11:       **[Maximum population.]**

12:       **if** $c(t_{r_i}) = 0$ **then**

13:          Assign $c(t_{r_i}) = 0.5$ if t_{r_i} is the referent with the largest population.

14:       **end if**

15:       **['One-referent-per-discourse'.]**

16:       **if** same toponym appears with disambiguator elsewhere **then**

17:          **if** that referent coincides with maximum-population referent **then**

18:             Propagate this referent to all instances with $c(t_{r_i}) = 0.9$

19:          **else**

20:             Propagate this referent with $c(t_{r_i}) = 0.8$

21:          **end if**

22:       **end if**

23:       **[Geometric minimality.]**

24:       { toponym still unresolved }

25:       find longest common path prefix p in the spatial ontology in which all toponyms t_u are unambiguous

26:       **for** each toponym t_u with $c(t_{r_i}) < 0.7$ **do**

27:          **if** referent for t_u in p coincides with maximum-population referent **then**

28:             Propagate this referent to all instances with $c(t_{r_i}) = 0.75$

29:          **else**

30:             Propagate this referent with $c(t_{r_i}) = 0.65$

31:          **end if**

32:       **end for**

33:       Choose referent t_{r_i} with maximum confidence $c(t_{r_i})$.

34:    **end for**

35: **end for**

Algorithm 8 describes the toponym resolution method employed in the SPIRIT prototype.
It allows optional manual involvement in the sense that the human operator can set a 'preferred
country' parameter (line 1), a useful feature if the place of publication of a newspaper is known
from the meta-data of its articles, for instance. Candidates are looked up (line 3) and sorted
using a set of four criteria. First, the number of words in a window spanning from two words
to the left of the toponym to eight words to the right in common with the words in the path
description of candidate referents is looked at (lines 6-7), which is equivalent to matching to
local patterns with some wildcards.[8] Second, the number of parts in the hierarchical path,
e.g. $|England > UK > Europe| = 3$ is considered (line 8). Third, candidate referents that
originate from SABE are always preferred to those from the Ordnance Survey gazetteer, which
in turn are preferred over those originating from TGN ('*source preference order*'). Last but
not least, the country preference parameter, if present, is considered in the sorting step (line 9).
The pre-defined source preference order of the three gazetteers is again invoked to break ties
(lines 11-13). Finally, the highest-ranking referent is assigned (line 14).

For evaluation, a sample of 130 documents were selected from the 900,000 Web pages that
form the SPIRIT collection. No details of the annotation process (such as inter-annotator agreement) are given, but in technical terms the implementation is based on GATE markup. Clough
(2005) reports an accuracy of 89%. It is somewhat difficult to compare the evaluation results
with others due to the selection of countries, which appears to be motivated by the countries
of the members of the SPIRIT project rather than by experimental objectives. Furthermore,
the documents chosen for evaluation were filtered based on having 'between 5 and 10 unique
footprints' (Clough, 2005, p. 27), which unfortunately means that the evaluation results are not
based on the natural statistical distribution as far as degree of toponym ambiguity is concerned.

Zong et al. (2005): Assigning Spatial Metadata to Web Page Regions.   Zong et al. (2005)
report on a method for assigning spatial meta-data to parts of Web pages. They use the GATE
ANNIE named entity tagger, but enhance its default gazetteer 6,713 of toponyms (useful only
for recognition, as GATE contains no referent information) with about 60,000 entries from the
US Census 2000 gazetteer. The system is thus US-centric, and since its purpose is to assign
spatial meta-data to regions of Web pages, toponym resolution is just a means to an end. They
use evidence sources mentioned in this chapter, and a tiny set of 760 toponyms is evaluated by
manual inspection of tagging results. Zong et al. (2005) report 88.9% resolution accuracy, but a
problem with their evaluation is that the test set was chosen to comprise only pages containing
between 32-199 occurrences of toponyms. It is not clear why this was done, nor what the
impact on the evaluation is. A large proportion of pages in a naturally distributed sample will
likely feature less than 32 toponym instances.

---

[8]Note the difference between this fixed 10-token window around toponyms and the sliding window of varying
length defined so as to include a certain number of toponyms in Algorithm 7.

Algorithm 12 TR in the SPIRIT system (Clough 2005).

1: c = read preferred country parameter from command line.

2: **for** each toponym t **do**

3:      look up all candidate referents from { TGN; SABE; OS }.

4:      **[Sort.]**

5:      **for** each candidate referent r_t **do**

6:          **['local context'.]**

7:          Compute overlap o between hierarchical path description and local context window of size [-2;+8].

8:          d = length of hierarchical path.

9:          Sort candidate referents in a list by decreasing score $r_{t\,score}$, taking into account:

          $- o$ (matching words),

          $- d$,

          $-$ resource preference $SABE \prec OS \prec TGN$,

          $- c$.

10:     **end for**

11:     **if** score $r_{t\,score}$ for two referents is equal **then**

12:         resolve ties using the preference $SABE \prec OS \prec TGN$.

13:     **end if**

14:     Assign referent r_t with highest $r_{t\,score}$.

15: **end for**

Overell and Rüger (2006): WikiDisambiguator. Overell and Rüger (2006) describe the *WikiDisambiguator* system, an ongoing attempt to combine many of the heuristics described here in order to disambiguate toponyms with respect to unique identifiers from TGN. Using manually annotated ground truth data (1,694 locations from a random article sample of the online encyclopedia *Wikipedia*), they report 82.8% resolution accuracy. A random baseline of 58.6% on the same task suggests a relatively simple task setting. Wikipedia uses a special form of markup that can be exploited to guide the extraction of referents for toponyms, including hyperlinks and subject categories with structured data.

3.3 Comparative Analysis

We have described early approaches to toponym resolution. Despite the fact that some methods are very different from others in spirit, heuristics or knowledge sources re-occur and are used by several authors. We attempt to systematically factor out these common sources of evidence for subsequent individual evaluation and recombination so as to form new, superior methods. Where examples are given, these use the gazetteer service described in the next chapter, and the toponyms to be resolved are underlined.

/H0/ Assign unambiguous referent. Assign all referents r_i to toponyms t_j where there is exactly one candidate, i.e. no ambiguity with respect to the gazetteer used exists. This trivial processing step is used by all systems, and is usually done first.

Example:

Bad Bergzabern $\mapsto \langle 49.11; 7.99 \rangle$

Ashe $\mapsto \langle 43.95; 39.28 \rangle$.

Used by:

used by all methods described here (typically invoked first by toponym resolution systems)

/H1/ 'Contained-in' qualifier following. Assume $t_1, t_2, \ldots, t_T$ are toponyms and $r_1, r_2, \ldots, r_R$ are referents. Try to match the local regular patterns:

t_1, t_2 $\qquad$ t_1, t_2, t_3

$t_1 \; \text{in} \; t_2$ $\qquad$ $t_1 \; (t_2)$

t_1 / t_2 $\qquad$ $t_1 ; t_2$

If a pattern matches, and it is the case that exactly one candidate referent r of t_1 exists such that r_1 is spatially contained in r_2, where r_2 is a candidate referent of t_2, then assign that referent r to t_1. Proceed accordingly to resolve t_2 using t_3.

Example:

London (UK) $\mapsto \langle 51.5; -0.1166 \rangle$

> *London (Ontario, Canada)* $\mapsto \langle 42.98; -81.25 \rangle$
>
> *Cambridge, MA, USA* $\mapsto \langle 42.24444; -71.8125 \rangle$
>
> *Cambridge, England, GB* $\mapsto \langle 51.73; -2.37 \rangle$.

Used by:

Hauptmann and Olligschlaeger (1999);

Smith and Crane (2001);

Li et al. (2003);

Rauch et al. (2003);

Amitay et al. (2004);

Clough (2005) (using wildcard patterns corresponding to a window of 2 words to the left and 8 words to the right).

/H2/ Superordinate mention. If a toponym t_1 is to be resolved, and a second toponym t_2 which can refer to a country r_c, appears elsewhere in the same document, and it further holds that one candidate referent of t_1 is located in country r_c, then assign t_1 to the referent in that country. This is essentially a 'long distance' version of the local pattern constraint above.

Example:

> *... USA ... Boston ...* $\mapsto \langle 2.35833; -71.06028 \rangle$
>
> *... Boston ... UK ...* $\mapsto \langle 52.9833333; -0.0166667 \rangle$
>
> *... Paris ... France ...* $\mapsto \langle 45.63; 5.73 \rangle$
>
> *... Texas ... Paris ...* $\mapsto \langle 33.66; -95.56 \rangle$.

Used by:

Hauptmann and Olligschlaeger (1999);

Pouliquen et al. (2004).

/H3/ Largest population. Assign the referent with the largest population size, as looked up in a (typically incomplete) authority list. Rather than making a hard assignment, Rauch et al. (2003) use a *soft* version of this heuristic in their confidence-based framework: 'confidence of a place p is decreased by an amount proportional to the logarithm of the ratio of the population of p to the population of all places with the name n.'

Example:

Paris $\mapsto \langle 48.8666667; 2.3333333 \rangle$, i.e. assume Paris, France, the population of which is 2,107,700 (as of 2004) instead of Paris, TX, USA (25,898 inhabitants as of 2000)

Boston $\mapsto \langle 2.35833; -71.06028 \rangle$, i.e. assume Boston, MA, USA, which has a population of 577,100 according to the World Gazetteer, instead of Boston, England, United Kingdom, which hast just 36,300 inhabitants according to the same source.

Used by:

Rauch et al. (2003);

Amitay et al. (2004);

Pouliquen et al. (2004).

/H4/ One referent per discourse. Assume that all toponyms with identical surface form in a
document also share the same referent, i.e. all the resolved referents are propagated to
those with the same surface string in a text. This follows the 'one sense per discourse'
heuristic bias suggested for Word Sense Disambiguation (WSD) by Gale et al. (1992).

Example:

... *Paris, TX* ... *Paris* ... $\mapsto \langle 33.66083; -95.55528 \rangle$, i.e. assume both 'Paris-es' refer to
the same location (Paris, Texas, USA) in the document in which they co-occur, despite
the fact that one is not qualified explicitly.

Used by:

Hauptmann and Olligschlaeger (1999);

Leidner et al. (2003);

Li et al. (2003);

Amitay et al. (2004);

Schilder et al. (2004) (using a variant, one *country* per discourse);

Pouliquen et al. (2004)

Pouliquen et al. (2006).

/H5/ Geometric minimality (minimal bounding polygon/distances). Assign those referents
to all toponyms that minimise the convex hull or pairwise distances, of all referents in a
document, respectively.

This heuristic takes all possible interpretations for each referent into account and opti-
mises using spatial proximity as a criterion.

This heuristic is elaborated further in Chapter 5.

Example:

... *Berlin* ... *Potsdam* ... $\mapsto \langle 52.5166667; 13.4 \rangle$ (Berlin, Germany)

... *Fairburn* ... *Berlin* ... $\mapsto \langle 43.96806; -88.94333 \rangle$ (Berlin, WI, USA).

Similarly,

{ West *Berlin*; Bishops; Dicktown } $\mapsto$ Berlin, NJ, USA

{ Kensington; *Berlin*; New Britain } $\mapsto$ Berlin, CT, USA

{ Copperville; *Berlin*; Gorham } $\mapsto$ Berlin, NH, USA

{ Moultrie; *Berlin* } $\mapsto$ Berlin, GA, USA

{ *Berlin*; Prouty } $\mapsto$ Berlin, IL, USA

{ *Berlin*; Berlin Center; Cherryplain } $\mapsto$ Berlin, NY, USA

{ Medberry; *Berlin* } $\mapsto$ Berlin, ND, USA.

Used by:

Leidner et al. (2003) (first described for TR using convex hull; see Section 5.3);

Li et al. (2003) (first described for TR using pairwise distances);

Rauch et al. (2003) (the authors claim they use proximity, but do not give details);

Amitay et al. (2004).

/H6/ Singleton capitals. If a toponym t_1 occurs only once in a text, and if exactly one of the candidate referents is a capital (e.g. according to some geopolitical database such as the *CIA World Factbook*), then choose this capital as the interpretation for t_1.

Example:

Washington $\mapsto$ $\langle 38.895; -77.03667 \rangle$ (select Washington, DC, the capital of the United States of America)

Madrid $\mapsto$ $\langle 40.4; -3.68 \rangle$ (always pick Madrid, the capital of the Spain, as opposed to any of the other possible Madrids).

Used by:

Schilder et al. (2004).

/H7/ Ignore small places. Reduce (prune) the size of the gazetteer database, based on the size of population. This decreases ambiguity, but obviously also recall, so this is a simplification of the problem rather than a real solution. However, as Pouliquen et al. (2004) demonstrate, the technique can be helpful in some applications.

Example:

Washington $\mapsto$ 35 candidate referents in the USA alone, after filtering out those locations that are not known to have more than half a million inhabitants there remains 1 candidate referent, namely Washington, DC, with a population of 572,059 (as of 2000).

Used by:

Pouliquen et al. (2004).

/H8/ Focus on geographic area. Ignore referents that lie outside a given polygon by thinning out the gazetteer (data reduction), which corresponds to setting a static geographic context based on application considerations to simplify the task. Like the previous idea, this is a pseudo-technique. Alternatively, it is possible to apply this focus selection not statically, but dynamically, i.e. by first assigning unambiguous ('sure-fire') toponyms, then determining the geographic focus for the whole document based on these partial assignments, in order to subsequently filter out interpretations that are outside of this focus. As an example of a static focus scenario, consider a system dedicated to the analysis of

Russian news, which could be provided with a gazetteer in which locations outside of Russia are pruned so as to increase the precision of the system as far as locations inside Russia are concerned.

As an example of a dynamic focus scenario, in a global geographic newspaper indexing software, the system may be informed by a document's country of publication, and this knowledge may be used to restrict gazetteer lookup to entries within the realm of the document's country.

Example:

Springfield $\mapsto$ In a system with a world wide gazetteer, we would need to choose from 125 candidate referents; but after removing all non-US entries from the gazetteer (US-specific, static/offline tuning), a mere 63 candidate referents remain.

Berlin $\mapsto \langle 54.03; 10.45 \rangle$ (unambiguously assigned) in a system focussing on the country Germany only; otherwise, without a geo-focus, the system would have to choose from a total of 45 candidate referents (populated places) worldwide, obviously a much harder task.

Used by:

Pouliquen et al. (2004) (static focus on Europe);

Pouliquen et al. (2006) (dynamic focus).

/H9/ **Distance to unambiguous textual neighbours.** To resolve a toponym t_1, consider the W surrounding, *unambiguous* toponyms on either side in the discourse. Assign the referent which is geographically the closest to (the centroid of) all of them as the interpretation for t_1. Note that the utility of this heuristic decreases as the ambiguity of the gazetteer increases, since in a situation without unambiguous toponyms, the heuristic is no longer applicable.

Example:

... *Trumpington* ... *Madingley* ... *Cambridge* ... *Fletching* ... *Arrington* ... $\mapsto$ $\langle 52.2; 0.1166667 \rangle$, i.e. Cambridge, UK, is chosen (here $W = 2$)

Bad Bergzabern ... *Landau* ... *Dörrenbach* $\mapsto \langle 49.2075; 8.1133 \rangle$, i.e. Landau (*in der Pfalz*), Palatine, Germany is preferred over Landau (*an der Isar*), Bavaria, Germany (here, a context $W = 1$ is used).

Used by:

Smith and Crane (2001) (for $W = 4$).

/H10/ **Discard off-threshold.** Compute the geographic focus (centroid) for the toponyms mentioned in the document. Eliminate all candidate referents that are more than 2 standard deviations away from it.

This can be seen as a dynamic version of /H8/ (online centroid based pruning).

Example:

... Tonbridge ... Rainham ... Leeds ... Birling ... ↦ ⟨51.2333333; 0.6166667⟩, i.e. select not the more popular Leeds in the English midlands, since it it much further away than 2 standard deviations from the centroid, but rather the Leeds near Maidstone in the south of England.

Used by:

Smith and Crane (2001).

/H11/ Frequency weighting. Give higher importance (weight) to more frequent toponyms in a text. This is a meta-heuristic that can be applied to the treatment of toponyms combined with other heuristics when comparing decisions for multiple toponyms, especially to avoid ties in scoring.

Example:

Edinburgh ... Glasgow and Edinburgh ... Edinburgh ... ↦ give higher weight to Edinburgh than to Glasgow when applying other heuristics (e.g. for centroid computation).

Used by:

Smith and Crane (2001);
Li et al. (2003).

/H12/ Prefer higher-level referents. If a toponym can refer to two candidate referents, one of which is a continent, and the other one a country, pick the one that belongs to a higher-level category in a spatial taxonomy with earth as its root and cities as its leaves (i.e., country-level is higher level than city-level, independent of population size).

If a toponym can refer to two referents, one of which is a country, and the other one a state, pick the higher-level unit one.

If a toponym can refer to two referents, one of which is a state, and the other one a county, pick the higher-level unit one.

If a toponym can refer to two referents, one of which is a county, and the other one a city, again pick the higher-level one. The length of the hierarchical path (the shorter, the more global) can also be used as a numerical feature.

Example:

Africa ↦ assign the continent Africa rather than the cities Africa, Mexico, Africa, IN, USA, or Africa, OH, USA.

Used by:

Smith and Crane (2001);
Clough (2005).

/H13/ Feature type disambiguator. If the patterns

t_1 t_2 t_2 in t_1

t_2 near t_1 t_2 of t_1

t_2 on t_1

match, where t_1 is a toponym and t_2 is a term which is indicative of a feature type (*city, capital, country, county, town, province, ...*), then eliminate those candidate referents that are known to be *not* of type t_2. This is a negative constraint.

Example:

city of Scotland $\mapsto$ eliminate UK country interpretation (among other locations, 21 US cities are called *Scotland*, e.g. Scotland, Alabama).

Used by:

Li et al. (2003);

Rauch et al. (2003);

Schilder et al. (2004).

/H14/ Textual-Spatial Correlation. Assume that textual proximity is strongly positively correlated with spatial proximity, and assign referents accordingly.

Note that unlike /H5/, this takes *textual* distance into account, and unlike /H2/, the two toponyms can be, but need not be in a meronymic relationship.

It is also worth noting that this source of evidence is not actually restricted to toponym–toponym co-occurrence relationships, since arbitrary toponym–*term* correlations can also provide disambiguation cues. For example, the term *Theresa* is positively correlated with the assignment *Calcutta* $\mapsto \langle 22.5697222; 88.3697222 \rangle$, i.e. a mention of Calcutta is be more likely to be grounded in India when *Mother Theresa* is mentioned nearby.

This type of evidence can be implemented using significance tests, pointwise mutual information, or likelihood ratios, for example.

Example:

If *Paris* and *France* (and/or *Versailles*) are in close textual proximity to each other, then assign *Paris* $\mapsto$ Paris, France.

Used by:

Li et al. (2003);

Rauch et al. (2003).

/H15/ Default Referent. Use existing knowledge where available about the most salient referent in typical discourse and assign referents accordingly.

Note that unlike /H3/, this heuristic draws directly on human intuitions about the salience (as opposed to population size).

Example:

Assume *Washington* to refer to the capital city of Washington, DC, USA, rather than the US state Washington despite the fact that more people live in the latter.

Note that while population size is a very obvious indicator, it does not always yield reliable results: 'Cambridge' may refer to the famous English University town or to Cambridge, MA, USA, but both Cambridges have similar population size (just above 100,000).

Another possible indicator of salience is the area covered by the populated settlement (city, town, village).

Used by:

Li et al. (2003) (using defaults from the TIPSTER gazetteer).

/H16/ Preference order. When using several gazetteers in parallel, there may be evidence of superior authoritativeness between these datasets. This fact can be used to define a static order of priority between them. For example, if we are using SABE, OS and TGN together in a system, we may follow Clough (2005), who as a rule prefers SABE entries over OS entries, which in turn are preferred over TGN entries.

In general, given a set of different gazetteers covering the same geographic area, the more gazetteers that a given toponym occurs in the more salient it will typically be.

Example:

Assume *Washington* has a SABE entry that refers to the capital city of Washington, DC, USA, and OS had a British Washington entry, then we can simply ignore the OS entry and stick to the SABE entry by default, because we always assume SABE $<$ OS $<$ TGN (read '$<$' as 'has priority over').

Washington $\mapsto \langle 38.895; -77.03667 \rangle$, i.e. Washington is always Districy of Columbia, because SABE contains that referent, and the SABE gazetteer takes priority over the OS gazetteer.

Stanford $\mapsto \langle 37.42417; -122.165 \rangle$, i.e. a Stanford in California, if specified in SABE, has priority over its British 'rival' place, $\langle 51.1; 1.033 \rangle$, as specified in OS.

Used by:

Clough (2005).

Figure 3.6 summarises these findings and tries to group these sources of evidence for resolution decision making in a taxonomy. We distinguish between linguistic knowledge (left) and world knowledge (right); unambiguous toponyms do not require any resolution knowledge, so they do not belong to either category. Linguistic heuristics are either local (/H1/ and /13/), discourse-level (/H2/, /H4/, /H5/, and /H14/), or global and statistical (/H11/) in nature. Discourse heuristics can be instances of the *minimality principle* Gardent and Webber (2001), such as 'one referent per discourse', 'minimal bounding polygon' (Leidner et al. (2003)) and also 'distance to unambiguous neighbours'. World knowledge, on the other hand, encompasses population size related heuristics (/H3/, /H7/) and other indicators of salience (such as 'being a capital' for /H15/) as well as ontological relationships (/H2/). The final, quite large sub-group comprises knowledge about spatial distribution. Some heuristics draw on both spatial and linguistic knowledge, turning the taxonomy into a more complex graph where leaf nodes can have multiple parent nodes. This form of visualisation should not be seen as the only possible way to present the outcome of the analysis of the knowledge used in past work; rather, it is merely intended to provide a synopsis that facilitates relating the various heuristics and knowledge sources.

3.4   Chapter Summary

In this chapter, we have reviewed the existing literature on toponym resolution. Table 3.2 (on page 112) summarises the state of the art in TR. It compares the various research systems in terms of their gazetteer sizes (number of entries), the chosen spatial representation for toponym referents (numerical coordinates or symbolic taxonomy paths), and whether or not named entity tagging was used. Where available, separate quality measures for named entity recognition and toponym resolution are given.[9] Where an evaluation is mentioned, the sample size (number of toponyms in the test set) is given. The table also recapitulates the described limitations of the systems.

Two observations are most striking: firstly, the evaluation of existing TR methods is sadly lacking, which is a primary motivation behind this thesis. Secondly, proposed systems and methods are very different in nature: implementation idiosyncrasies and differences in gazetteer size, granularity and spatial representation do not allow a direct comparison.

In the absence of formal specifications or easily available implementations, I also have devised semi-formal reconstructions of the described algorithms in the form of pseudo-code in this chapter.

We have systematically described the sources of evidence for a particular referent to be chosen from a set of candidates in the existing algorithms surveyed. The resulting repertoire

---

[9]We follow established convention in using P for Precision, R for Recall, F for the geometric mean between P and R, A for Accuracy, and E for Error rate; see Manning and Schütze (1999) for the standard definitions of these metrics.

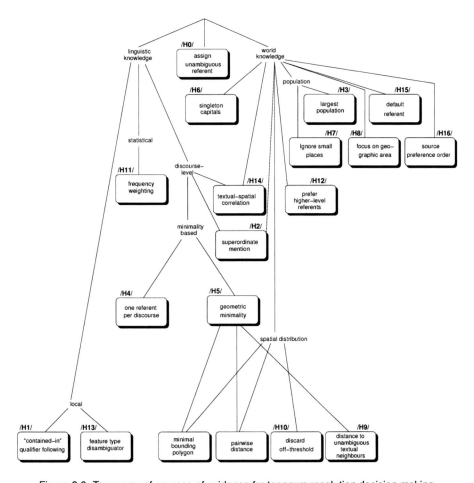

Figure 3.6: Taxonomy of sources of evidence for toponym resolution decision making.

of knowledge sources and heuristic biases is shown in Table 3.3 on page 114.[10] Interestingly, apart from local disambiguation patterns (/H1/) and the 'one referent per discourse' heuristic (/H4/), there is not a large degree of overlap of the knowledge sources employed between those approaches. We will be using this inventory of heuristics later in this thesis to evaluate their relative utility, and to show that combining them in a principled fashion yields a method that outperforms the state of the art and has useful applications. But first, we need to concentrate on curating a dataset for such an evaluation, which is the topic of the next chapter.

---

[10]At the beginning of this thesis project, only the first two of the publications listed in Table 3.3 existed, which shows the increase of interest that toponym resolution has been receiving.

	Hauptmann and Olligschlaeger (1999)	Smith and Crane (2001)	Bilhaut et al. (2003)	Li et al. (2003)	Rauch et al. (2003)
Gazetteer size	80,000	>1,000,000	10,000	237,916	unknown
Representation for referents	(lat/lon)	(lat/lon)	hybrid (AVMs)	lat/lon + path	lat/lon
NE tagging used?	yes (custom)	yes (rules)	no	yes	yes
Evaluation sample size N	357	unknown	–	149	–
Toponym Recognition P R $F_{\beta=0.5}$ A E	unknown	unknown	unknown	unknown	unknown
Toponym Resolution P R $F_{\beta=0.5}$ A E	unknown	0.89-0.99 0.89-1.00 0.81-0.96	unknown	0.96	unknown
Limitations	now commercial	unknown	France only	commercial	commercial

Table 3.2: Summary of the state of the art in toponym resolution.

	Schilder et al. (2004)	Pouliquen et al. (2004)	Amitay et al. (2004)	Clough (2005)	Pouliquen et al. (2006)
Gazetteer size	36,000	85,000	75,000	915,949	85,000(?)
Representation for referents	path	lat/lon	path	path and lat/lon	lat/lon
NE tagging used?	yes (custom)	no	no	no (best)/ yes (GATE)	no
Evaluation sample size N	unknown (12 articles)	1,650 (en)	2,307 (news)	1,864 (130 docs.)	unknown (en: 40 docs.)
Toponym Recognition					
P		0.98			
R		0.88			
$F_{\beta=0.5}$				0.71	≈0.77
A	0.74				
E			0.154		
Toponym Resolution		unknown			
P					0.91
R					0.78
$F_{\beta=0.5}$					0.84
A	0.64			0.89	
E			0.069		
Limitations	German only	Europe only?	commercial	parts of Europe	Europe-optimised

Method	/H1/	/H2/	/H3/	/H4/	/H5/	/H6/	/H7/	/H8/	/H9/	/H10/	/H11/	/H12/	/H13/	/H14/	/H15/	/H16/
(Hauptmann and Olligschlaeger 1999)	■	■		■												
Smith and Crane (2001)	■															
Leidner et al. (2003)	■				■											
Li et al. (2003)	■			■	■											
Rauch et al. (2003)			■			■										
Schilder et al. (2004)	■		■	■			■	■			■					
Pouliquen et al. (2004)	■	■		■	■		■	■					■	■	■	
Amitay et al. (2004)									■	■		■	■			
Clough (2005)													■	■		
Pouliquen et al. (2006)	■										■	■				■

Works are given in chronological order.

The numbering of the heuristics follows the scheme introduced earlier in this chapter.

The method proposed in Leidner et al. (2003) will be described below in Chapter 5.

Table 3.3: Synopsis of heuristics used by previous work.

Chapter 4

Dataset

Next to a good dictionary,
the most generally useful book is a good gazetteer.
– W. G. Blackie (1855)

[Parts of a previous version this chapter have been published as 'Towards a Reference Corpus for Automatic Toponym Resolution Evaluation' in the Proceedings of the Workshop on Geographic Information Retrieval held at the 27th Annual International ACM SIGIR Conference (SIGIR 2004), Sheffield, UK (Leidner (2004b)) and in Computers, Environment and Urban Systems 30(4), pp. 400–417 (Leidner (2006a)).]

4.1 Introduction

This chapter addresses the problem of the absence of a standard benchmark for the toponym resolution task (pointed out by Leidner (2004a); Clough and Sanderson (2004); Pouliquen et al. (2006), among others) by proposing the first reference dataset for the task, created for the current investigation. A reference dataset requires the curation of two elementary parts:

- a *reference gazetteer* that lists the toponyms with associated spatial footprints and

- a *reference corpus* in which all toponyms in it are annotated with spatial footprint information from the reference gazetteer.

Using this reference dataset provides a means of control, i.e. using it for experiments leads to more comparable results. The absence of sufficient control has presented a barrier to progress in the field of TR to date, because there are too many variables that impact task difficulty and performance.

Section 4.2 describes criteria for corpus sampling and the resulting design decisions for choosing documents for annotation used in this thesis. Section 4.3 discusses the requirements that the annotation for this thesis project should meet. Section 4.4 describes the reference gazetteer that constitutes the basis for all annotation in this project. Section 4.5 then describes a new markup scheme devised for the task, a new toolkit developed to annotate datasets with geographic grounding information, and the annotation process that leads to the reference corpus presented in this thesis. Finally, Section 4.6 characterises the resulting annotated dataset, and Section 4.7 summarises and concludes this chapter.

4.2   Corpus Sampling

The first question when curating a reference corpus is the question of *corpus sampling*. In general, it is desirable to have a large, diverse collection of texts which is balanced and thus representative of typical text exposure of a well-defined audience. Unfortunately, this ideal can be unrealistic in the face of resource constraints. Nevertheless, we begin by stating criteria for the ideal case:

- **R1. Balance.** Intuitively, different text types are likely to exhibit specific distributions of toponyms, and this is likely to impact their grounding. Thus, it is desirable to curate a corpus that contains a wide range of text types such as news, travel reports, personal emails, and novels. Another dimension of diversity is the *geographic scope* of the places mentioned, e.g. from community-local over country-specific to global newspaper.

- **R2. Availability.** The text corpus used as a basis should exist already in online form.

- **R3. Shareability.** A prerequisite for the curation of a scientific reference resource is that it is possible to share it with other research groups so as to be able to evaluate improved algorithms against the same dataset to quantify progress. Unfortunately, copyright and licensing restrictions often limit the degree to which available resources can be shared across institutions.

- **R4. Named entity annotations.** Existing named entity annotation in gold-standard quality allows the investigation of the quality of toponym resolution methods independently of artefacts introduced by imperfect automatic named entity recognition and classification (i.e., a controlled component-based evaluation). Using a corpus that does not have pre-annotated named entity information implies a cost increase as two levels of markup have to be provided instead of just one.

- **R5. Corpus size.** The corpus has to be as large as possible. In practice, the size needs to be significant, yet small enough to be annotated with the limited resources available.

Based on these criteria, and taking into account time and budget constraints, two corpora that contain news prose were chosen, one global and another one regional, for subsequent annotation of toponyms with representations of the locations referred to. This means that requirement R1 had to be compromised as far as the text type balance is concerned, but is fully met as far as geographic score is concerned. News data was chosen as the basis mainly for two reasons: first, the availability of well-known news corpora pre-annotated for place names made this project practically feasible (R4), because the annotation could be restricted to choosing between the various candidate *referents* for a place name, rather than having to *identify* all toponyms in the text first. Second, news is arguably the text type that is publically available in the largest quantity while being relevant to a large target audience and for various purposes from political decision making to entertainment. Requirement R2 is easily satisfied, as all significant newspapers are nowadays created in electronic form before going to print, and most of them have an online Web presence. R3 is difficult in that newspaper reports are covered by copyright law and cannot be freely shared. However, the corpora chosen here are both already used by NLP researchers, so copyright clearances have been obtained in the past. R4 is difficult: only a small minority of news corpora are readily available with human-quality named entity annotation, and from this set two datasets have been selected to form a new corpus. The existing, human gold-standard named entity markup means this corpus can be used to assess toponym *resolution* accuracy without introducing noise by potential errors in the named entity *recognition* sub-task, thus allowing a controlled, *component-based evaluation*. As for the size (R5), again a compromise had to be made. The corpus created here contains two sub-corpora, one larger, global sub-corpus and a smaller regional sub-corpus. Both together comprise several hundred documents, which is a reasonably large collection for evaluation, although it would be desirable to create even larger annotated datasets due to the huge number of toponyms and the existence of millions of locations. It is evident that only a minority of these can ever be seen in datasets of practical size for a thesis. Next I describe the two sub-corpora in detail.

4.2.1 TR-CoNLL: Global News from REUTERS

The REUTERS Corpus Volume I (RCV1)[1] is a document collection containing all English-language news stories produced by REUTERS journalists between August 20, 1996 and August 19, 1997 (Rose et al. (2002)). These stories contain typical international newswire prose, and the documents vary in length from a few hundred to several thousand words. Among other uses, the RCV1 corpus is frequently used for benchmarking automatic text classification methods (Lewis et al. (2004)).

Its widespread use and the fact that it contains stories of global scope and interest, however, are not the main reason for considering using RCV1 as a resource to draw upon when

---

[1] http://about.reuters.com/researchandstandards/corpus/

```
┌─────────────────────────────────────────────────────────────────────┐
│  Thirty killed as floods plunge Lahore into chaos.                    │
│                                                                       │
│  ISLAMABAD 1996-08-24                                                 │
│                                                                       │
│  At least 30 people have been killed and about 100 injured in the     │
│  flood-hit Pakistani city of Lahore, newspapers reported on Saturday. │
│  They said 461 mm (18 inches) of rain had drenched the Punjab         │
│  provincial capital in 36 hours, turning streets into rivers,         │
│  knocking out power, water and telephone services, disrupting air     │
│  and rail traffic, and sweeping away houses and cars.                 │
│  Newspapers quoted witnesses as saying they had seen bodies floating  │
│  in the streets.                                                      │
│  Among the dead were five members of the religious Jamaat-i-Islami    │
│  party who drowned while trying to remove books from a basement       │
│  library.                                                             │
│  They said thousands of people had been made homeless after a         │
│  breach opened in the city canal, inundating residential areas.       │
│  Army troops were called in to evacuate residents of low-lying        │
│  areas to higher ground.  Officials said the Ravi and Chenab rivers,  │
│  which both flow through Punjab, were in high flood and emergency     │
│  services backed by troops were on full alert.                        │
└─────────────────────────────────────────────────────────────────────┘
```

Figure 4.1: Example document D307. Toponyms (named entities tagged LOCATION) in the original corpus are underlined.

sampling a toponym resolution evaluation corpus; rather, it is the fact that for a subset of it, gold-standard named entity annotation is already available. In 2003, the Conference on Natural Language Learning (CoNLL) offered a 'shared task' exercise in which international teams competed in applying machine learning methods to solve a natural language processing task comprising the automatic identification and appropriate labelling of location names in texts (Tjong Kim Sang and De Meulder (2003)). For this competitive evaluation, a subset of the RCV1 corpus was created in which all named entities were manually annotated in order to benchmark named entity tagging.

Here, a subset of 946 documents, henceforth called **TR-CoNLL**, was chosen from the news stories (specifically, the CoNLL training corpus in the file 'eng.train') for creating the first toponym resolution evaluation sub-corpus, resulting in 204,566 text tokens. The documents in this set cover REUTERS news from the date range 22 August 1996 to 31 August 1996.[2]

Figure 4.1 shows a typical story from the TR-CoNLL corpus. In general, despite its 'gold standard' status, the named entity annotation this dataset is not perfect in practice. The data was taken as is, however, i.e. no attempts were made to correct named entity tagging mistakes in the data.

4.2.2 TR-MUC4: FBIS Central American Intelligence Reports

The second sub-corpus, henceforth called **TR-MUC4**, comprises a subset of 100 documents used in MUC-4, the Fourth Message Understanding Contest (Sundheim (1992)).[3] This collection is made up from intelligence reports from the Foreign Broadcast Information Service (FBIS) covering Central America from August to December 1988. The sub-collection contains 30,051 tokens.

4.3 Annotation Desiderata

4.3.1 Referent Representation

Feature types. A gazetteer contains a set of toponyms with their associated feature type as well as spatial footprints. However, feature type inventories differ widely across applications. For example, an internal Edinburgh EDINA-LTG geo-parsing project (Matheson (2003)) used the categories `loc-boundary`, `loc-hydro`, `loc-manmade`, `loc-other` and `loc-physio` annotation. Clough and Sanderson (2004), on the other hand, propose the following feature types: `City`, `River`, `Mountain`, `Island`, `Region`, `Province`, `WaterRegion`, `Address`, `Zipcode`, `PhoneNumber`, `EmailAddress`, and `URL`. For this study, it was decided to concentrate on populated places (of all granularities), simply because they coincide with named entities of type `LOCATION` already annotated in the two corpora used. The reliance on existing named entity annotation is also the reason why no distinction was drawn between `LOCATION` and `GPE` (geopolitical entity).

 Spatial footprint. There have been several proposals for representing locations (Table 4.1 gives a summary): numerical *latitude/longitude coordinates* are the most widely used system. Some countries define a structured *national grid reference* system. *Polygon points* can be used to describe a location associated with a toponym more accurately, since e.g. cities have complex shapes. ISO 631 path identifiers like `de_mag` (for the city of Magdeburg, Sachsen-Anhalt, Germany) have also been proposed (Schilder et al. (2004)). Jiang and Steenkiste (2002) describe a hybrid notation for the representation of locations in a ubiquitous computing environment.

 For this project, numeric coordinates given as decimal latitude and longitude of the location centroids are used in conjunction with human-readable hierarchical path descriptions like `'London > United Kingdom > Europe'`. While a polygon representation would have been a

[2]Personal communication, Eric Tjong Kim Sang (2006-08-26).

[3]The author gratefully acknowledges the financial contribution of MetaCarta Inc., which made the annotation of this second sub-corpus possible.

```
-DOCSTART- -X- -X- O

EU NNP I-NP I-ORG
rejects VBZ I-VP O
German JJ I-NP I-MISC
call NN I-NP O
to TO I-VP O
boycott VB I-VP O
British JJ I-NP I-MISC
lamb NN I-NP O
. . O O

Peter NNP I-NP I-PER
Blackburn NNP I-NP I-PER

BRUSSELS NNP I-NP I-LOC
1996-08-22 CD I-NP O

The DT I-NP O
European NNP I-NP I-ORG
Commission NNP I-NP I-ORG
said VBD I-VP O
on IN I-PP O
Thursday NNP I-NP O

[...]
```

Figure 4.2: CoNLL format (excerpt).

Annotation with	Type	Structure
latitude/longitude	*numeric*	*flat*
grid references	symbolic	hierarchical
polygons	numeric	set (of flat)
ISO 631 path identifier	symbolic	hierarchical
Aura Location Identifier (ALI)	hybrid	hierarchical

Table 4.1: Different kinds of spatial annotation.

Name	Distributor	Coverage	Entries
Columbia	Columbia UP	Earth	165,000
Digimap	EDINA	UK	258,797
GNIS (Geographic Names Information System)	*U.S. Geographic Survey*	*USA*	*1,836,264*
GNS (GEPmet Names Server)	*U.S. NGA*	*Earth\USA*	*5,268,934*
TGN (Thesaurus of Geographic Names)	J. P. Getty Trust	Earth	1,300,000
UN LOCODE	UNECE	Earth	40,000
WFB	*U.S. CIA*	*Earth*	*267*

Figure 4.3: Gazetteer profiles.

better representation, unfortunately no free and comprehensive gazetteers are readily available that associate polygon footprints with place names on an earth-wide scale.

4.3.2 Problems of Gazetteer Selection

Existing gazetteers (see Figure 4.3 for some examples) vary along a large number of dimensions. The following six key criteria for gazetteer selection were taken into account for selecting a gazetteer compatible with the goals of this project:

1. *Gazetteer scope*: gazetteers vary in range from small communal (cadastral) databases over regional/national lists to worldwide scope. In this project, grounding shall be attempted on a global scale, which requires earth-wide scope.

2. *Gazetteer coverage*: to date, no gazetteer covers all places in existence; but whereas some are more comprehensive (like NGA GNS), others only have a very limited coverage (e.g. UN-LOCODE).

3. *Gazetteer correctness*: Gazetteers typically contain many wrong or outdated entries: for example, in 1996, South Africa changed its administration from four provinces to nine.[4] However, at the time the data snapshot was taken (May 2004), the then-current GNS edition still featured a London, Transvaal, South Africa, although Transvaal had long ceased to exist. Indeed, there are circa 20,000 changes per month carried out on the GNS gazetteer data alone. Gazetteers also suffer from measurement imprecision.

4. *Gazetteer granularity*: not all gazetteers aim to achieve completeness; some merely list the more popular or relevant places. A less fine-grained gazetteer may actually facilitate the toponym resolution task by providing a useful bias (in the same way that average humans living in New York are not familiar with minor Siberian villages), and too fine-grained databases yield 'noise', but sometimes unpopular places are in the media spotlight for a short term due to an important event (Shaw (2003)), and it is therefore desirable for a system to have very fine-grained geographic knowledge.

5. *Gazetteer balance*: a gazetteer that is balanced provides uniform degree of detail and correctness across all continents and regions.

6. Gazetteer *richness of annotation*: the amount and detail of information associated with the name of a place varies from mere longitude/latitude numbers to detailed type and population information.

For scientific study, the free availability of the source is also a key criterion, as stated in the introduction, since published performance results can only be replicated and improved on if the dataset used can be obtained and shared. Consequently, the Columbia Gazetteer and TGN had to be excluded on grounds of restricted availability. Digimap is limited to the UK, and also not free. UN LOCODE had to be discarded because of its insufficient coverage.

Note that unlike in traditional text span classification tasks, a grounding task must rely on an external knowledge source and thus suffers from a *interdependence* between gazetteer/ontology on the one hand and the document with instances to be marked up and grounded on the other hand: *the gazetteer is not simply an interchangeable system component, it gains reference status together with the corpus in which it is employed to look up the set of potential referents.*

This means that the gazetteer chosen to curate a reference corpus influences the outcome of any subsequent experiment: there can be a potential bias towards systems using the same gazetteer for resolving the toponyms. However, if systems are designed in a modular fashion, they could be provided with the gazetteer used for gold-standard curation for the purpose of evaluation of the resolution method only.[5] The role of a gazetteer in toponym resolution cor-

---

[4]Personal communication, Douglas E. Ross, National Geospatial Intelligence Agency, 2004-04-23.

[5]This would be a method evaluation rather than a component evaluation, since the system could still be deployed with another gazetteer.

Toponym / No. of Referents	WordNet	USGS	NGA	UN-LOCODE	World Gazetteer
Edinburgh	1	4	11	3	2
Sheffield	1	16	10	3	2
London	1	18	33	4	5
Berlin	1	29	95	8	2
Paris	1	24	31	6	7
New York	1	7	12	2	1
Aberdeen	4	19	22	6	4
Springfield	3	63	62	10	13
Victoria	3	26	250	6	15
Santa Ana	2	3	597	4	11
Cambridge	2	29	25	7	1
Macclesfield	0	1	4	1	1
Bad Bergzabern	0	0	1	1	0

Table 4.2: Comparison of gazetteer density.

responds to the role of *WordNet* (Fellbaum (2001)) in Word Sense Disambiguation (WSD) evaluations like SENSEVAL (Kilgarriff and Rosenzweig (2000)). Hill (2006) provides a detailed treatment of gazetteers in a geo-referencing context.

4.3.3 Gazetteer Ambiguity and Heterogeneity

Figure 4.4 shows a log-scale plot of the referential ambiguity inherent in the gazetteer, contrasted with the aforementioned smaller gazetteers. As is evident from the graph, using a tiny gazetteer such as UN-LOCODE or World Gazetteer represents an oversimplification of the TR problem, because they omit the most ambiguous (and therefore most difficult) cases. On the one hand, it is shown that a large number of toponyms are not ambiguous. On the other hand, some toponyms have more than 1,500 locations that they could potentially be referring to. Overall, the distribution is approximately exponential.

Note, however, that we cannot use the gazetteer alone to reason about the difficulty of toponym resolution as a task, because its difficulty not only pertains to the number of referents in the gazetteer (*potential ambiguity*, *type ambiguity*), but also to the distribution of instances in documents, i.e. whether the difficult cases also occur in texts and how often (*actual ambiguity*, *token ambiguity*), a question to which we will return later in this chapter.

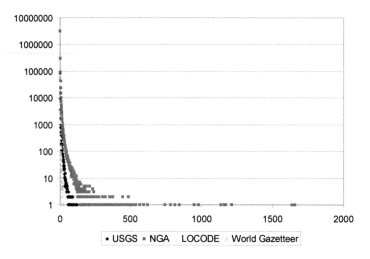

Figure 4.4: Gazetteer ambiguity (number of gazetteer entries as a function of the number of candidate referents).

Table 4.2 shows the number of referents for a selection of cities from a high-level perspective. As can be seen, the number of entries for many of them varies by orders of magnitudes across the gazetteers compared.

Table 4.3 shows the number of referents of the 40 most referentially ambiguous toponyms as taken from four gazetteers. Place names that occur in the top-40 in more than one gazetteer (i.e. entries shared across several gazetteers) are shown in bold type. We can witness *gazetteer heterogeneity*, i.e. both the degree of overlap in the top-40 ranks and the relative position of a toponym's number of referents across gazetteers vary dramatically. By implication, the choice of a particular gazetteer in a toponym resolver presents a crucial commitment and a variable that needs to be controlled in any comparative study.

4.4 Gazetteer

For this project, a new gazetteer (henceforth *TextGIS® Gazetteer*), was built from existing sources. The GNIS gazetteer of the U.S. Geographic Survey and the GNS gazetteers of the National Geospatial Intelligence Agency (NGA)[6] were used and supplemented by 267 *CIA World Factbook* (WFB) country centroids. Unlike the very large USGS and NGA datasets, the smaller CIA World Factbook's set of entries for countries was pre-processed manually in the following way to improve automatic matching of toponyms in text against gazetteer entries: for entries with multi-token (composite) names, such as

```
Bosnia and Herzegovina|44|00|N|18|00|E
```

in addition to the original entry, constituent entries were generated to accommodate the fact that there is a high likelihood for them to occur in newspaper text as well:

```
Bosnia and Herzegovina|44|00|N|18|00|E
Bosnia                 |44|00|N|18|00|E
Herzegovina            |44|00|N|18|00|E
```

If used together, these resources have world-wide scope, very good coverage, and the data can be freely shared.

In addition to coverage, another advantage of the design criteria for the *TextGIS® Gazetteer* is that the data can be freely shared, in accordance with the criteria mentioned in Section 4.2.

However, it is well known that the quality of publically available geo-data is only modest with respect to correctness compared to commercial sources. The NGA gazetteer alone

---

[6]Formerly known as NIMA (U.S. National Imaging and Mapping Agency).

USGS	Ref.	NGA	Ref.	UN-LOCODE	Ref.	World Gazetteer	Ref.
Midway	211	**San José**	1658	**Clinton**	16	Oktjabrskij	23
Fairview	202	**San Antonio**	1637	Newport	15	La Unin	16
Oak Grove	160	Santa Maria	1213	Plymouth	14	Victoria	15
Five Points	147	**Santa Rosa**	1168	Madison	14	**Santa Rosa**	15
Pleasant Hill	121	**San Pedro**	1159	**Georgetown**	14	**San Rafael**	15
Riverside	119	**San Juan**	1134	Milford	13	**San Juan**	15
Mount Pleasant	115	**San Francisco**	980	Kingston	13	**Santiago**	14
Bethel	109	**San Miguel**	950	Greenville	13	**San Pedro**	14
Centerville	108	San Isidro	845	Burlington	13	**Springfield**	13
New Hope	106	La Esperanza	814	Windsor	11	**San José**	13
Liberty	98	**Santa Cruz**	784	**Washington**	11	Pervomajskij	13
Union	95	**San Rafael**	744	Oxford	11	**Clinton**	13
Pleasant Valley	91	**Santa Rita**	625	Hamilton	11	**Santa Cruz**	12
Shady Grove	89	**Santa Ana**	597	Franklin	11	San Marcos	12
Salem	89	Buenavista	571	Columbia	11	**San Luis**	12
Pleasant Grove	87	Aleksandrovka	569	Ashland	11	San Carlos	12
Oakland	87	Hoseynabad	541	**Springfield**	10	**San Antonio**	12
Greenwood	86	Gradina	535	**Salem**	10	Santa Ana	11
Pine Grove	84	**San Vicente**	531	Rochester	10	**San Pablo**	11
Oak Hill	79	Mikhaylovka	523	**Richmond**	10	**San Miguel**	11
Shiloh	78	Aliabad	505	Marion	10	**San Lorenzo**	11
Georgetown	78	Ivanovka	503	Jackson	10	**San Francisco**	11
Concord	75	**Buenos Aires**	487	Danville	10	San Fernando	11
Lakeview	74	Buena Vista	487	Chester	10	**Buenos Aires**	11
Cedar Grove	74	**San Luis**	484	Auburn	10	**Washington**	10
Glendale	72	Kamenka	478	Arlington	10	**Santa Bárbara**	10
Antioch	71	Nikolayevka	458	Alexandria	10	Pueblo Nuevo	10
Hopewell	68	Quebrada Honda	451	Troy	9	Guadalupe	10
Friendship	68	**San Pablo**	448	Newton	9	Concepcin	10
Sunnyside	67	**San Lorenzo**	446	Monticello	9	Zaragoza	9
Spring Hill	66	El Carmen	446	Monroe	9	**San Vicente**	9
Lakewood	66	Santo Domingo	445	Milton	9	**Santa Rita**	9
Buena Vista	64	Berezovka	441	Livingston	9	Santa Luca	9
Springfield	63	San Martin	439	Lexington	9	San Nicols	9
Stringtown	62	**Santa Bárbara**	437	Lebanon	9	San Ignacio	9
Harmony	62	Ojo de Agua	435	Fairfield	9	**Richmond**	9
Highland	61	**Santiago**	424	Canton	9	Neustadt	9
Oakdale	60	Santa Isabel	420	Aurora	9	Hidalgo	9
Highland Park	59	La Laguna	419	Woodstock	8	**Georgetown**	9
Riverview	58	El Porvenir	418	Winchester	8	Trinidad	8

Table 4.3: Most referentially ambiguous toponyms with respect to four different gazetteers.

undergoes thousands of corrections per month and there are many near-duplicates.[7]

Also, for completeness' sake it ought to be mentioned that the particular gazetteer mix is much less suited for studies of grounding historic text (which is an important application, but not the focus of this thesis).

4.5 Document Annotation

4.5.1 A Simple Markup Scheme

This section describes *Toponym Resolution Markup Language* (TRML), the XML-based markup scheme which is implemented by the tool-chain described below.

XML was chosen because of its W3C recommendation status and the resulting widespread tool support. For these same reasons, stand-off XML, which was initially considered due to its clean separation of data and markup (Carletta et al., 2003), had to be discarded: Web browsers do not at the time of writing support stand-off XML for rendering, it has no standard status, and there is also no validation support by available XML parsers.

An important criterion for the design of a successful toponym markup scheme was that *document structure* should be preserved. Otherwise, discourse conventions, such as introducing a news story by specifying the main location and the source of the information below the headline, could not be utilised by the resolution method. Furthermore, the scheme was to be kept simple to ease implementation and to reduce adoption barriers for other research groups.

As a result, TRML offers the following tags for the markup of text. First, a document can be marked up structurally. Documents are wrapped in a <doc> tag. Optionally paragraphs can also be marked up as <p> (however, the CoNLL subset of RCV1 used here does not contain paragraph information.). Sentence boundaries are indicated by the <s> content element. Sentences comprise either word tokens (sometimes called *w-units*), <w>, or toponyms (<toponym>), which in turn contain one or more <w> elements.

The word token content element <w> has attributes for part of speech (pos), for indicating the non-recursive phrase type or *chunk* (chk), and for named entity boundary and type (ne).

Each <toponym> content element contains a <candidates> element that contains a set of the alternative candidate referents (<cand>).

Each of these locations has an identifier and carries information about origin of the data (src), i.e. whether an entry originates from the NGA gazetteer, for instance. Longitude and latitude coordinates are stored in decimal form in the long and lat attributes, respectively. The

---

[7]Note that for the purpose of evaluating algorithms for toponym resolution, correctness of the entries matters much less compared to consistency between the gazetteer used in the resolution system and the gazetteer used for the annotation of the evaluation corpus.

A production system could be evaluated using the static gazetteer snapshot presented here but would be likely to use the most recent version of the data when deployed.

```
<doc id="d1">
 <s id="s1">
  <w tok="EU" pos="NNP" chk="I-NP" ne="I-ORG" />
  <w tok="rejects" pos="VBZ" chk="I-VP" ne="O" />
  <w tok="German" pos="JJ" chk="I-NP" ne="I-MISC" />
  <w tok="call" pos="NN" chk="I-NP" ne="O" />
  <w tok="to" pos="TO" chk="I-VP" ne="O" />
  <w tok="boycott" pos="VB" chk="I-VP" ne="O" />
  <w tok="British" pos="JJ" chk="I-NP" ne="I-MISC" />
  <w tok="lamb" pos="NN" chk="I-NP" ne="O" />
  <w tok="." pos="." chk="O" ne="O" />
 </s>
 <s id="s2">
  <w tok="Peter" pos="NNP" chk="I-NP" ne="I-PER" />
  <w tok="Blackburn" pos="NNP" chk="I-NP" ne="I-PER" />
 </s>
 <s id="s3">
  <toponym did="1" sid="3" tid="1" term="BRUSSELS">
    <w tok="BRUSSELS" pos="NNP" chk="I-NP" ne="I-LOC" />
    <candidates>
      <cand id="c1" src="NGA" lat="-23.3833333" long="29.15"
            humanPath="Brussels &gt; (SF04) &gt; South Africa" />
      <cand id="c2" src="NGA" lat="-24.25" long="30.95"
            humanPath="Brussels &gt; (SF04) &gt; South Africa" />
      <cand id="c3" src="NGA" lat="-24.6833333" long="26.6833333"
            humanPath="Brussels &gt; (SF04) &gt; South Africa" />
      <cand id="c4" src="NGA" lat="-27.1" long="24.6666667"
            humanPath="Brussels &gt; (SF01) &gt; South Africa" />
      <cand id="c5" src="NGA" lat="-27.15" long="24.75"
            humanPath="Brussels &gt; (SF01) &gt; South Africa" />
      <cand id="c6" src="NGA" lat="50.8333333" long="4.3333333"
            selected="yes"
            humanPath="Brussels &gt; (BE02) &gt; Belgium" />
      <cand id="c7" src="USGS_PP" lat="38.94944" long="-90.58861"
            humanPath="Brussels &gt; Calhoun &gt; IL &gt; US &gt; North America" />
      <cand id="c8" src="USGS_PP" lat="44.73611" long="-87.62083"
            humanPath="Brussels &gt; Door &gt; WI &gt; US &gt; North America" />
    </candidates>
  </toponym>
  <w tok="1996-08-22" pos="CD" chk="I-NP" ne="O" />
 </s>
 <s id="s4">
  <w tok="The" pos="DT" chk="I-NP" ne="O" />
  <w tok="European" pos="NNP" chk="I-NP" ne="I-ORG" />
  <w tok="Commission" pos="NNP" chk="I-NP" ne="I-ORG" />
  <w tok="said" pos="VBD" chk="I-VP" ne="O" />
  <w tok="on" pos="IN" chk="I-PP" ne="O" />
  <w tok="Thursday" pos="NNP" chk="I-NP" ne="O" />
[...]
```

Figure 4.5: TRML format (excerpt).

`humanPath` attribute contains the human-readable hierarchical geographic path description for the annotators, and the `selected` attribute finally stores the referent chosen by them.

Figure 4.5 gives an example fragment of valid TRML to illustrate the elements described.[8]

4.5.2 Tool-Chain and Markup Process

This section describes the design implementation of the *Toponym Annotation Markup Editor* (*TAME*), the tool that constitutes the annotation system (Figure 4.6), and the mark-up process it supports.

The following requirements were defined, from which the design decisions that led to TAME were derived:

- **R1. Low cost.** The time to develop and support an annotation tool should be minimal. Ideally, an existing generic tool could be configured to allow toponym reference annotation.

- **R2. Ease of use.** The annotation should be easy to learn and it should be convenient to carry out the task.

- **R3. Annotation speed.** A large number of annotation decisions should be possible in a short amount of time when using the tool.

- **R4. Distribution.** The tool should be usable from various sites to allow for cross-organisational annotation projects.

- **R5. Moderation.** Problematic or questionable annotation decisions should be markable for moderation.

- **R6. Cross-platform.** The tool should be executable on at least the GNU/Linux and Microsoft Windows operating systems.

A Web-based design appears to satisfy Requirements R1, R2, R4 and R6 at the same time: Web applications are easily implemented and users have become used to using Web browsers to perform various tasks. The Web is accessible from all important computer platforms and from any computer connected to the Internet. Web applications do not offer the same performance as local applications, but the benefits outweigh a slight compromise of R3.

The CoNLL data (Figure 4.6, number 1) comes in tabular plain-text format (Figure 4.2), where the first column contains a token (word or part of a multi-token word), the second column contains a part-of-speech tag, the third column contains a chunk-tag and the fourth and

---

[8]Note how difficult it is to judge whether two gazetteer entries for locations called *Brussels* in South Africa truly stand for separate places, or whether they refer to the same place using incorrect/imprecise coordinate information. In Chapter 6, it is described how the evaluation takes this into account.

final column contains a named entity tag in BIO-format (Tjong Kim Sang and De Meulder (2003)). Sentence boundaries are represented by empty lines, and the start of a new document is indicated by a -DOCSTART- pseudo-token. This format does not lend itself to elegant extension or processing with modern tools based on structured data modeling standards (Sall (2002)).

Therefore, the TRML markup language for toponym resolution was specified based on XML (Yergeau et al. (2004)), and a converter was implemented in *Perl* which transforms the CoNLL format into TRML (2). During this conversion, an SQL-based gazetteer server is consulted on the fly (3) to look up the set of candidate referents for each toponym (i.e. for each named entity instance of type LOC, for 'location'). This server is implemented using the RDBMS *SQLite* (Newman (2005)) and takes about 1.5 GB of persistent storage. It delivers gazetteer entries very efficiently (4). The result of the process is a set of independent XML document instances that can be served to annotators anywhere on the Internet over HTTP (Fielding et al. (1999)) by a Web server (5-8). However, raw XML data containing numerical coordinates would be of little use to human annotators. This is traditionally solved by converting a set of XML document instances to static HTML. Here, another route was taken: an XSLT style sheet (Clark (1999)) was implemented (9) that translates TRML into XHTML (Pemberton (2002)) dynamically on the client.

XHTML forms are used to offer the actual annotation interaction to the human annotator, who simply selects a referent from a list of candidates presented in a drop-down menu (Figure 4.7). Selecting one out of a set of textual path descriptions such as London > United Kingdom > Europe hides the numerical longitude/latitude coordinates from the annotators. The coordinates are thus associated with the paths in the TRML internally, but not rendered visibly. Sometimes, identical labels are created based on the information provided in the gazetteer, in which case annotators chose the first entry and flagged the choice 'for moderation'.

Very rarely it might happen that a toponym has more than one referent even within the smallest administration region, such as 'London', which has three potential referents in South Africa alone, one in the Northern Province, and two in Mpumalanga.[9] Such cases require expert moderation, and annotators were told to mark them as such. In fact, it is unlikely for human annotators to have the expertise to cope with such instances even in the presence of more fine-grained hierarchical information, as sub-units of most countries other than the annotators' home country will not be known. However, luckily no such cases occurred in the two sub-corpora described here. Appendix B contains the guidelines that the annotators were provided with. In addition, they were instructed to maintain an electronic file where they were expected to record noteworthy observations, and a second browser window where they could consult

---

[9]Personal communication, Douglas E. Ross, National Geospatial Intelligence Agency, 2004-04-23.

	TR-CoNLL	TR-MUC4
Corpus size (in tokens)	204,566	30,051
Number of documents	946	100
Toponym instances	6,980	278
Unique toponyms	1,299	135
Annotator agreement κ	0.9350	0.7840
Human annotators employed	4	2

Table 4.4: Evaluation corpus profiles.

a Web search engine where they could search for further evidence in case the referent for a toponym was not immediately obvious from the context.

When displayed in a standard Web browser, the document instances are also validated automatically on the fly to ensure correctness (10), making the system immune to syntactic conversion errors. The advantage of this procedure is that no auxiliary sets of HTML files have to be maintained and updated after system modification.[10]

Cases where human annotators are uncertain about their annotation decision can be flagged for moderation using a check-box. After the annotation of a document is complete, submission transfers the results back to the server via CGI (Coar and Robinson (1999)), where the chosen referents are flagged in the Annotation Store. This completes the document annotation cycle (11-12).

100% of TR-MUC4 was annotated in parallel by 2 annotators, and the results were manually adjudicated, whereas TR-CoNLL toponyms were only annotated by one annotator, apart from an $N = 658$ toponym sample to measure agreement. Annotation (see below) was adjudicated for the 100 document subset for which more than one annotation result was available.

Annotators. The human annotators were native English PhD students in Informatics and one professional annotator (a native speaker of Greek), all with average knowledge of geography as relevant for typical news items such as the documents from the corpus described here. They reported the task was defined reasonably well and could be carried out conveniently using the Web based tool with the relatively brief path descriptions (occasionally, multiple entries with identical path descriptions were flagged 'for moderation').

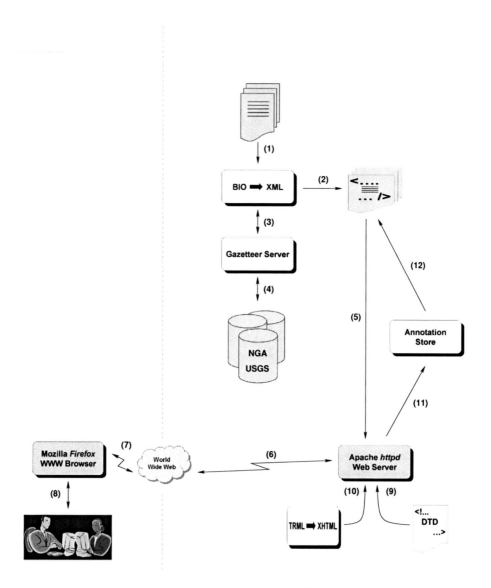

Figure 4.6: The TAME system architecture.

Figure 4.7: TAME, the Toponym Annotation Markup Editor (screen capture).

4.6 Result: Corpus Profile

This section describes the two resulting sub-corpora. Table 4.4 summarises some characteristics.

4.6.1 TR-CoNLL

The resulting annotated corpus comprises 946 documents containing 6,980 toponym instances (tokens) annotated with their path descriptions and latitude/longitude coordinates and 1,299 toponym types (resulting in a type-token ratio of 18.61% for toponyms compared to 11.55% for all corpus terms). The corpus contains 13,991 distinct unique candidate referents. The ten most frequent toponyms are *U.S.* (303 occurrences), *Germany* (141 occurrences), *Britain* (130 occurrences), *Australia* (129 occurrences), *France* (122 occurrences), *England* (122 occurrences), *Spain* (110 occurrences), *Italy* (98 occurrences), *LONDON* (92 occurrences), and *China* (91 occurrences). The prominence of the upper-case form of the British capital city among highest-frequent countries is caused by the fact that the REUTERS news office in London is mentioned in many of the corpus articles. Overall (and ignoring case) there are 184 occurrences of *London*, 48 occurrences of *Paris* and one occurrence of *Edinburgh*.

---

[10]On the client, TRML is shown when a 'View Source' command is issued in the Web browser instead of the XHTML seen by the user.

4.6.2 TR-MUC4

However, we were also interested in studying the robustness of TR methods by comparing news of varying difficulty. I conjectured that the TR-CoNLL corpus, as global news, would be simpler to deal with than more regional news items. Consequently, a second sub-corpus was created (**TR-MUC4**) by taking 100 MUC-4 documents (Sundheim (1992)), whose focus is on Central America, and annotating them in a way compatible with the aforementioned corpus (Table 4.4 compares the two corpora).[11] Note that the human inter-annotator agreement is remarkably lower for TR-MUC4 than for TR-CoNLL. This is caused by the mention of small Central American villages that the annotators had difficulty disambiguating, despite the fact that they were aided by an Internet search engine to retrieve additional information where necessary.

4.6.3 Inter-Annotator Agreement

To establish the reliability of the annotation task for humans (*inter-annotator agreement*), Cohen's κ, a statistic used to measure inter-annotator agreement between a group of two or more annotators designed to factor out agreement by chance (Krippendorf, 1980; Siegel and Castellan Jr, 1988), was used:

$$\kappa = \frac{P(A) - P(E)}{1 - P(E)}, \tag{4.1}$$

where $P(A)$ is the probability that the k annotators agree and $P(E)$ is the probability that the annotators would be expected to agree by chance (Siegel and Castellan Jr, 1988, p. 284-291). Agreement was found to be very high at $\kappa = 0.935$ (Table 4.4). Thus, the current methodology and tool set can be expected to produce only very small annotator-specific idiosyncrasies. The discrepancy between the agreement found here on the one hand and the much lower agreement typically reported in the WSD literature on the other hand could be expected, since the task of assigning a name to a location is intuitively easier than the task of discriminating between different word senses (i.e., *WordNet* synsets) that are much less tangible to the annotator, as required in the WSD task.

Figure 4.8 shows a map of the geographic distribution of the resolved toponyms in the TR-CoNLL, created with GMT (Wessel and Smith, 2004). Obviously, the majority of places reported in stories by global news agencies like REUTERS are located Western Europe and the USA.

Initial experiments were carried out (Leidner (2006e)) without any inspection of the data (i.e. test data was handled as entirely unseen data to avoid potential bias). Some error analysis

---

[11]This annotation effort was financially supported by MetaCarta Inc., whose contribution is gratefully acknowledged.

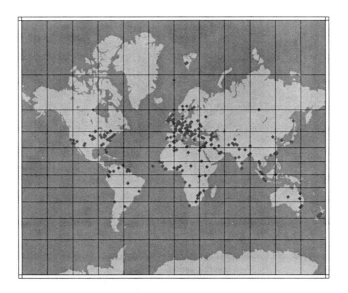

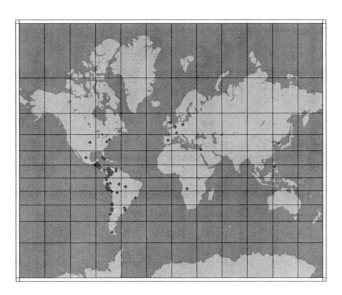

Figure 4.8: Geographic distribution of the locations in TR-CoNLL (top) and TR-MUC4 (bottom).

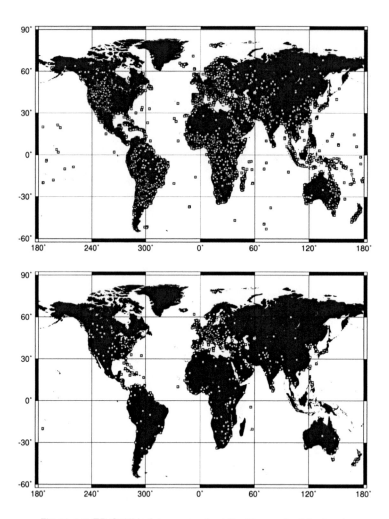

Figure 4.9: TR-CoNLL: from unresolved (top) to resolved (bottom).

done post-hoc revealed, however, that the resulting corpus was of limited use in its raw form because a large number of documents did not contain English prose, but only cricket tables, tables of contents, or other 'noise' (from the linguist's point of view).[12] To exclude potential adverse effects caused by this noise, I decided to manually select a number of documents that contained 'real' English prose text, using the following criteria:

1. textual: eliminate documents without any prose text, including

   - sport results tables (files containing mostly cricket, some football and tennis tables);

   - lists of the performance of financial indices (files containing only number sequences);

   - 'press digest' clippings (files containing only long lists of phrases separated by dashes);

   - table of contents (files that seem to contain meta-data); and

2. length: eliminate files that contain only very short prose texts (i.e. just headlines, or stories with not more than three 80-character lines of text in total).

Unfortunately, applying these criteria required time-intensive manual skim-reading of the corpus. A sample of 154 TR-CoNLL documents meeting the above criteria was obtained this way (cf. Appendix D for a list), which forms the basis of the evaluation experiments described in Chapter 6. This does not mean that the remaining documents from the collection (946 documents overall) all contain cricket tables, but merely that only a controlled sub-sample could be manually inspected for reasons of time. In contrast, no problems with noise were encountered with TR-MUC4, which was therefore used in full.[13]

4.6.4 Toponym Distribution in Documents

Figure 4.10 shows a toponym distribution map of a sample document from TR-CoNLL.[14] It is typical of both corpora in that it reveals that toponyms usually occur in clusters or bursts, i.e. given that we have just seen one place name mentioned, there is a higher probability that we will observe the same (BEIRUT—BEIRUT) or another one (LEBANON—SYRIA) in its immediate textual proximity. Figure 4.11 shows the distribution of toponyms in TR-MUC4 and the TR-CoNLL sample.

Figure 4.10: Toponym distribution in discourse of TR-CoNLL document D19.

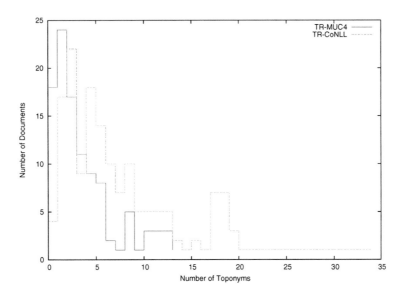

Figure 4.11: Number of documents in the sample as a function of toponym occurrences.

4.6.5 Referential Ambiguity in the Corpora

In Figure 4.12, the number of toponym instances is plotted as a function of the number of referents for TR-CoNLL (top) and TR-MUC4 (bottom), respectively, in order to compare the difficulty of the toponym resolution task for the two corpora. TR-CoNLL contains a larger number of toponym instances than TR-MUC4. While many of the toponyms in TR-CoNLL are ambiguous, they tend to be much less so than those in TR-MUC4 on average. Looking at the most ambiguous toponyms in either corpus we observe that those in TR-MUC4 have many more referents on average than those in TR-CoNLL (also note the scale of the x-axis).

Label bias. There is a very strong *label bias* in both corpora towards what can be considered the *most salient referent*, especially in TR-CoNLL where it amounts to label 'monoculture': a cursory check revealed that no mentions of London, Ontario, Canada or Paris, Texas, USA were found in either corpus. This can be attributed to the statistical distribution of refer-

---

[12]It is surprising that this fact has not been discussed in the CoNLL literature using the same data to train NERC taggers, since it is very likely to affect the utility of the data for NERC quite negatively as well.

[13]The results for an evaluation of *all* documents in TR-CoNLL, irrespective of whether they constitute "clean prose" prose or not, is included in Appendix E for completeness.

[14]This map was generated with the TextGIS® program `trdist`.

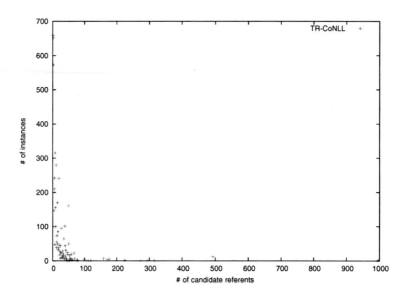

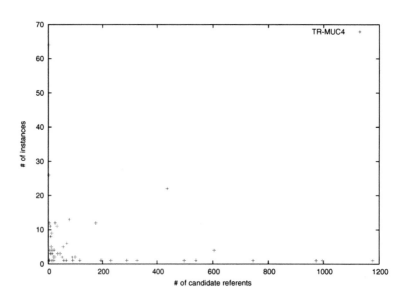

Figure 4.12: Distribution of referent frequency.

ents combined with the still fairly limited size of the dataset.

Key finding. This finding suggests that at least for global news, the real challenge in toponym disambiguation is not be the *discrimination* between alternatives that actually occur in text (since all instances of Londons and almost all instances of Paris in the datasets presented here point to a single referent), but to discover suitable *default referents*. Whereas for the more frequent toponyms like *London*, these defaults will be seen in the annotated corpora, where the task then degrades to a simple lookup procedure where actual knowledge about the defaults is available, typically referents have to be chosen without ever seeing them again in a reference dataset. Also, especially in the case of TR-MUC4, there may not be an obvious most salient referent to the non-expert human (which of the over 1,600 places called *Santa Ana* is the most prominent one?).

4.7 Chapter Summary

This chapter described the curation of a reference corpus for the toponym resolution task comprising two sub-corpora, TR-CoNLL and TR-MUC4. Design issues regarding corpus sampling, gazetteer influence, and markup schemes were discussed. TRML, a new proposal for a markup language, and *TAME*, an editor which implements document annotation supporting it, were presented. Then the annotation process and the resulting dataset was characterised. Finally, the reliability of the human annotators for the task as defined was established. A strong label bias was observed in the data, and the average ambiguity in TR-MUC4 was much higher than in TR-CoNLL.

Chapter 5

Methods

Take a method and try it.
If it fails, admit it frankly, and try another.
But by all means, try something.
  – Franklin D. Roosevelt

[Parts of this chapter have been published in Leidner et al. (2003) and Leidner (2006e).]

5.1 Introduction

This chapter describes two automatic toponym resolution methods in detail, one replicated in full from the literature, the other one novel.[1] Then the TextGIS® software platform is presented, which was built to implement and evaluate both of them. A re-implementation ensures that both methods, old and new, make use of a shared infrastructure, which controls for implementation idiosyncracies. Thus, differences in performance are caused by differences in the algorithm as opposed to by factors such as the choice of a gazetteer or the type of pre-processing.

5.2 The *PERSEUS* Resolver Replicated: Focus & Sliding Window

Smith and Crane's method in the *PERSEUS* digital library system (Smith and Crane (2001)) works as shown in Algorithm 1. First a bitmap representing the globe is populated with all referents for all mentioned toponyms in a document, weighted by frequency of mention (lines 5-10). Then, the geometric centroid of all potential referents is computed, and all candidates with a distance greater than two standard deviations from it are discarded (lines 11-16). After this

---

[1] First presented in Leidner et al. (2003).

pruning step, the centroid is updated (lines 17-18). Then for each toponym instance in the document, a sliding window containing four toponyms to the left and to the right—unambiguous or previously uniquely resolved—is constructed (lines 19-25). For each referent, a score based on the spatial distance to other resolved toponyms in the context window, the distance to the document's geographic centroid, and its relative importance is computed (lines 23-24). Relative importance is determined using an order of feature types (country interpretations carry more weight than city interpretations). Finally, the candidate with the highest score is selected (line 24).

5.3 A New Algorithm Based on Two Minimality Heuristics

Motivation. The method described in the previous section, like other state of the art techniques, is focused on maximising precision, at the cost of recall. In the case of *PERSEUS*, the resolution of all toponyms is not even attempted (it's a partial algorithm). However, some applications, notably in political situation analysis, demand high recall, since they are used to pre-fetch documents that are then further investigated by human analysts. In such a context, processing a spurious document causes a low overhead in time, but missing a document can have serious consequences. This section proposes a novel algorithm (henceforth *LSW03* for short) that tries to increase recall, while still maintaining reasonable precision. It is also motivated by principles from linguistic pragmatics.

Core idea. When ambiguous place names are used in conversation or in text, it is usually clear to the hearer what specific referent is intended. First, speaker and hearer usually share some extra-linguistic context and implicitly adhere to *Grice's Cooperative Principle* (and the 'maxims' that follow from it), which require a speaker to provide more identifying information about a location that the recipient is believed to be unfamiliar with (Grice (1975)). Secondly, linguistic context can provide clues: an accident report on the road between Perth and Dundee promotes an interpretation of Perth in Scotland, while an accident on the road between Perth and Freemantle promotes an interpretation of Perth in Western Australia. Computers, which are bound to select referents algorithmically, can exploit linguistic context more easily than extra-linguistic context, but even the use of linguistic context requires some heuristic reasoning. To make use of discourse context in resolving ambiguous toponyms we apply two different *minimality heuristics* (Gardent and Webber (2001)). Neither heuristic is logically necessary, and hence both are simply *interpretational biases*.

First minimality heuristic: 'One-referent-per-discourse' ($\mathcal{H}_4$). The first minimality heuristic we borrow (slightly modified) from work in automatic word sense disambiguation (Gale et al. (1992)), calling it 'one referent per discourse'. It assumes that a place name mentioned in a discourse refers to the same location throughout the discourse, just as a word

---

Algorithm 13 Smith and Crane (2001): centroid-based toponym resolution (PERSEUS).

1: **[Initialize + $\mathcal{H}_0$.]**

2: resolve trivial (unambiguous) toponyms

3: **['Contained-in' qualifier following ($\mathcal{H}_1$).]**

4: match patterns that resolve some toponyms based on local context (e.g. *Oxford, England, UK*)

5: let M be a 2-dimensional, $1°$-resolution map $[\pm 180; \pm 90]$

6: **for** all possible toponyms t in a document **do**

7:     **for** all possible referents t_r of t **do**

8:         store $freq(t)$ in M at coordinates for t_r

9:     **end for**

10: **end for**

11: **[Centroid and pruning ($\mathcal{H}_{10}$).]**

12: compute the centroid c of weighted map M

13: calculate standard deviation σ from c

14: **for** each point associated with any t_r in M **do**

15:     Discard all points that are more than 2σ away from c

16: **end for**

17: **[Centroid re-computation.]**

18: re-compute centroid c

19: **[Sliding window.]**

20: **for** each toponym instance t in document **do**

21:     construct a context window w with ± 4 unambiguous or uniquely resolved toponym to the left and to the right of t.

22:     **for** each candidate referent t_r of t **do**

23:         **[Scoring ($\mathcal{H}_{9,11,12}$).]**

24:         compute candidate score $s(t_r)$ based on:

           – proximity to other toponyms in w,

           – proximity to c, and

           – relative salience

           (i.e. $s(Spain) > s(Madrid)$)

25:     **end for**

26:     pick as referent un-discarded candidate

        $t_r^* = \arg\max_{t_r} s(t_r)$ unless $s < \theta$

27: **end for**

---

is assumed to be used in the same one sense throughout the discourse. In a more algorithmic view, a resolved toponym can be seen to propagate its interpretation to other instances of the same toponym in the same discourse or discourse segment, e.g.

$$\ldots \text{London}_{\boxed{1}} \ldots \text{London}_{\boxed{2}}, \text{UK} \ldots \text{London}_{\boxed{3}} \ldots$$
$$\Rightarrow \boxed{1} \equiv \boxed{2} \equiv \boxed{3} \rightsquigarrow \texttt{London > England > UK.}$$

Second minimality heuristic: spatial minimality ($\mathcal{H}_5$). The second minimality heuristic assumes that, in cases where there is more than one toponym mentioned in some span of text, the smallest region that is able to ground the whole set is the one that gives them their interpretation.[2] This can be used to resolve referential ambiguity by proximity: i.e., not only is the place name *Berlin* taken to denote the same Berlin throughout a discourse unless mentioned otherwise, but so does a *Potsdam* mentioned together with a *Berlin* uniquely select the capital of Germany as the likely referent from the set of all candidate Berlins.[3] For example,

$$\{ \textit{Paris}; \text{Gennevillier}; \text{Versailles} \}$$
$$\Rightarrow \quad \text{Paris} \rightsquigarrow \texttt{Paris > France, but}$$
$$\{ \text{Bonham}; \textit{Paris}; \text{Windom} \}$$
$$\Rightarrow \quad \text{Paris} \rightsquigarrow \texttt{Paris > TX > USA.}$$

To illustrate this 'spatial minimality' heuristic graphically, consider Figure 5.1: assume that a mention of place A in a text could either refer to A' or A''. If the text also contains terms that ground unambiguously to I, J, and K, then we may assume the referent of A to be A' rather than A'', because the former interpretation leads to a smaller spatial context than the latter, indicated in the figure by the surrounding polygon (i.e., the dashed polygon $IJA''K$ has a larger area than the preferrable smaller-area convex hull IJK).

---

[2]Probably the smaller the span, the more often this heuristic will be valid.
[3]Despite the fact that most places named *Berlin* are in the United States.

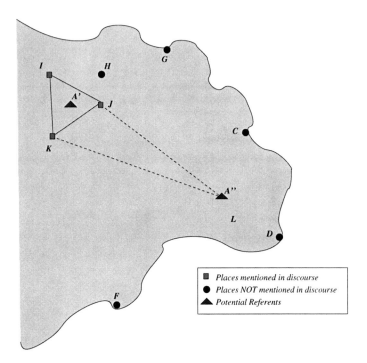

Figure 5.1: Illustration of the spatial minimality principle.

To use this novel 'spatial minimality' heuristic, we start by extracting all place names using a named entity recognizer. We then look up the 'confusion set' of potential referents for
each place name, e.g. for *Berlin*: { Berlin, FRG (German capital); Berlin, WI, USA; Berlin,
NJ, USA; Berlin, CT, USA; Berlin, NH, USA; Berlin, GA, USA; Berlin, IL, USA; Berlin, NY,
USA; Berlin, ND, USA; Berlin, NJ, USA }. Each member of the set of potential referents
is associated with its spatial coordinates (longitude/latitude), using a gazetteer. Then the toponym resolution method as outlined in Algorithm 5.3 can be applied. Before the minimality
heuristics can be executed, we resolve countries (lines 4-9) and apply resolution rules based
on local disambiguation patterns (line 10-11). This is necessary to avoid the scenario depicted
in Figure 5.2: an 'Israel' in Nicaragua is wrongly chosen because that choice minimizes the
minimal bounding rectangle (to an area of $\approx 3,686\,km^2$ as indicated by the asterisk at the top
right). [4] So while in practice, the core algorithm (lines 19-25) is preceded by other heuristics, which provide *sure-fire anchors* for the minimality approach to build on, for the sake of
demonstration, Figure 5.2 shows a trace of the core steps working in isolation. In this exam-

---

[4]In the current implementation, a Minimum Bounding Rectangle (MBR) approximation is used. If runtime is
not an issue, a full *minimal bounding polygon* or *convex hull* implementation can be used (cf. (O'Rourke, 1998, p.
63–100) for a description of efficient algorithms).

Algorithm 14 Leidner et al. (2003): minimality-based toponym resolution (*LWS03*).

1: **[Initialize + $\mathcal{H}_0$.]**

2: resolve trivial (unambiguous) toponyms

3: let S be the cross-product of all candidate referents for each of the N toponyms in a document

4: **['Country' ($\mathcal{H}_{12}$).]**

5: **for** each toponym t **do**

6:    **if** t_i has a country interpretation **then**

7:       pick the country interpretation

8:    **end if**

9: **end for**

10: **['Contained-in' qualifier following ($\mathcal{H}_1$).]**

11: match patterns that resolve some toponyms based on local context (e.g. *Oxford, England, UK*)

12: **['One-referent-per-discourse' ($\mathcal{H}_4$).]**

13: **for** each toponym t **do**

14:    **if** t appears resolved elsewhere **then**

15:       Propagate the resolvent to all unresolved instances

16:    **end if**

17: **end for**

18: **[Search.]**

19: **for** each N-tuple $C \in S$ **do**

20:    **[Scoring.]**

21:    create MBR H_C that contains all centroids in tuple C

22:    compute area $A(H_C)$

23: **end for**

24: **[Spatial minimality ($\mathcal{H}_5$).]**

25: pick candidate tuple C^* with minimal MBR area:

$C^* = \arg\min_C A(H_C)$ as referents

---

ple, there are three toponyms in the document ($N = 3$), *Israel, El Salvador, U.S.*, shown in the bottom part with their associated candidate references from the reference gazetteer. The cross-product (or set of triples) of all candidate readings is formed, which is shown in the middle part, where the candidate interpretation triples, i.e. what token is assigned what candidate referent c_i, are displayed followed by the area of the associated Minimal Bounding Rectangle. Since the toponym *US* is not ambiguous, the same interpretation (`token_37->c1`) is included in all candidate interpretation tuples. Then the interpretation triple with the smallest area is chosen. Note that the area computation can be approximated for efficiency gains (it need not take the curvature of the geoid into account), since it is only used to discriminate between competing interpretations. Even so, it can sometimes happen that a tie occurs, as is the case in this example (there is another 'solution' with the same area). Currently, the first interpretation is greedily selected. Note that the algorithm has a disadvantage for very large documents that contain many toponyms in the sense that since its asymptotic time complexity grows exponentially with the number of toponyms: $O(N) = c^N$, where N is the number of toponyms and c is the largest number of candidate referents in the gazetteer for any toponym. The implementation described below avoids such explosions by cutting off after investigating a number of candidates specified by a threshold. Another solution would be to process the document passage by passage, where passages could be specified as windows of a number of lines or sentences of text or by using paragraphs.

```
N=3: ( |4|  |7|  |1| )


token_17->c4 token_30->c7 token_37->c1   6429.48
token_17->c4 token_30->c6 token_37->c1   3686    * <------------------------ SELECTED INTERPRETATION
token_17->c4 token_30->c5 token_37->c1   6232.25                            (SMALLEST BOUNDING BOX AREA)
token_17->c4 token_30->c4 token_37->c1   6237.1
token_17->c4 token_30->c3 token_37->c1   6230.63
token_17->c4 token_30->c2 token_37->c1   6238.72
token_17->c4 token_30->c1 token_37->c1   3686
token_17->c3 token_30->c7 token_37->c1   8674.35
token_17->c3 token_30->c6 token_37->c1   8199.88
token_17->c3 token_30->c5 token_37->c1   8408.25
token_17->c3 token_30->c4 token_37->c1   8414.8
token_17->c3 token_30->c3 token_37->c1   8406.07
token_17->c3 token_30->c2 token_37->c1   8416.98
token_17->c3 token_30->c1 token_37->c1   8199.88
token_17->c2 token_30->c7 token_37->c1   8732.83
token_17->c2 token_30->c6 token_37->c1   5006.5
token_17->c2 token_30->c5 token_37->c1   8464.94
token_17->c2 token_30->c4 token_37->c1   8471.52
token_17->c2 token_30->c3 token_37->c1   8462.74
token_17->c2 token_30->c2 token_37->c1   8473.72
token_17->c2 token_30->c1 token_37->c1   5006.5
token_17->c1 token_30->c7 token_37->c1   16872.4
token_17->c1 token_30->c6 token_37->c1   11785.7
token_17->c1 token_30->c5 token_37->c1   16354.8
token_17->c1 token_30->c4 token_37->c1   16367.6
token_17->c1 token_30->c3 token_37->c1   16350.6
token_17->c1 token_30->c2 token_37->c1   16371.8
token_17->c1 token_30->c1 token_37->c1   11785.7


Israel  LOC
      c1       -8.3     157.55  Israel > Solomon Islands
      c2       31.5     34.75   Israel
      c3      -24.6578  33.8678 Israel > Gaza > Mozambique
     >c4       12.8628 -86.8456 Israel > Chinandega > Nicaragua <----------- SELECTED INTERPRETATION

El Salvador     LOC
      c1        6.2333 -75.5667 El Salvador > Antioquia > Colombia
      c2      -26.3167 -69.7167 El Salvador > Atacama > Chile
      c3      -26.2333 -69.65   El Salvador > Atacama > Chile
      c4      -26.3    -69.5    El Salvador > Atacama > Chile
      c5      -26.25   -69.6167 El Salvador > Atacama > Chile
     >c6       10.2333 -83.9    El Salvador > Heredia > Costa Rica <-------- SELECTED INTERPRETATION
      c7      -28.2833 -64.9667 El Salvador > Santiago del Estero > Argentina

U . S . LOC
     >c1       38       -97     United States <---------------------------- SELECTED INTERPRETATION
```

Figure 5.2: Spatial minimality algorithm at work (trace).

Now we can apply the one-referent-per-discourse heuristic by propagating all contextually resolved interpretations to all instances of the same toponym that are yet unresolved (line 12-17). We then compute the cross-product of all the confusion sets (lines 18-23). Each member of the cross-product contains one potential referent for each place name, along with its spatial coordinates. For each member of the cross-product, we compute the area of the polygon (or MBR[5]) bounding all the potential referents (line 21-22), and select as the most likely intended interpretation the one with the smallest area (line 24-25). The resulting behaviour is shown in Figure 5.3: depending on contextually mentioned other places, a different Berlin is selected. The value of this approach will be assessed quantitatively in the next chapter.

{ *Berlin*; Potsdam } ↦ Berlin, FRG (Germany)
{ Fairburn; *Berlin* } ↦ Berlin, WI, USA
{ West *Berlin*; Bishops; Dicktown } ↦ Berlin, NJ, USA
{ Kensington; *Berlin*; New Britain } ↦ Berlin, CT, USA
{ Copperville; *Berlin*; Gorham } ↦ Berlin, NH, USA
{ Moultrie; *Berlin* } ↦ Berlin, GA, USA
{ *Berlin*; Prouty } ↦ Berlin, IL, USA
{ *Berlin*; Berlin Center; Cherryplain } ↦ Berlin, NY, USA
{ Medberry; *Berlin* } ↦ Berlin, ND, USA

Figure 5.3: Toponym resolution with spatial minimality: examples.

5.4 Machine Learning Methods

5.4.1 Introduction

Figure 5.4 shows an instantiation of the general regime of supervised machine learning for the toponym resolution task. Given a human-tagged gold-standard corpus for training, a set of features are computed that characterise the properties of each example instance (i.e. of each candidate referent for any particular toponym occurrence) thought to be relevant for the decision making by the human system designer. For each candidate referent, a set of feature values forming a *feature vector* are computed, and the set of feature vectors for all training examples is then fed into a *learning algorithm* that induces a model of the toponym resolution decision making knowledge. A machine-learning based toponym resolver then uses this model as a basis for prediction to resolve toponyms in unseen raw text.

---

[5]One can alternatively approximate this by computing the sum of pairwise point-point distances, or symbolically, using a hierarchical gazetteer's relations, such as `in-region-of`.

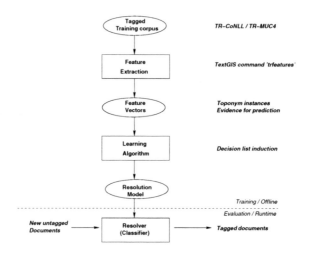

Figure 5.4: Supervised machine learning for toponym resolution.

5.4.2   Decision Tree Induction (DTI)

Decision trees are tree data structures used for automatic classification.[6] They can be constructed from data for which the solution (ground truth) is known by iteratively 'growing' new decision nodes labelled with decision predicates that partition the training dataset according to a so-called *splitting criterion*, so as to narrow down the classification choices when the resulting decision tree is interpreted. Usually the splitting criterion is an information-theoretic measure such as *information gain*, the difference of the *entropy* of the mother node and the weighted sum of the entropies of the child nodes (Manning and Schütze, 1999, pp. 572 f.). Black (1988) applied decision tree learning to WSD for five words, trained on 2,000 samples per word extracted from a corpus of Canadian parliament records. For the experiments on toponym resolution reported in Chapter 6, the decision tree induction implementation provided by the *WEKA* machine learning toolkit (Witten and Frank (2005)) was used.

---

[6]See (Duda et al., 2000, pp. 395-406), (Hastie et al., 2001, pp. 266-272), (Witten and Frank, 2005, pp. 97-105), or (Manning and Schütze, 1999, pp. 578-583) for more detailed accounts.

Features. The following features may, for example, be computed from the documents in order to predict the location referents for each toponym (Figure 5.5):

- 3 tokens to the left,

- the toponym itself,

- 3 tokens to the right, and

- the candidate referent ID with the largest population (or NIL if no information available).

Left context	toponym	right context	maximum population referent	ground truth referent
1990 invasion of	*Kuwait*	*, Zhirinovsky said*	NIL	**c2**
Iraq and blamed	*Moscow*	*for delaying establishment*	c10	**c5**

```
"1990","invasion","of","Kuwait",".","Zhirinovsky","said","NIL",c2
"trade","sanctions","on","Iraq","and","blamed","Moscow","NIL",c1
"Iraq","and","blamed","Moscow","for","delaying","establishment","c10",c5
"good","ties","with","Baghdad",".","&dquo;","Our","NIL",c1
"economic","embargo","on","Iraq","and","resume","trade","NIL",c1
"trade","ties","between","Russia","and","Iraq",",","NIL",c1
"between","Russia","and","Iraq",",","&dquo;","he","NIL",c1
".","Zhirinovsky","visited","Iraq","twice","in","1995","NIL",c1
"referendum","held","on","Iraq","&equo;s","presidency",",","NIL",c1
"in","Europe",".","GENEVA","1996-08-23","European","champions","NIL",c6
"and","Fenerbahce","of","Turkey",".","Juventus","meet","NIL",c5
"meet","United","in","Turin","on","September","11","NIL",c2
"to","Galatasaray","of","Turkey","and","Spain","&equo;s","NIL",c5
```

Figure 5.5: TR-CoNLL feature vectors: structure (top) and examples (bottom).

However, preliminary supervised learning experiments using decision tree induction provided by the *WEKA* package (Witten and Frank (2005)) were disappointing. Due to *data sparseness*, i.e. the phenomenon that most events are hardly ever seen in the training data, and the uneven class distribution that is heavily biased towards a most salient referent (which is, however, not known to the machine without giving it access to further knowledge or rules). This leads to led to *overfitting* of induced models, i.e. instead of inducing a generic decision rule tree, the training set simply gets memorised. For this reason, no learning results are reported for this approach in the next chapter. Instead, an alternative suggestion for future work will be suggested in the next section.

5.4.3 Outlook: Learning Voting Weights

In tasks like TR where supervised learning is difficult because of *data sparseness* and class distribution bias, a combination of knowledge-intensive approaches and learning-based approaches can be attempted. In the case of toponym resolution, the heuristics can be combined in a learning regime, for example using a *linear classifier*, as follows. Given an *ensemble* of N classifiers $C_1, \ldots, C_N$, and a set of associated weights $w_1, \ldots, w_N$, we can apply them in a *weighted voting* regime (Gangardiwala and Polikar (2005); Littlestone and Warmuth (1994)). For TR, we can re-use the existing TR heuristics as 'voters' (although they are not statistical in nature, they can opt for a category each) C_i in a similar way (Figure 5.6).

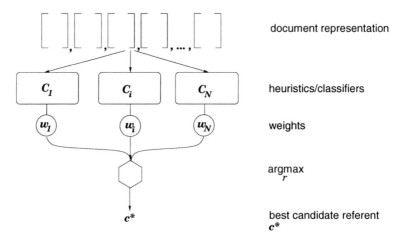

Figure 5.6: Heuristic ensembles with weights.

The category of the voted interpretation can then be computed as

$$c^*(\vec{f}) = \arg\max_{r \in \mathcal{R}} \sum_{i:C_i(\vec{f})=r} w_i, \qquad (5.1)$$

and the weights w_i can be learnt from a held out portion of an annotated dataset.

While the implementation of such an approach is left for future work, it is expected to outperform existing approaches, including the ones evaluated in the next chapter.

5.5 The TextGIS® Toolkit: Design and Implementation

This section describes the design and implementation of TextGIS® (Leidner (2006d)), the toolkit built for experimentation with toponym resolution and for developing applications in this thesis and beyond. In the first part, some general issues in Software Architecture for Language Engineering (SALE)[7] are raised, and in the second part the concrete choices made when designing TextGIS® are described.[8]

5.5.1 Introduction: Software Architecture for Language Engineering

All applications should to be *efficient*. In language processing, where approximate rather than complete solutions are the state of the art, *accuracy* is another quality criterion for good software. In addition to these rather obvious factors, Leidner (2003a) identifies the following:

- *productivity:* the amount of results that a researcher or developer can accomplish when (re-)using a certain software;

- *flexibility:* the ease with which many diverse tasks can be accomplished when (re)-using a piece of software;

- *robustness:* in general, the property of a system to work under extreme conditions. In NLP, the property of a system to yield only a minimal decay in quality (for example, as measured in terms of precision/recall) when applied across a range of different text types, registers or domains.

- *scalability:* the ability of a piece of software to be (re-)used in a very large software system, comprising many sub-components.

Whereas the evaluation of linguistic effectiveness of NLP methods has recently become an integral part of most NLP research, to date the *architectural evaluation* of the software, e.g. using the criteria above is often neglected. It should also be recognised as vital part of language engineering, including an assessment of *standard compliance*, *rapid deployability*, *maintainability* and *flexibility* of design, because the quality of the architecture determines its capability to be re-used, likelihood of adoption by third-party developers, and productivity of adopters when integrating components in new applications.

---

[7]A phrase coined in Cunningham (2000).

[8]For the figures in this section, the *Unified Modeling Language* (*UML*) is used, an industry standard defined by the Object Management Group (OMG) for the analysis and design of software systems (Jacobson et al. (1999)).

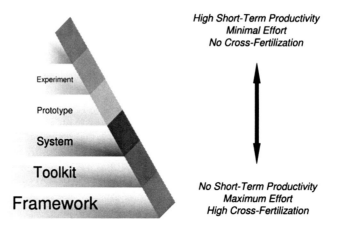

Figure 5.7: Developer productivity versus re-usability in software systems (Leidner (2003a)).

Figure 5.7 shows the tradeoffs that researchers face when creating software as part of the scientific process. On the top of the pyramid that represents the invested initial effort, there are experiments, for which researchers manipulate data semi-interactively, often by forming ad-hoc *UNIX* pipelines until the desired output data has been computed. This is a powerful paradigm for exploration and keeps the initial effort at a minimum (thus yielding high short-term productivity), however the result is not suitable for easy re-use, so there is little expected *cross-fertilisation* between the current and future projects and in the long term, lack of re-use may actually lead to higher overall effort. The other extreme are *frameworks*, highly complex software infrastructures that provide automatic code generation or template-based wizards, GUI-based development environments and development support tools, but come at price of enforcing the adoption of certain programming styles. Therefore, often, different frameworks are not interoperable. NLP researchers should strive towards development of *toolkits*, i.e. versatile, small-footprint, re-usable component APIs that foster re-use by third parties, but that do not require the effort required for building a full framework. On the horizon, NLP *composition languages* (Krieger (2003)) and *workflow systems* for NLP services (Grover et al. (2004)) could be the ingredients to the solution of problems of productivity and re-use. Based on these considerations, it was decided to devise a new toolkit for toponym resolution.

5.5.2 Design

To implement the algorithms presented earlier in this chapter, a new, robust and flexible software toolkit for the experimentation with toponym resolution methods and for building applications was designed. The layered and modular architecture of the result, TextGIS®, is depicted in Figure 5.8. An *Infrastructure Layer* provides access to functionality for database access, mapping, named entity tagging and some generic tools (generic API[9]). An *Interface Layer* provides a useful abstraction over details of the representation of data and linguistic markup. It also offers access to non-linguistic knowledge such as population information. The *Resolution Strategy Layer* provides a repertoire of pre-defined resolution strategies, including those compared in this paper. Finally, an *Application Layer* offers tools to perform conversion to various output formats such as RDF, XHTML with links to satellite images, and tools for performance evaluation.

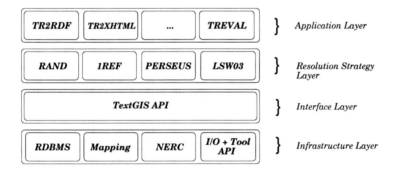

Figure 5.8: System architecture of the TextGIS® toolkit.

5.5.3 Implementation

The TextGIS® system was implemented in standard C++ (ISO (1998)) to allow an interface-based design while retaining high runtime performance. The TextGIS® API comprises a class hierarchy with various support functionality and a main class, `TextGIS`, which provides a rich set of methods that each operate on objects representing text documents annotated with named entities and sets of candidate locations for toponyms (Figure 5.10). Using this API, the heuris-

---

[9]Application Programming Interface.

tics in Table 5.1 (a subset of the full inventory that was extracted from past work in Chapter 3) were developed. The re-implementation of *PERSEUS* and a new implementation of *LSW03* were then built on top of both the API. Easy re-use of the aforementioned heuristics was possible without modification of the code base. New strategies for toponym resolution can also be easily added; they can utilise the functionality in the TextGIS® API, and their minimal requirement is that they implement a `resolve()` method that works on a TextGIS® corpus object and a `getName()` method providing its own name (Figure 5.9).

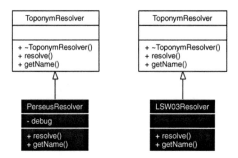

Figure 5.9: All resolution strategies implement the `ToponymResolver` C++ interface.

($\mathcal{H}_0$)	(Resolve unambiguous)
$\mathcal{H}_1$	"Contained-in" qualifier following
$\mathcal{H}_2$	Superordinate mention
$\mathcal{H}_3$	Largest population
$\mathcal{H}_4$	One referent per discourse
$\mathcal{H}_5$	Geometric minimality
$\mathcal{H}_9$	Textual distance to unambiguous neighbors (in tokens)
$\mathcal{H}_{10}$	Discard off-threshold
$\mathcal{H}_{11}$	Frequency weighting
$\mathcal{H}_{12}$	Prefer higher-level referents

Table 5.1: Implemented heuristics.

5.6   Chapter Summary

In this chapter, a detailed reconstruction of the toponym resolution method from the *PERSEUS* digital library was given. The complete system was replicated to serve as a baseline for the evaluation in the next chapter. Then a new method was described, which is based on two

Figure 5.10: TextGIS, the main class of the TextGIS API.

minimality heuristics, 'one referent per discourse' and 'smallest bounding polygon'. Next, the application of two well-known machine learning methods to the toponym resolution task were described, decision tree learning and learning of heuristic weights. Finally, an account of the design and implementation of the TextGIS® software toolkit was given, which was conceived to evaluate the methods in a comparable setting and for future experimentation.

Chapter 6

Evaluation

Only what you can measure,

can you improve.

– Anonymous

[Parts of an earlier version of this chapter have been published in the technical report Leidner (2006e).]

6.1 Introduction

In this chapter, it is shown how traditional performance metrics can be adapted for assessing the quality of a particular toponym resolution algorithm. In addition, task-specific metrics are proposed that take into account the severity of a decision error. Then a set of heuristics and evidence sources previously applied to the automatic toponym resolution task as well as the two methods described in the previous chapter, PERSEUS, because it is a well-known and state-of-the-art system, which can be seen as a system-level baseline, and another method, LSW03, developed by the author of this thesis.[1] Both methods are evaluated in two settings, using human-quality toponym recognition and automatic toponym recognition, respectively. Finally, the impact of the results is discussed.

In this thesis, the focus is on the impartial, comparative evaluation of several heuristics and systems in controlled conditions rather than proposing one single method and claiming superiority.

---

[1]LSW03 was first described in Leidner et al. (2003).

6.2   Evaluation Methodology

Errors in toponym processing can happen at the levels of toponym identification (whether or not a term is the name of a place), toponym classification (what type of place it is, in the case of multiple geographic feature types[2]) or resolution (which location it is). In order to learn about resolution quality, we need to control for errors introduced by processing steps that precede the resolution proper. In the following series of experiments, we therefore begin by measuring resolution quality on a gold standard dataset in which toponyms are already marked up, i.e. an *oracle study* is presented. However, while such an isolated component evaluation enables us to learn about the properties of the resolution methods, it has the drawback of being an artificial setting. It is thus complemented by a more realistic scenario in which toponym tagging is carried out by an automatic named entity tagger. Both evaluations taken together allow a better judgment as to which method ought to be employed in a real-word application.

6.2.1   Adapting Traditional Evaluation Metrics

To assess the quality of a toponym resolution method, we first need to define metrics that quantify either the success or, negatively, the amount of decision errors that happen when applying the method to a particular dataset. An instance of *London*, after having been identified as a toponym by the NERC stage is either found in the gazetteer or not, resulting in $0...n$ candidate references or possible readings. If the toponym lookup in the gazetteer fails (i.e., if 0 candidate referents are returned due to incomplete gazetteer coverage), the toponym remains *unresolved* (and is, in fact, *unresolvable* by the subsequent toponym resolution step in the sense that coordinates have to be obtained from somewhere). Otherwise, a mapping to coordinates is attempted, which can lead to one of the following three outcomes (Figure 6.1):

- *correct*: the coordinates selected by the system represent the intended referent of the toponym;

- *incorrect*: the coordinates do *not* represent the intended referent of the toponym; or

- *unresolved*; the system decided not to make a choice of a referent.

---

[2]But recall that, in this thesis, a single notion of *populated place* is used, i.e. we are not discussing natural features like rivers or artefacts such as airports here, for instance.

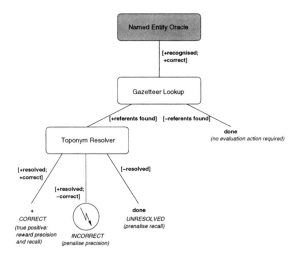

Figure 6.1: Three cases in TR evaluation.

In information retrieval and natural language processing, the metrics *Accuracy* (A), *Error* (E), *Precision* (P), *Recall* (R) and *F-Score* (F) are widely used to assess the quality of methods for automatic retrieval and annotation (Manning and Schütze (1999)). We therefore recapitulate these here, adapting our terminology to the task at hand.

If T_N is the total number of *resolvable* toponyms in a text document or corpus, T_C is the number of correctly resolved toponym occurrences, T_I is the number of incorrectly resolved toponym occurrences, T_U is the number of toponym occurrences whose candidate referents are unresolved, and T_R is the number of resolved toponym occurrences, then we can define:

DEFINITION 1 (ACCURACY) :

*The **Accuracy** A is the proportion of all toponyms resolved to the correct location (i.e. to the location given in the gold standard):*

$$A = \frac{T_C}{T_N} = \frac{T_C}{T_C + T_I + T_U} \tag{6.1}$$

Note that unresolvable toponyms (T_X) are not added to the denominator, because they cannot be resolved in principle due to either the incompleteness of the gazetteer (no candidate referents found) or the fact that in the gold standard an annotator forgot to annotate a toponym. There is not much point adding in T_X because both factors are constant across the experiments and because we want to benchmark the methods rather than the gazetteer. For convenience, we define accuracy over a document to be 1 if $T_N = 0$, i.e. when no toponyms exist in a document or corpus. This is helpful to avoid dealing with undefined values when averaging results. The number of unresolvable toponyms, i.e. those whose candidate referent list remains empty due to

unsuccessful gazetteer lookup, are not counted towards T_N nor T_U, since the resolution methods
are sought to be assessed here, not the gazetteer (which is constant across the experiments
reported here anyway). The dual of accuracy is error:

DEFINITION 2 (ERROR) :

*The **Error** E is the proportion of all toponyms resolved to an incorrect location (i.e. to a location different from the one given in the gold standard), or that remain unresolved:*

$$E = \frac{T_I + T_U}{T_N} = \frac{T_N - T_C}{T_N} = 1 - A \qquad (6.2)$$

Again for convenience, we define $E := 0$ for $T_N = 0$. Although very intuitive, these two
classical metrics are often substituted by other metrics because accuracy and error can be misleading metrics to judge classification quality in the presence of category bias: if a system
needs to decide between two classes, and one class occurs in 90% of the cases, whereas the
other class gets assigned in only 10% of the cases, even trivial strategies (such as always assigning the most frequent category) undeservedly result in a very high accuracy (90% in this
example). To avoid this, precision, recall and F-score are commonly used in NLP:

DEFINITION 3 (PRECISION) :

***Precision** P is the ratio of the number of correctly resolved toponym instances and the number
of toponym instances that the system attempted to resolve (either correctly or incorrectly):*

$$P = \frac{T_C}{T_C + T_I} \qquad (6.3)$$

A system has high precision if the ratio of the number of toponym instances whose resolution was both attempted by the system and successfully achieved (numerator), and the total
number of toponym instances, is high.

DEFINITION 4 (RECALL) :

***Recall** R is the ratio of the number of correctly resolved toponym instances and the number of
all toponym instances:*

$$R = \frac{T_C}{T_N} \qquad (6.4)$$

A system has high recall if the ratio of the number of toponym instances whose resolution
was both attempted by the system and successfully achieved (same numerator as precision),
and the number of toponym instances whose resolution was attempted and succeeded or was
not attempted (denominator), is high.[3] Note that for this task, the recall definition is identical

---

[3]Note that in Leidner (2006e), *coverage* was used instead of recall, and a combined metric was formed using
precision and coverage, the *T-score*. However, this approach has subsequently been abandoned in favour of the
account presented here because the desired tradeoff relationship that exists between P and R does not exist between

with the definition of accuracy above.

Precision and recall are complementary metrics: a system that achieves high precision has a high proportion of correct decisions in relation to all system decisions, even if it might not commit to deciding about certain toponym instances, whereas a system that achieves high recall has a high proportion of correct decisions in relation to correct decisions and non-decisions. In order to provide a convenient combined measure (Jardine and van Rijsbergen (1971)) introduced *F-score*, which has a parameter β that allows for the weighting of P against R:

DEFINITION 5 (F-SCORE (JARDINE AND VAN RIJSBERGEN (1971))) : *Given a precision of P and recall of R, the **F-Score** F_β is defined as:*

$$F_\beta = \frac{(\beta^2 + 1)PR}{\beta^2 P + R} \tag{6.5}$$

For equal weight, F-score becomes the harmonic mean between precision and recall. It is then defined as follows:

DEFINITION 6 (F1-SCORE (JARDINE AND VAN RIJSBERGEN (1971))) : *The **F1-Score** (F1 for short) is the harmonic mean of precision and recall.*

$$F1 = F_{\beta=1} = \frac{2PR}{P + R} \tag{6.6}$$

The $\beta = 1$ variant is sometimes referred to as simply the *F-score* for short. In many evaluation settings, F-score is the only single metric worth optimising (see also van Rijsbergen (1979) for a more background account). Table 6.1 shows an example calculation using the metrics as defined above.

In Toponym resolution evaluation, the question of deciding whether a particular method's resolution decision is equal to the human decision or not is sometimes not easy. In many natural language processing tasks such as part-of-speech tagging, all that is necessary is a test for string equality: the word *duck* gets assigned a word class string like NN (common noun) by the human and either the system assigns NN as well, or there was an error. In contrast, when comparing the many candidate referents in toponym resolution, the right choice depends on the particular representation chosen. Here, latitude and longitude of any referent are compared in addition to the toponym itself when comparing places, and quite often, a toponym has more than one referent with coordinates that are almost, but not exactly identical. This may be due to measurement imprecision or rounding errors that occurred during floating point calculations. Unfortunately, the size of the gazetteer (about 7 million entries) prohibits manual correction.[4]

P and C, and because the definition of coverage does not refer to the gold standard. The numbers in Leidner (2006e) are therefore not comparable with the numbers presented in this chapter.

[4]Recall that a snapshot of the gazetteer data was taken for this study before the start of the annotation phase was used, since NGA continue to perform about 20,000 corrections per month (Chapter 4).

Toponym Occurrence	Correct (T_C)	Incorrect (T_I)	Resolved (T_R)	Unresolved (T_U)
London		●	●	
Ontario	●		●	
Paris	●		●	
Paris	●		●	
Buffalo				●
New York				●
Sum:	3	1	4	2

$$A = R = \frac{3}{6} = 0.50 \qquad P = \frac{3}{3+1} = 0.75$$

$$E = \frac{1+2}{6} = 0.50 \qquad F_{\beta=1} = \frac{2 \times 0.75 \times 0.60}{0.75+0.60} = \frac{0.9}{1.35} \approx 0.67$$

Table 6.1: Toponym resolution evaluation: calculation example.

As a solution, the following procedure was applied. An equality threshold θ is used to account for near-matches. For example, a threshold $\theta = 1$ means that if two gazetteer entries have latitude/longitude coordinates that differ by less than one degree (about[5] 110 km), then the two gazetteer entries are considered variants of each other (i.e., they could be merged) if the locations they represent share the same toponym, rather than being considered to represent two different locations near each other and bearing the same name. In other words, $\theta = 1$ implies there is only one place with the same name in each $1°$ latitude/longitude grid cell. The same effect as this lenient equality test could have been accomplished by pre-processing the gazetteer before starting any annotation work. However this would have implied committing to a particular value for θ. In contrast, by defining a parametrised equality predicate, we can change our θ setting at any time to study the impact of the approximation. Here, results are reported using $\theta = 1$.

In evaluation, the computing of averages leaves room for the choice between *micro-averaging* on the one hand, in which the individual scores per decision are added up across the whole dataset and divided by the number of decisions (here, instances of toponyms that could be resolved), and *macro-averaging* on the other hand, in which the average for each document is computed separately, and the average of the method is the arithmetic mean of the per-document scores. Here, both kinds of averages are reported to make it easier for subsequent authors to compare results.

---

[5]Note that this statement is a crude approximation since due to the shape of the earth, one degree latitude is (i) not a constant, and (ii) the average distance between points that are one degree longitude away from each other is not the same as the average distance of points one degree latitude away from each other.

6.2.2 Task-Specific Evaluation Metrics

There are many different legitimate ways to evaluate TR performance. Also, the task formulation adopted here, namely choosing a single toponym referent assumed to be the correct one, is by no means the only possible way to cast the TR problem, and alternatives may require different evaluations. I propose two metrics here, *RMSD* and *sliding ratio*. While I will not use them for the comparative evaluation in this chapter,[6] their discussion may help the current discussion of how to evaluate geographic information retrieval results (Leidner (2006b)).

RMSD. As stated earlier, since the extension of geographic terms encompasses the continuous geographic space on earth, it would be beneficial for evaluation purposes to discard the notion of binary judgments (i.e., giving up rating using the crude 'correct'/'incorrect' distinction) in favour of a smoother scheme that weights smaller discrepancies between a system's toponym resolvent (i.e. the candidate assigned by the system) and the referent in the gold standard less heavily than larger ones.

Many measures have been proposed as performance metrics for numeric predictions (Witten and Frank, 2005, Table 5.8 on p. 178), and the following proposal is derived from Root Mean Square Error (*ibid.*), because of its intuitive appeal. I suggest *Root Mean Squared Distance*, the root of the arithmetic mean of the squared toponym resolution error with respect to a document or corpus, where error is measured as *geoid distance* from the ground truth in kilometers:[7]

DEFINITION 7 (ROOT MEAN SQUARED DISTANCE, RMSD) :
Given the geoid distance $\Delta(\cdot,\cdot)$ *between a set of N ground-truth location centroids* $\vec{g} = (g_1,\ldots,g_N)$ *and a set of automatically tagged location centroids* $\vec{d} = (d_1,\ldots,d_N)$ *in a document or corpus,*

$$\text{RMSD}(\vec{d},\vec{g}) = \sqrt{\frac{1}{N}\sum_{i=1}^{N}[\Delta(d_i,g_i)]^2} \tag{6.7}$$

is called **Root Mean Squared Distance (RMSD).**

A strength of this definition is that the average per-document (or per corpus) *distance* is, quite literally, a distance (in the geographic sense) from the truth according to the gold standard. The dual correct/incorrect dichotomy is replaced by a more fine-grained (in fact, continuous) penalty for errors, so that using RMSD, a resolution error to the wrong candidate 5,000 km away gets penalised more than to a similarly wrong candidate only 10 km away from the ground truth. Another strength is that RMSD is mathematically well-behaved in that it closely resembles root mean squared error.

---

[6]RMSD is already implemented in TextGIS®, whereas the sliding ratio is not implemented, as it would require both a major software re-design and also a different way of gold standard annotation (ranking-based).

[7]Recall that $\Delta(\cdot,\cdot)$ is the geoid distance described in Chapter 2.

Another big advantage of RMSD is that, unlike precision, recall, and F-score, its adoption actually makes the gold standard corpus immune from the dependency that otherwise exists between gazetteer and corpus[8], because the use of RMSD implies the only coupling between gazetteer and gold standard annotation is via the extensional latitude/longitude semantics. So if a developer had developed his or her own toponym resolver independently from the reference gazetteer developed for this thesis, the gold standard could still be used to assess that new system as long as it was capable of assigning coordinates in latitude/longitude to toponyms, as that is the only basis of evaluation with RMSD. Even an approximate match of the coordinates would be given credit by the metric. In contrast, using the precision, recall, and f-score family of metrics to score the selection of a particular gazetteer entry commits to a particular gazetteer that contains these entries.

However, one disadvantage of RMSD as defined here is that unlike F-score, it is not worth optimizing for if used as the only metric, since low recall is not penalised directly by it. Another caveat is that the metric's usefulness is dependent on the application scenario. While suitable for some applications like geographic Web search, other applications may not benefit from it, namely whenever resolving a toponym to the wrong candidate with the right name nearby causes the same *cost* as resolving the toponym to a wrong candidate further away.

It would be beneficial to develop RMSD further into a single combined metric worth optimising for (like F-score), but retaining its unique advantages outlined above.

Sliding ratio. For systems that output a *ranking* (like in a retrieval system) ordering candidate toponym referents from better to worse instead of giving simply a Boolean projection as output (i.e. selecting a single correct referent among the candidate set of referents), we can compare the system ranking to a gold-standard ranking using the *sliding ratio score SR* (Pollack (1968), cited after (Belew, 2000, pp. 134)):

DEFINITION 8 (SLIDING RATIO SCORE (POLLACK (1968))) : *The **sliding ratio score** SR is the ratio*

$$SR = \frac{\sum_{i=1}^{Rank_1(d_i,q) \leq NRet_q}}{\sum_{i=1}^{Rank_2(d_i,q) \leq NRet_q}}, \tag{6.8}$$

where $Rank_1$ and $Rank_2$ are the system ranking and the *gold ranking*, respectively, $NRet$ is the number of resulting referents returned by the system, and $Rel(d,q)$ is a measure for the quality of referent d to toponym q. The system ranking can be compared with the gold-standard by computing a list of geo-spatial distances between the selected referent from the gold-standard and each of the (other) candidate referents (gold ranking), i.e. using a $Rel(d,q) = \Delta(\cdot,\cdot) < \theta$ threshold cutoff for $Rel(d,q)$, so.[9] That is, positions in the ranking agree if and only

---

[8]See p. 122.

[9]The use of the parameters d and q indicates that the original formulation in Belew (2000) was intended for document retrieval, where d stands for document and q stands for query.

if the distance from gold standard referent to system output candidate referent does not exceed θ. The more positions in the ranking agree in this way, the higher the score SR. Similarly, a geographic information system that ranks documents using a notion of geographic relevance in addition to topical relevance may be evaluated using the sliding ratio score on the document level.

TR-CoNLL $N = 1018$	(gold NERC)	P	R	$F_{\beta=1}$	significant? $\mathcal{H}_x$ v RAND	significant? $\mathcal{H}_x$ v $\mathcal{H}_{0+3}$
—	RAND	0.3035	0.3035	0.3035	n/a	n/a
$\mathcal{H}_{0+3}$	MAXPOP	**0.6676**	0.2328	0.3452	▲	–
$\mathcal{H}_0$	1REF	**1.0000**	0.1434	0.2509	▼	▼
$\mathcal{H}_{0+1}$	LOCAL	0.9451	0.1523	0.2623	▼	▼
$\mathcal{H}_{0+2}$	SUPER	0.3333	0.0943	0.1470	▼	▼
$\mathcal{H}_{0+1+5}$	YAROWSKY	0.9023	0.1542	0.2634	▼	▼
$\mathcal{H}_{0+4}$	**MINIMALITY**	0.5832	**0.2652**	**0.3646**	▲	–
$\mathcal{H}_{0+1,9-12}$	PERSEUS	0.3651	0.2328	0.2843	–	▼
$\mathcal{H}_{0+1,4+5,12}$	**LSW03**	**0.3925**	**0.3389**	**0.3637**	▲	–

Table 6.2: Micro-averaged evaluation results for TR-CoNLL on human oracle NERC tags (subset). MINIMALITY and LSW03 have the highest absolute scores (for R and F1) and significantly outperform RAND, but not MAXPOP. LSW03 outperforms PERSEUS in absolute terms (for all three metrics).

6.3 Component Evaluation Using a Named Entity Oracle ('in vitro')

Tables 6.2 and 6.3 show the TR component evaluation results for TR-CoNLL and TR-MUC4, respectively. The tables comprise three parts: at the top, results for two baselines, RAND and MAXPOP, are given. RAND selects a random referent if at least one referent was found in the gazetteer. MAXPOP picks the candidate referent with the largest population (if known by consulting World Gazetteer population data). The second part reports the performance of individual heuristics from Table 5.1 (Chapter 5). 1REF is the trivial strategy that only resolves non-ambiguous toponyms, and the other heuristics were introduced earlier, as were the two complete systems, *PERSEUS* and *LSW03*, that form the last part of the table. For each heuristic or system, precision, recall and F_1-score are reported.[10]

Statistical Significance. When comparing experimental results of one method with another, we have to be careful with the conclusion that the method that achieves the higher score is more effective in general than the other one, since higher results may be due to chance ef-

---

[10]Recall that TR-CoNLL uses a subset of documents guaranteed to contain prose, as discussed in the description of the dataset. The results for an evaluation of *all* documents in TR-CoNLL, prose or not, is included in Appendix E for completeness in order to demonstrate that no undue negative bias is introduced by the 'prose only' TR-CoNLL sample reported on in this chapter. As you can see there, LSW03 compares even more favourably against PERSEUS on the full TR-CoNLL dataset. In fact, LSW03 is the *only* method that is able to significantly outperform the strong MAXPOP baseline *and* PERSEUS in terms of F1-score (on TR-CoNLL, full dataset, oracle NERC setting, cf. Table E.1 on page 228).

TR-MUC4	(gold NERC)	P	R	$F_{\beta=1}$	significant? $\mathcal{H}_x$ v RAND	significant? $\mathcal{H}_x$ v $\mathcal{H}_{0+3}$
$N = 235$						
—	RAND	0.2723	0.2723	0.2723	n/a	n/a
$\mathcal{H}_{0+3}$	**MAXPOP**	**0.6645**	**0.4298**	**0.5220**	▲	n/a
$\mathcal{H}_0$	**1REF**	**1.0000**	0.1532	**0.2657**	–	▼
$\mathcal{H}_{0+1}$	LOCAL	0.8409	0.1574	0.2652	–	▼
$\mathcal{H}_{0+2}$	SUPER	0.4082	0.0851	0.1408	▼	▼
$\mathcal{H}_{0+1+5}$	YAROWSKY	0.8222	0.1574	0.2642	–	▼
$\mathcal{H}_{0+4}$	**MINIMALITY**	0.3333	**0.2085**	0.2565	–	▼
$\mathcal{H}_{0+1,9-12}$	**PERSEUS**	**0.5929**	0.2851	**0.3851**	▲	▼
$\mathcal{H}_{0+1,4+5,12}$	LSW03	0.3750	**0.3191**	0.3448	△	▼

Table 6.3: Micro-averaged evaluation results for TR-MUC4 on human oracle NERC tags. Despite its simplicity MAXPOP significantly outperforms all heuristics and complex systems on this dataset.

fects. Statistical *significance tests* can be used to reject the hypothesis – traditionally called H_0 – that findings obtained are due to chance. A measure p is used to quantify how much evidence we have to reject H_0, and $p < 0.05$ or less is considered by convention to be significant evidence to do so ('significant at the 5% level'). Accordingly, the last two columns in the tables presented here report whether the F-score of a heuristic or method is statistically significant from the two baselines RANDOM (left column) and MAXPOP (right column), respectively, as reported by a *binomial test* (Dalgaard (2002)). Arrows pointing upwards indicate strong (▲, $p < 0.01$) or weak statistical significance (△, $p < 0.05$), respectively, when comparing a method against a baseline, whereas arrows pointing downwards indicate that a method performs significantly worse than the baseline (▼, and ▽, respectively). Otherwise, results are not statistically significant (indicated by '–').

Utility of Heuristics. The random baseline RAND achieves F=30% and F=27% on the two datasets, respectively. RAND is not a partial algorithm, i.e. a random referent is always chosen, except of course where gazetteer lookup yields no results. This latter case is not penalised here since we only want to evaluate the resolution algorithms, and the gazetteer used remains constant. Therefore, precision and recall values and F-score coincide here. Note that RAND is not that weak a baseline since for unambiguous toponyms, it automatically always picks the correct referent. The 1REF (pseudo-)heuristic has a precision of 1 since is resolves only unambiguous toponyms, and its recall is approximately 15%-16% for both datasets. 1REF is applied as a first step in all experiments reported here. As the low number implies, there is a high number of ambiguous toponym instances occurring in both datasets. Local patterns (LOCAL) have very high precision, and quite expectedly so since they utilise explicit disambiguators in the toponym's environment. However recall is very low (less than 16%) given that the corpus contains news: intuitively, professional journalists could be expected to comply with an in-house editorial style that uses explicit disambiguators as often as possible to avoid confusing the reader. As expected, MAXPOP achieves very good precision relatively speaking, but its recall is not always good, since population data is simply not available for many locations in the gazetteer. In contrast to its name, the 'superordinate mention' heuristic (SUPER) has very low performance on both sub-corpora. YAROWSKY seems to have very high precision and low recall at first sight, but this is misleading: note that YAROWSKY is defined as $\mathcal{H}_0$ followed by $\mathcal{H}_1$ (LOCAL contextual patterns) plus $\mathcal{H}_5$, 'assume one referent per discourse', so that it can use the toponyms resolved by LOCAL as anchors that are propagated through the documents. Without LOCAL, YAROWSKY could not ever become active, since for a referent to be propagated there needs a non-trivial resolution result in the first place, and its scores would fall to the level of 1REF. Unfortunately, here it does not reach the performance of LOCAL, which is fully contained in YAROWSKY (see first column). MINIMALITY is the strongest individual heuristic in terms of F1-score on TR-CoNLL and the only heuristic that significantly outperforms RAND, but not MAXPOP. None of the heuristics (apart from MINIMALITY, first introduced in Leidner et al. (2003), on TR-CoNLL) are in fact alone able to beat the MAXPOP baseline in F-score in a $\beta = 1$ setup.

Performance of Systems. When comparing *PERSEUS* with *LSW03*, the performance of both systems is low due the difficulty of the TR task on world-wide scope, where a resolver sometimes has to decide among 1,600 candidate referents. The systems' F-scores in general range between 28% and 39% across the datasets studied here. On TR-CoNLL (prose subset), LSW03 is superior to PERSEUS with respect to all three metrics in absolute terms, but on the TR-MUC4 data, PERSEUS has a lead in terms of precision and F-score. LSW03 has consistently better recall than PERSEUS (staying ahead between 3%-11% in absolute terms, depending on the corpus), and the latter cannot even beat RANDOM on TR-CoNLL.

PERSEUS' drawback is low recall, especially where documents are short and thus less likely to contain many toponyms (recall its core part requires a window of four *unambiguous* or resolved toponyms to serve as anchors). Overall, LSW03 has achieved its design objective of higher recall, which is important for some applications (e.g. intelligence analysis), whereas the overall score of both methods may not yet be sufficient for satisfactory deployment in many applications yet.

Note, however, that the merits and disadvantages of a method depend on the weighting between precision and recall, which is reflected in the β weighting factor of the F-score. A

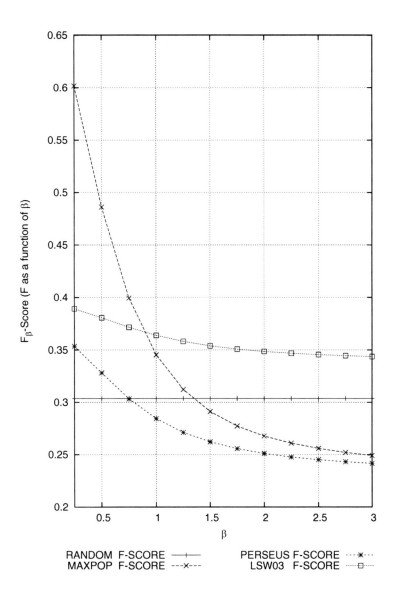

Figure 6.2: Performance of the two systems and two baselines on TR-CoNLL as a function of the F-score's β parameter on gold standard data. The more emphasis is placed on recall, the closer (and lower) MAXPOP and PERSEUS get in F-score. Obviously, LSW03 outperforms both baselines as well as PERSEUS for $\beta > 0.9$, and the more so the higher recall is weighted. LSW03 is thus superior in applications where missing a relevant item comes at a high price, such as patent search or intelligence analysis.

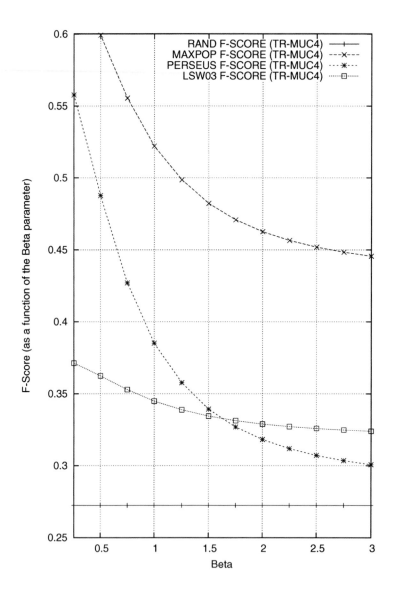

Figure 6.3: Performance of the two baselines and two systems on TR-MUC4 as a function of the *F*-score's β parameter on gold standard data. MAXPOP by far outperforms other methods for all weightings between P and R considered. LSW03 beats PERSEUS for β > 1.65.

suitable choice of β very much depends on the application, but then again we are attempting a component evaluation rather than a task-based evaluation. Consequently, F_β is also reported here as a function of β instead of fixing a single β value such as $\beta = 1$ in the F1-score (which tells but a small part of the story).[11] Figures 6.2 and 6.3 show the two system's F-score for a range of β weights. Precision and recall are not shown, since they do not depend on the parameter β and would only show as flat lines.

The RANDOM baseline has moderate recall and identical precision. LSW03 beats it on both datasets for all values of β, whereas PERSEUS' F-score remains below the random baseline for all $\beta > 0.6$ when run against TR-CoNLL. On TR-MUC, both methods stay on top of RANDOM for all β. We can observe that for TR-CoNLL-like data, and perhaps even in general when documents tend to be short, LSW03 may be the method of choice. The same holds for applications with high recall requirements. In the TR-MUC4 oracle experiment, from $\beta > 1.6$ LSW03 beats PERSEUS, but for smaller values the opposite holds. The TR-MUC4 oracle experiment is also the only case where PERSEUS recall is higher than RAND recall. Where high precision at the expense of low recall is sought ($\beta < 1.6$), for example in Web search like applications, PERSEUS is superior, as long as documents are longer and thus more likely to contain more toponyms. Overall, LSW03 appears to be more resilient across variation of β and robust across datasets ($F \in [32\%; 39\%]$), unlike PERSEUS consistently staying above the baseline.

6.4 Component Evaluation Over System Output ('in vivo')

In the previous section, evaluation results were given using a named entity tagging *oracle*, i.e. the toponym resolution task was carried out on (near-)perfect toponym annotation. While this is useful in order to learn about the true merits of TR methods in a controlled fashion, any real life application will be confronted by imperfect toponym recognisers. This section provides a second series of evaluation results that replace the perfect named entity annotation by a state-of-the-art automatic named entity tagging methods in order to study TR degradation effects caused by real-life conditions. The objective of the evaluation design is to assess how the toponym resolution methods fare in a controlled situation, where the only variable is the choice of using either the gold standard named entity tags (as in the oracle experiment in the previous section) or real-life automatic named entity tags, as described in this section.

---

[11] This way of reporting supports the selection of an algorithm for a particular kind of application, because it shows which method works best for which weighting between P and R.

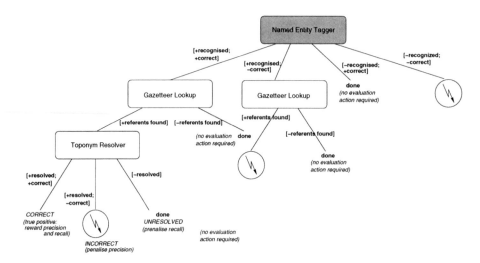

Figure 6.4: Errors can be introduced at three levels.

When toponyms are recognised automatically, errors can be introduced at three different levels, namely the named entity tagging phase, the gazetteer lookup phase, and the toponym resolution proper (Figure 6.4). We are interested here in the additional TR errors introduced when gold standard named entity tags (toponym tags) are replaced by output from an automatic tool. After the named entity tagger tags a word token, there are four possible situations:

1. [+recognised;+correct]: the text contained a toponym in the current position and that decision was indeed correct. Next, the gazetteer lookup can either successfully retrieve a list of referents ([+referents found]), which in turn leads to three possible outcomes for the toponym resolver, which correspond to the three distinct cases from the 'in vitro' evaluation discussed on page 160, namely

   - *correct* ([+resolved;+correct]),
   - *incorrect* ([+resolved;-correct]) or
   - *unresolved* ([-resolved]).

   If the gazetteer does not retrieve a list of candidate referents ([-referents found]), then no penalty needs to be given.

2. [+recognised;-correct]: a *false positive* occurred. For example the English preposition *For* could be mis-recognised as a toponym in the song-line *For He's a Jolly Good Fellow*, which leads to the retrieval of several candidate referents, including a place in Norway called *For* (penalised as *incorrect*). If no referents could be looked up from the

gazetteer, no toponym resolution is carried out, which means no further harm can be done.

3. [-recognised;-correct]: the current token is not a toponym, so we can proceed with the next token and no action needs to be undertaken.

4. [-recognised;-correct]: a *false negative* occurred, i.e. the named entity tagger has overlooked a toponym. Consequently, the resolution cannot be attempted, but it should have been (*incorrect*).

After considering all possible cases that may occur in the evaluation, the named entity tagger that is used is described next.

6.4.1 Using a Maximum Entropy NERC Model

C&C (Curran and Clark (2003a,b); Clark and Curran (2004)) is an NLP toolkit for sequence tagging and parsing. It is based on the *Maximum Entropy (MaxEnt)* machine learning framework. A MaxEnt model comprises a set of binary features or *contextual predicates* $f_i(x,y)$ that describe properties of a word token under consideration together with its context. For example, a feature could have the value 1 if and only if the word token to the left of the current word token starts with a capital letter, otherwise 0. Word tokens x_i are learnt to be associated with a label or category y (such as 'toponym' = LOC), using a probability model of the form

$$p(y|x) = \frac{1}{Z(x)} \exp\left(\sum_{i=1}^{n} \lambda_i f_i(x,y)\right) \qquad (6.9)$$

(Curran and Clark (2003a)) which is maximally uniform, maximising the information-theoretical entropy while remaining consistent with the information in the training data, but non-committal with regard to any unseen information. For each feature a weight λ_i is acquired in the training phase. $Z(x)$ is a normalisation factor. In tagging mode, the induced model is then used for sequence labelling by searching for the tag sequence $y_1 \dots y_n$ that maximises the conditional probability

$$p(y_1 \dots y_n | w_1 \dots w_n) \approx \prod_{i=1}^{n} p(y_i|x_i), \qquad (6.10)$$

i.e. the probability of the tag sequence $y_1 \dots y_n$, given a sequence of n word tokens $w_1 \dots w_n$.

The experiments reported here use *C&C*'s *ner* named entity tagger version 0.96.[12] Curran and Clark (2003b) report a performance of $F_{\beta=1} = 84.89\%$ for English named entities and $F_{\beta=1} = 87.66\%$ for toponyms (category LOC only). Note that these figures were obtained on CoNLL 2002/2003 shared task data (Tjong Kim Sang and De Meulder (2003)), whereas in this section the default NERC model that comes with the *C&C* software distribution is used, which

---

[12] Available from http://svn.ask.it.usyd.edu.au/trac/candc/wiki (accessed 2006-10-03).

was trained on MUC-7 data instead. This is important since for methodological reasons, we cannot use the same data for training and testing (TR-CoNLL is derived from CoNLL).

Since no performance numbers have been published for the MUC-7 model distributed with *C&C* (Curran and Clark (2003b) only report on a model trained on CoNLL data), and since the CoNLL data is available for testing and has gold standard named entity labels, an evaluation of the MUC-7 model on CoNLL was first carried out to assess the named entity tagger's ability to tag toponyms. The `eng.train` portion of the CoNLL 2003 Shared Task data was used. Results are shown in Table 6.5. As it turns out, for all named entity types, the MUC-7-trained model degrades dramatically on the CoNLL dataset.

CoNLL (eng.train)	Precision	Recall	$F_{\beta=1}$
LOC	**62.61%**	**55.70%**	**58.95%**
ORG	35.45%	18.95%	24.70%
PER	69.98%	64.82%	67.30%
Overall	59.66%	47.12%	52.66%

Table 6.4: *C&C* NERC performance on CoNLL 2003 `eng.train` trained on default MUC-7 model.

This leaves us with the question of how automatic toponym resolution quality may suffer from (and on top of) an imperfect named entity tagging process. For example, the village *Quebrada del Oro* (6 referents) is wrongly split by *C&C* into 'Quebrada' (20 ref.) and 'Oro' (31 ref.), increasing ambiguity and introducing noise at the same time. Tables 6.5 and 6.6, respectively, show the evaluation results on the TR-CONLL corpus obtained for the various heuristics and evidence sources (top) as well as some (re-)implemented systems (bottom) using the C&C MaxEnt tagger to recognise toponyms before attempting to resolve them. Figures 6.5 and 6.6 show F-score, plotted again as a function of the β parameter for TR-CoNLL and TR-MUC4, respectively.

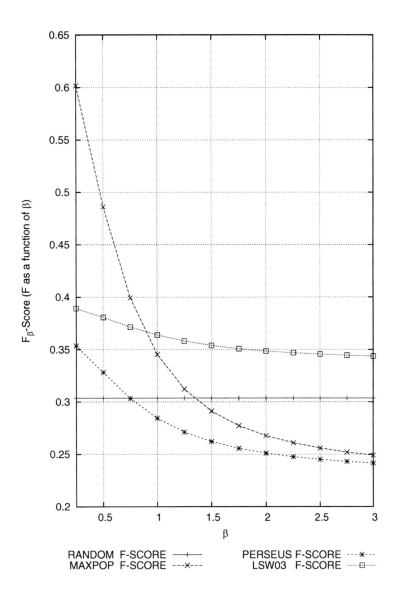

Figure 6.5: Performance of the two systems and two baselines on TR-CoNLL ('clean prose'-only subset) as a function of the F-score's β parameter using MaxEnt toponym tagging. PERSEUS' performance stays well under the MAXPOP baseline, but they show convergent behaviour for large values of β. LSW03 outperforms the MAXPOP baseline in scenarios where high recall is vital.

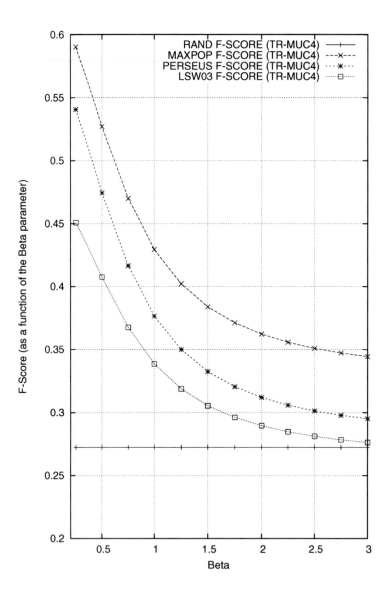

Figure 6.6: Performance of the two systems on TR-MUC4 as a function of the F-score's β parameter using MaxEnt toponym tagging. MAXPOP outperforms its competitors for all β settings.

TR-CoNLL $N = 629$	(MaxEnt NERC)	P	R	$F_{\beta=1}$	significant? $\mathcal{H}_x$ v RAND	significant? $\mathcal{H}_x$ v $\mathcal{H}_{0+3}$
	RAND	0.3481	0.3481	0.3481	n/a	n/a
$\mathcal{H}_{0+3}$	**MAXPOP**	**0.6641**	0.2766	**0.3905**	–	n/a
$\mathcal{H}_0$	1REF	**1.0000**	0.1574	0.2720	△	▼
$\mathcal{H}_{0+1}$	LOCAL	0.9908	0.1717	0.2927	▼	▼
$\mathcal{H}_{0+2}$	SUPER	0.3538	0.0731	0.1212	▼	▼
$\mathcal{H}_{0+1+5}$	YAROWSKY	**0.9910**	0.1749	0.2973	▼	▼
$\mathcal{H}_{0+4}$	**MINIMALITY**	0.4985	**0.2591**	**0.3410**	–	▼
$\mathcal{H}_{0+1,9-12}$	**PERSEUS**	**0.3802**	0.2576	0.3071	▽	▼
$\mathcal{H}_{0+1,4+5,12}$	**LSW03**	0.3800	**0.3323**	**0.3545**	–	–

Table 6.5: Micro-averaged evaluation results for TR-CoNLL (subset) on MaxEnt-tagged data. MAXPOP has highest absolute precision and F1-score overall, though not significantly different from LSW03 (at the 5% level), while PERSEUS' 5% lower absolute F1 performance means it is outperformed by MAXPOP.

On MaxEnt tagger output for TR-MUC4, LSW03 and PERSEUS show similar trends for different β weights. In general the effect of exchanging gold standard NERC data for real-life MaxEnt model output is surprisingly small, in general just a few percent, and can be in either direction. Where scores go slightly up, this is due to the automatic MaxEnt tagger not being able to recognise infrequent place names, and where these are ignored it implies a penalty for the toponym tagging (not shown here), but actually precludes a potential source of failure for the toponym resolution layer on top of it due to the experimental setup (in a more task-oriented setting, this may have to be adapted, but note that we are interested in controlling for NERC errors here when evaluating the *resolution* processing layer). Also, using automatic toponym recognition 'underneath' the toponym resolution changes the number N of toponym instances in the data (due to false positives and false negatives): for example, for TR-CoNLL (subset), contrast $N = 1018$ (gold standard) with $N = 629$ when replacing oracle tags with C&C's MaxEnt tagging.

TR-MUC4 $N = 250$	(MaxEnt NERC)	P	R	$F_{\beta=1}$	significant? $\mathcal{H}_x$ v RAND	significant? $\mathcal{H}_x$ v $\mathcal{H}_{0+3}$
	RAND	0.2489	0.2200	0.2335	n/a	n/a
$\mathcal{H}_{0+3}$	**MAXPOP**	**0.6212**	**0.3280**	**0.4293**	▲	n/a
$\mathcal{H}_0$	1REF	**1.0000**	0.1240	0.2206	–	▼
$\mathcal{H}_{0+1}$	LOCAL	0.8205	0.1280	0.2215	–	▼
$\mathcal{H}_{0+2}$	SUPER	0.1833	0.0440	0.0710	▼	▼
$\mathcal{H}_{0+1+5}$	**YAROWSKY**	0.7727	**0.1360**	**0.2313**	–	▼
$\mathcal{H}_{0+4}$	MINIMALITY	0.4714	0.1320	0.2062	–	▼
$\mathcal{H}_{0+1,9-12}$	**PERSEUS**	**0.5738**	**0.2800**	**0.3763**	▲	–
$\mathcal{H}_{0+1,4+5,12}$	LSW03	0.4714	0.2640	0.3385	▲	▼

Table 6.6: Micro-averaged evaluation results for TR-MUC4 on MaxEnt-tagged data. MAXPOP has highest absolute performance also on automatic named entity tags (F1-score statistically on par with PERSEUS, but significantly outperforming every other method). MAXPOP and PERSEUS are significantly superior to LSW03 in this setting.

6.5 Discussion

The previous sections have evaluated the performance of various heuristics and two fully implemented toponym resolution systems.

The performance of both methods studied here still leaves open much room for improvement, as our evaluation on world-scale scope shows.

Most obviously, MAXPOP is a very strong baseline that is easy to implement, although in some contexts population data may not be readily available. Both systems could benefit from incorporating MAXPOP's knowledge in some form.

It would also be interesting to combine the two methods implemented so as to inherit from LSW03 high robustness in the light of noise (and potentially in document length) and geographic score and from PERSEUS its superior precision and recall on the more difficult regional dataset TR-MUC4, where the sliding window approach seems more succesful than MINIMALITY. For instance, future methods could be applied selectively, taking into account the nature of the data (global versus regional geo-focus, length).

In general, the situation in TR seems to be similar to WSD, where the performance of methods is hampered by data sparseness (most events will never be seen in any single document or manageable corpus). In contrast to WSD, however, geographic space can be modelled using a numerical latitude/longitude grid that allows heuristics such as the ones studied above to be applied (taking into account distance relationships), where the semantic space of word senses has no obvious counterpart.

Impact. The findings in this chapter have some consequences for the principled construction of future systems: the order in which heuristics are implemented should ideally be guided by their expected utility. Where resources are limited, the language engineer should implement LOCAL and MAXPOP first, and he or she can safely ignore SUPER. YAROWSKY also seems to be low-payoff from the evidence seen (it performs lower than LOCAL alone, which contains it). Where high recall is required, spatial MINIMALITY, the core ingredient of LSW03, appears favourable, and is to be recommended especially where toponyms are rare in documents, for example due to their length.

6.6 Chapter Summary

In this chapter, I have presented results of the first evaluation of different toponym resolution methods from the literature on the *same evaluation dataset* under controlled conditions. Using well-established metrics including F-score adapted from IR, I have given evaluation results for toponym resolution strategies in two settings, namely (i) when applying the methods on gold-standard ('oracle') named entity tags (to measure the quality of the resolution in an ideal scenario), and (ii) on automatic named entity tags as produced by a a state-of-the-art maximum entropy model.

To the best of the author's knowledge, this represents the first study of the robustness of toponym resolution methods in the face of named entity recognition and classification errors that inevitably exist in any real system. Furthermore, this thesis is also the first evaluation study to apply toponym resolution based on a large-scale (earth-wide) gazetteer to a non-trivial number of documents, TR-CoNLL representing global news and TR-MUC4 representing regional news, respectively. While both sub-corpora represent the news genre, their different geographic scope was shown to impact the evaluation results for all systems, and more so than exchanging oracle NERC tags with automatic MaxEnt tags to identify the toponyms.

The main surprise in the results is the very different behaviour exhibited by *PERSEUS* on the two sub-corpora (it is much more useful on MUC-style text than on CoNLL-style, despite the fact that both belong to the news genre), and main confirmation of the positive, recall-enhancing effect that the spatial minimality heuristic (MINIMALITY) developed for this thesis brought to bear as part of the LSW03 method (Leidner et al. (2003)), because its geometric nature means that it is applicable where not textual context or knowledge other than latitude/longitude is available.

The overall performance of TR methods when using global (earth-wide) gazetteers still leaves much to be desired, but on the other hand it is not yet clear what levels of performance are required to build useful applications. In any case, different applications will require different properties from a method, some focusing more on precision, others focusing more on recall, and there is no overall clear winner. The strength of MAXPOP was to be expected, as quite similarly in WSD the choice of a default referent (most common sense) is very hard to outperform.

The best properties of the two methods could perhaps be combined by selecting the one known to be better depending on text type (length, number of toponyms) and geographical scope. Another means of combination would be to borrow PERSEUS' sliding window technique and integrate it into LSW03. Incorporating MAXPOP is an obvious addition to both methods.

More generally, I claim that the use of an oracle experiment over a reference dataset with known inter-annotator agreement and using different methods implemented in the same software environment as described in this thesis introduces a level of control that makes it much less likely that any observations are idiosyncracies of the way the software was built (for instance different treatment of uppercase/lowercase in two systems under comparison may already impact results) or differences in the gazetteers, and this has not been systematically addressed before.

In the next chapter, we will look at several types of applications that will support the claim of usefulness of automatic toponym resolution further. They can also serve as examples to think about more task-based evaluation, which is beyond the scope of the present thesis and left for future work.

Chapter 7

Applications

Use the technology which the engineer has developed,
but use it with a humble and questioning spirit.
Never allow technology to be your master, and never
use it to gain mastery over others.
– Marina Lewycka (2005),
*   A Short History of Tractors in Ukrainian*

[Parts of this chapter have been published as Leidner et al. (2003), Leidner (2003b), Leidner (2005a) and Leidner (2006b).]

While the focus of this thesis is on evaluation of toponym resolution, this chapter presents four proof-of-concept applications that demonstrate further the importance of toponym resolution, and, by implication, the importance of methods developed and evaluated in the previous chapters. Specifically, here it is shown how toponym resolution can (i) link text and space by automatically creating hypertext that connects toponyms to the locations on maps that they refer to, (ii) aid the generation of visual summaries, (iii) enable the spatial exploration of events, (iv) increase performance in text search and (v) allow for precise answering of spatial questions.

7.1 Visualization: Bridging Text and Space by Hyperlinking to Satellite Images

Text documents are the primary medium in which any kind of intelligence is stored, retrieved and processed. Quite often, geographic maps are used to relate events reported in textual form to the location in which they occurred, in order to find causal links between nearby incidents, and to consider 'what-if' scenarios. For example, a political analyst studying drug trafficking in South America will have to read regular intelligence reports covering individual incidents

187

in order to write high-level briefs that assess certain aspects of the status quo, which are then used by policy makers as a basis for their decisions. One important tool of the analysis process are *thematic maps*, and using toponym resolution we can compute thematic maps that link text and space in the most literal sense: Figure 7.1(a) shows a sample document from TR-MUC4 describing a drug-related arrest in Peru. Toponyms recognised in the prose can be resolved to coordinates in latitude/longitude format, which allows one to create automatic hyperlinks (underlined text in yellow boxes) to mapping applications (in this case, Google Maps[1]) that situate the locations referred to in the document to satellite images (b) and country borders on a map (c). In this example, the satellite footage actually reveals that the arrest happened near a river, which demonstrates that by virtue of linking text and space, we can obtain valuable additional information that is not contained in the text alone.

7.2 Summarisation: Generating Map Surrogates for Stories

The usefulness of visual representations to convey information is widely recognized (cf. Larkin and Simon (1987)). In this section, we demonstrate how toponym resolution applied to a document can be used to to create a graphical summary that represents the 'spatial aboutness' of its narrative (we use the term 'surrogate' to refer to a partial representation of a text). In a case study, toponym resolution allows us to create a custom map centered around an event reported, because we can compute *where* the event happened.

Two news stories were selected from online newspapers on the same day (2003-02-21): one story (Appendix G.1) reports the tragic death of a baby from London in a Glasgow hospital despite flying it to a Glasgow specialist hospital in the Royal aircraft, and the other story (Appendix G.2) describes the search of the Californian police for a pregnant women from Modesto, CA, USA, reported missing.[2]

Figure 7.2 shows textual surrogates of the two documents in the form of a synopsis of all place names found in the documents: an analyst who wants to get a quick overview over the locations involved in some item of news reportage might find such a surrogate helpful to decide its local interest or relevance, although the source would then still have to be skim-read.

---

[1]`http://www.maps.google.com/` (accessed 2006-09-11).
[2]Sadly, the woman was later found dead, and her husband was found guilty of murdering her.

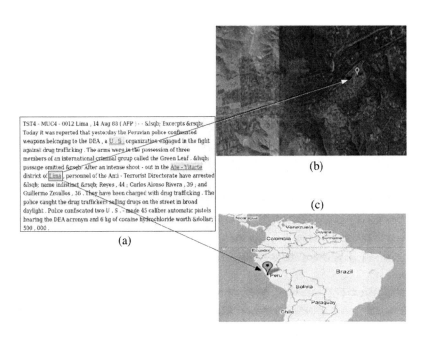

Figure 7.1: Hyperlinking toponyms in a text document with maps and satellite images.

Story G.1

... Scotland ... Tooting ... London ... Glasgow ... London ... Glasgow ... Northolt ... Glasgow ... Britain ... Prestwick ... Tooting ... Glasgow ... UK ... Glasgow ...

Story G.2

Modesto ... Southern California ... Modesto ... Los Angeles ... Sacramento ... Berkeley Marina ... Fresno ... Oakland ... Modesto ... Los Angeles ... Southern California ... Modesto ... Southern California ... New York ... Long Island ...

Figure 7.2: Textual geo-spatial document surrogates for the stories in Appendices G.1 and G.2.

We now compare this 'baseline' textual surrogate to a graphical map representation based on the process depicted in Figure 7.3): an unconstrained news item is fed into a simple named entity tagger for place names based on the UN-LOCODE gazetteer.[3] It recognizes location names, resolves multi-referential place names and looks up the coordinates:

```
Scott, more than a dozen news crews from <ENAMEX type="LOCATION" longitude=
"-118.25" latitude="34.05">Los Angeles</ENAMEX> to <ENAMEX type="LOCATION"
longitude="121.5" latitude="38.583333">Sacramento</ENAMEX> camped out front.
```

From the text we obtain a vector of types of all spatial named entities with their frequency of occurrence in the text:

---

[3]For the experiment reported here, some additional data was used from http://www.astro.com/cgi/aq.cgi?lang=e (accessed 2006-09-11).

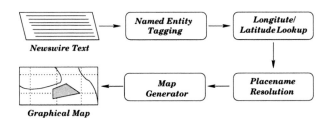

Figure 7.3: Map surrogate generation process.

$$
\begin{pmatrix}
UK: & 1 \\
Scotland: & 1 \\
Tooting: & 2 \\
London: & 2 \\
Glasgow: & 5 \\
Northolt: & 2 \\
Prestwick: & 1 \\
Britain: & 1
\end{pmatrix}
,
\begin{pmatrix}
Modesto: & 3 \\
Southern\,California: & 2 \\
LosAngeles: & 2 \\
Sacramento: & 1 \\
Berkeley: & 1 \\
Fresno: & 1 \\
Oakland: & 1 \\
NewYork: & 1 \\
LongIsland: & 1
\end{pmatrix} .
$$

For simplicity, we drop those that correspond to regions (which are represented by sets of points) and feed the remaining list of point coordinates (corresponding to villages and cities) into a map generator to generate a Mercator projection of the geographical area that includes all the points, plus 10% of the surrounding area. For this, The Generic Map Tools (GMT)[4] were used (Wessel and Smith (2004)) via HTTP.[5] On the custom map, we plot a filled polygon given by the resolved toponyms, which represents the location of the actions described in the narrative in visual form. Place names that are too small to be contained in the gazetteer (e.g. Tooting/Northold) are ignored.

Figure 7.4 and Figure 7.6 show the resulting maps for the stories in Appendix G.1 and Appendix G.2, respectively. Clearly, such a visual surrogate is superior with respect to comprehension time than the textual surrogate presented before.

It is further interesting to see what happens if we leave out the final paragraph for the map creation (Figure 7.5): we obtain a 'zoomed-in' version of the map. This turns out to be the case for many stories and is due to the convention of news reportage to close a report with linking the narrative to similar events in order to present the event in a wider context.

7.3 Exploration: Geo-Spatial News Browsing

Google Earth (Google, Inc. (2006a)) is a commercial application that allows virtual navigation of the globe in real-time, combining three-dimensional modeling and rendering techniques with satellite imagery covering the whole planet. It provides functionality for defining so-called place marks, electronic signposts that mark and label salient places, and enables the user to 'fly' across the (virtual) earth, zooming in on arbitrary locations. A flexible tool, it is employed by archaeologists, real estate surveyors, political analysts and hobbyists alike.

---

[4]http://gmt.soest.hawaii.edu/ (accessed 2006-09-11).
[5]http://stellwagen.er.usgs.gov/mapit/ (accessed 2006-09-11).

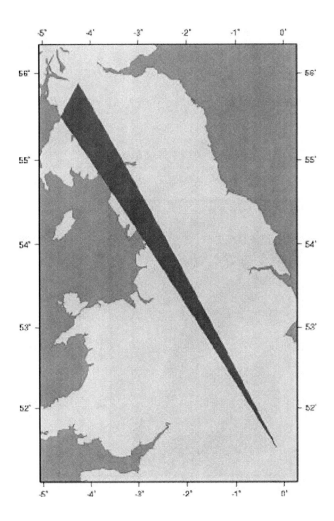

Figure 7.4: Automatic visualization of story G.1: a baby flown from London to Glasgow for medical treatment dies there.

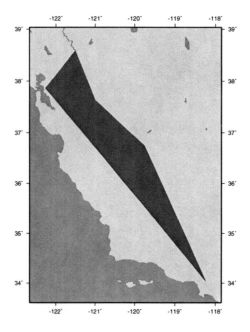

Figure 7.5: Automatic visualization of story G.2: a pregnant woman is missing in Modeno, CA (local view; final paragraph excluded).

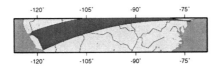

Figure 7.6: Story G.2: the final paragraph places the event in context (global view; complete story).

Google Earth supports interoperability with third-party software using the KML (Keyhole Markup Language), an XML-based language that allows for the enrichment of its built-in models with additional external information (Google, Inc. (2006b)).

TextGIS® supports KML export, which enables the bridging of the two media text and space. But unlike the study in the previous section, where a map is generated based on information contained in a document, here we take a given earth model as input and enrich it with place marks that indicate events (Figure 7.7 shows a sample KML fragment generated). Users can then click on the place mark icon to see a 'snippet', a tiny textual excerpt of the document context surrounding the toponym that is grounded.[6]

Figure 7.8 shows the TextGIS®-Google Earth demo in action. The grounded news events from the TR-MUC4 corpus were converted into KML and imported, and the user sees the locations at which the events reported are situated. By clicking on a place mark icon with the mouse, a pop-up window gives details of the event and links back to the full document in case the user desires to read more about it. In this case, the news event behind the place mark describes the terrorist attack on an airport in South America.

---

[6]At the time of writing, a nearly identical application was independently built by Pouliquen et al. (2006). So while I cannot claim to be the first to publish this particular application, the fact that a team at the EU's Joint Research Centre (JRC) have built the same application arguably supports my case for the importance of toponym resolution and its systematic evaluation in a standard setting.

```
<?xml version="1.0" encoding="UTF-8"?>
<kml xmlns="http://earth.google.com/kml/2.0">
 <Document>
   <Folder>
     <name>Linguit(R) TextGIS(R) Folder</name>
     <open>1</open>
     <Folder>
       <description>Linguit(R) TextGIS(R) analysis result</description>
       <name>d35.tr</name>
       <open>1</open>
       <Placemark>
         <description>
           <![CDATA[ <h1>Jucuapa</h1><p> ... reports state that a National Guard
             officer was killed while fighting an FMLN attack near <b>Jucuapa</b>
             . Another report indicates that the authorities have identified the
             corpse of policeman David Diaz ... <p>
             Go to <a href="file://d35.tr">Source document</a>. <p> ]]>
         </description>
         <name>Jucuapa</name>
         <LookAt>
           <longitude>-85.9833</longitude><latitude>12.8667</latitude>
           <range>300</range><tilt>46</tilt><heading>49</heading>
         </LookAt>
         <visibility>0</visibility>
         <Style>
           <IconStyle>
             <Icon>
               <href>root://icons/palette-3.png</href>
               <x>96</x><y>160</y><w>32</w><h>32</h>
             </Icon>
           </IconStyle>
         </Style>
         <Point>
           <extrude>1</extrude>
           <altitudeMode>relativeToGround</altitudeMode>
           <coordinates>-85.9833,12.8667,50</coordinates>
         </Point>
       </Placemark>
     [...]
   </Folder>
 </Document>
</kml>
```

Figure 7.7: Generated KML for TR-MUC4 document D35.

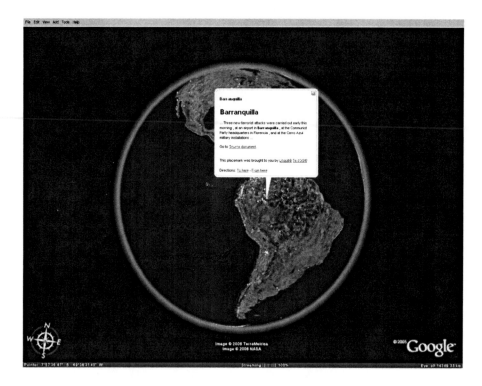

Figure 7.8: TextGIS® integration with Google Earth.

7.4 Search: Spatial Filtering for Document Retrieval

Since all human activity relates to places, a large number of information needs also contain a geographic or otherwise spatial aspect. People want to know about the *nearest* restaurant, about the outcome of the match football match *in Manchester*, or about how many died in a flood in *in Thailand*. Traditional IR however, does not accommodate this spatial aspect enough: place names or geographic expressions are merely treated as strings, just like other query terms. This chapter presents a general technique to accommodate geographic space in IR, and presents an evaluation of a particular instance of it carried out within the CLEF 2005 evaluation (Gey et al. (2006)).

7.4.1 Method: Geo-Filtering Predicates

This section describes the method used in this study. There are four essential processing steps. A document retrieval engine (IR) retrieves a set of documents relevant to the queries and groups them in a ranked list. A named entity tagging phase (NERC) then identifies all toponyms. Afterwards a toponym resolution (TR) module looks up all candidate referents for each toponym (i.e, the locations that the place name may be referring to) and tries to disambiguate the toponyms based on a heuristic. If successful, it also assigns the latitude/longitude of the centroid of the location to the toponym. For each document-query pair a geo-filtering module (CLIP) then discards all locations outside a Minimum Bounding Rectangle (MBR) that is the denotation of the spatial expression in the query. Finally, based on a so-called *geo-filtering predicate*, it is decided whether or not the document under investigation is to be discarded, propagating up subsequent documents in the retrieval engine's original ranking. Below, each phase is described in detail.

7.4.1.1 Document Retrieval (IR).

The document retrieval engine provides access to the indexed GEOCLEF document collection. No stop-word filtering or stemming was used at index time, and index access is case-insensitive. The IR engine is used to retrieve the top 1,000 documents for each evaluation query from the collection using the Vector Space Model with the TF*IDF ranking function (Gospodnetić and Hatcher (2005) p. 78 f.)

$$score(d,q) = \sum_{\forall t in q} tf(t,d) \, idf(t) \, lengthNorm(t,d).$$ (7.1)

The *Lucene* 1.4.3 search API was used for vector space retrieval (Cutting (2006); Gospodnetić and Hatcher (2005)), including *Lucene*'s document analysis functionality for English text without modification (i.e., no fields, phrasal indexing or the like was used).

Frequency	Toponym	Frequency	Toponym	Frequency	Toponym
18,452	**Scotland**	5,391	Metro	3,817	Bosnia
13,556	U.S.	4,686	Germany	3,548	France
9,013	**Los Angeles**	4,438	City	**3,388**	**Valley**
9,007	United States	4,400	London	3,273	Russia
7,893	California	**4,140**	**Glasgow**	3,067	New York
7,458	Japan	4,347	China	**2,964**	**Edinburgh**
7,294	Europe	4,235	Washington	2,919	Mexico
6,985	**Orange County**	4,013	England	2,782	**Southern California**
5,476	Britain	3,985	America		

Table 7.1: List of the most frequent toponyms in the GEOCLEF corpus. Toponyms in bold type are artifacts of the Glasgow/California bias of the corpus.

7.4.1.2   Named Entity Tagging (NERC).

For named entity tagging, we use a state-of-the-art Maximum Entropy classifier trained on MUC-7 data (Curran and Clark (2003b)).[7] Tagging 1,000 retrieved documents is a very expensive procedure; in a production system, this step would be carried out at indexing time. Therefore, the retrieved documents are actually pooled across runs[8] before tagging proceeded in order to speed up processing.

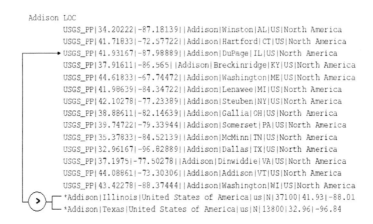

```
Addison LOC
        USGS_PP|34.20222|-87.18139||Addison|Winston|AL|US|North America
        USGS_PP|41.71833|-72.57722||Addison|Hartford|CT|US|North America
        USGS_PP|41.93167|-87.98889||Addison|DuPage|IL|US|North America
        USGS_PP|37.91611|-86.565||Addison|Breckinridge|KY|US|North America
        USGS_PP|44.61833|-67.74472||Addison|Washington|ME|US|North America
        USGS_PP|41.98639|-84.34722||Addison|Lenawee|MI|US|North America
        USGS_PP|42.10278|-77.23389||Addison|Steuben|NY|US|North America
        USGS_PP|38.88611|-82.14639||Addison|Gallia|OH|US|North America
        USGS_PP|39.74722|-79.33944||Addison|Somerset|PA|US|North America
        USGS_PP|35.37833|-84.52139||Addison|McMinn|TN|US|North America
        USGS_PP|32.96167|-96.82889||Addison|Dallas|TX|US|North America
        USGS_PP|37.1975|-77.50278||Addison|Dinwiddie|VA|US|North America
        USGS_PP|44.08861|-73.30306||Addison|Addison|VT|US|North America
        USGS_PP|43.42278|-88.37444||Addison|Washington|WI|US|North America
        *Addison|Illinois|United States of America|us|N|37100|41.93|-88.01
        *Addison|Texas|United States of America|us|N|13800|32.96|-96.84
```

Figure 7.9: Toponym resolution using the maximum-population heuristic.

7.4.1.3   Toponym Resolution (TR).

Complex methods have been proposed for resolving toponyms to locations (see Chapter 5 of this thesis; Smith and Crane (2001); Leidner et al. (2003); Amitay et al. (2004)), using graph search, statistics, spatial distance and discourse heuristics, among other techniques. However, for the first GEOCLEF, which forms the basis of this section, I decided to apply a very basic technique first, since the experiments reported in this section historically preceed the completion of the TextGIS® implementation and the comparative evaluation. Therefore, population data was used as sole predictor of default referents (i.e., only the 'maximum-population heuristic' $\mathcal{H}_3$).

For looking up the candidate referents, the large-scale gazetteer described in Chapter 4 (Leidner (2006a)) as primary gazetteer, supplemented by the *World Gazetteer*[9] for population information (as secondary gazetteer). The algorithm used to resolve toponyms to referents

---

[7]The named entity tagger does not use location gazetteers internally and has been reported to perform at an F-score of 87.66% for locations (Curran and Clark (2003b)).

[8]In TREC/CLEF terminology, a *run* is a single experiment submitted to an evaluation exercise.

[9]http://worldgazetteer.com/ (accessed 2006-09-11).

works as follows: first, we look up the potential referents with associated latitude/longitude
from the primary gazetteer. Then we look up population information for candidate referents
from the secondary gazetteer. In order to relate the population entries from the *World Gazetteer*
to corresponding entries of the main gazetteer, we defined a custom equality operator ($\doteq$)
between two candidate referents for a toponym T_{R_i} such that $R_1 \doteq R_2$ holds if and only if there
is a string equality between their toponyms ($T_{R_1} = T_{R_2}$) and the latitude and longitude of the
candidate referents are in the same 1-degree grid (i.e., if and only if $[R_{1_{lat}}] = [R_{2_{lat}}] \wedge [R_{1_{long}}] =
[R_{2_{long}}]$). If there is no population information available, the toponym remains unresolved.
If there is exactly one population entry, the toponym is resolved to that entry. If more than
one candidate has population information available, the referent with the largest population is
selected.

Figure 7.9 shows the algorithm at work. In the example at the top a case is shown where
only population information (prefixed by an asterisk) for one referent is available. This is used
as evidence for that referent being the most salient candidate, and consequently it is selected.
Note that the coordinates in the two gazetteers need to be rounded for the matching of corresponding entries to be successful. Out of the 41,360 toponym types, population information
was available in the World Gazetteer for *some* (i.e., more than zero) candidate referents only
for 4,085 toponyms. This means that using only the population heuristics, the upper bound for
system recall is $R = 9.88\%$, and for F-Score $F = 9.41\%$, assuming perfect resolution precision.

7.4.1.4 Geographic Filtering (CLIP).

We use a *filtering-based approach* in which we apply traditional IR and then identify locations
by means of toponym recognition and toponym resolution. We can then filter out documents or
parts of documents that do not fall within our geographic area of interest. Given a polygon P
described in a query, and a set of locations $L = \ell_1 \ldots \ell_N$ mentioned in a document, let Δ_i be an
N-dimensional vector of geographic distances on the geoid between the N locations in a text
document d (mentioned with absolute frequencies f_i) and the centroid of P. Then we can use
a *filtering predicate* GEO-FILTER(f, Δ) to eliminate the document if its 'spatial aboutness' is
not strong enough:

$$\text{SCORE}'(d,P) = \begin{cases} \text{SCORE}(d) & \text{GEO-FILTER}(f_d, \Delta_d, P) \\ 0 & \text{otherwise} \end{cases} \tag{7.2}$$

In filtering the decision is simply between passing through the original IR score or setting it to
0, thus effectively discarding the document from the ranking. Here are the definitions of three
simple GEO-FILTER predicates:

1. ANY-INSIDE. This filter is most conservative and tries to avoid discarding true positives
   at the risk of under-utilizing the discriminative power of geographic space for IR. It only

filters out documents that mention no location in the query polygon P:

$$\text{ANY-INSIDE}(f_d, \Delta_d, P) = \begin{cases} true & \exists_{\ell \in d} : \ell \in P \\ false & \text{otherwise} \end{cases} \tag{7.3}$$

2. MOST-INSIDE. This filter is slightly more aggressive than ANY-INSIDE, but still allows for some noise (locations mentioned that do not fall into the geographic area of interest as described by the query polygon P). It discards all documents that mention more locations that fall outside the query polygon than inside:

$$\text{MOST-INSIDE}(f_d, \Delta_d, P) = \begin{cases} true & |\{\ell \in d | \ell \in P\}| > |\{\ell \in d | \ell \notin P\}| \\ false & \text{otherwise} \end{cases} \tag{7.4}$$

3. ALL-INSIDE. This filter is perhaps too aggressive for most purposes; it discards all documents that mention even a single location that fall outside the query polygon P, i.e. all locations must be in the geographic space under consideration:

$$\text{ALL-INSIDE}(f_d, \Delta_d, P) = \begin{cases} true & \forall_{\ell \in d} : \ell \in P \\ false & \text{otherwise} \end{cases} \tag{7.5}$$

In practice, we use Minimal Bounding Rectangles (MBRs) to approximate the polygons described by the locations in the query, a strategy which trades runtime performance against retrieval performance. More specifically, we computed the union of the Alexandria Digital Library and ESRI gazetteers (Table 7.2) to look up MBRs for geographic terms in the GEOCLEF queries.[10] In cases of multiple candidate referents (e.g. for *California*), the MBR for the largest feature type was chosen (i.e. in the case of California, the U.S. membership state interpretation). Latin America was not found in the Alexandria Gazetteer. A manual search for South America also did not retrieve the continent, but found several other hits, e.g. South America Island in Alaska. Holland was recognized by the Alexandria Gazetteer as a synonym for the Netherlands. While this corresponds to typical layperson usage, formally speaking Holland refers to a *part* of the Netherlands. The ESRI server returned two entries for *Caspian Sea*, one as given in the table, another with MBR (41.81; 50.54), (42.21; 50.94)—since they share the same feature type they could not otherwise be distinguished.

Finally, the software module CLIP performs geographic filtering of a document given an MBR, very much like the clipping operation found in typical GIS packages, albeit on unstructured documents, not bitmaps. It would of course have been beneficial for the retrieval performance if the MBRs that were not available in the ESRI and Alexandria gazetteers had been gathered from elsewhere, as there are plenty of sources scattered across the Internet. However, then the experimental outcome would perhaps no longer reflect a typical *automatic* system.

---

[10]On the query side, manual disambiguation was performed.

Expression	Alexandria MBR	ESRI MBR
Asia	(0; 0), (90; 180)	—
Australia	(-45.73; 111.22), (-8.88; 155.72)	(-47.5; 92.2), (10.8; 179.9)
Europe	(35.0; -30.0), (70.0; 50.0)	(35.3; -11.5), (81.4; 43.2)
Latin America	—	(-55.4; -117), (32.7; -33.8)
Bosnia-Herzegovina	(42.38; 15.76), (45.45; 20.02)	—
Germany	(46.86; 5.68), (55.41; 15.68)	(47.27; 5.86), (55.057; 15.03)
Holland	(50.56; 3.54), (53.59; 7.62)	(51.29; 5.08), (51.44; 5.23)
Japan	(30.1; 128.74), (46.26; 146.46)	(24.25; 123.68), (45.49; 145.81)
Rwanda	(-3.01; 28.9), (-1.03; 31.2)	(-2.83; 28.85), (-1.05; 30.89)
UK	(49.49; -8.41), (59.07; 2.39)	(49.96; -8.17), (60.84; 1.75)
United States	(13.71; -177.1), (76.63; -61.48)	(18.93; -178.22), (71.35;-68)
California	(32.02; -124.9), (42.51; -113.61)	—
Scotland	— (56.0; -4.0)	(54.63; -8.62), (60.84; -0.76)
Siberia	— (60.0; 100.0)	—
Scottish Islands	—	—
Scottish Trossachs	— (49.63; -104.22)	—
Scottish Highlands	— (57.5; -4.5)	—
Sarajevo	— (43.86; 18.39)	(43.65; 18.18), (44.05; 18.58)
Caspian Sea	— (42.0; 50.0)	(45; 48.41), (42.40; 48.81)
North Sea	— (55.33; 3.0)	(58.04; 1.02), (58.44; 1.42)

Table 7.2: Minimal bounding rectangles (MBRs) from the Alexandria and ESRI gazetteers. MBRs are given as pairs of points, each with lat/long in degrees. A dash means that no result was found or that a centroid point was available only.

7.4.1.5 Query Expansion with Meronyms.

Query expansion is typically used as a Recall-enhancing device, because by adding terms to the original query that are related to the original terms, additional relevant documents are retrieved that would not have been covered by the original query, possibly at the expense of Precision. Here, I experimented with meronym query expansion, i.e. with geographic terms that stand in a spatial 'part-of' relation (as in 'Germany is part of Europe'). *WordNet* 2.0 was used to retrieve toponyms that stand in a meronym relationship with any geographic term from the query. The version used contains 8,636 part-of relationships linking 9,799 synsets. The choice of WordNet was motivated by the excessive size of both gazetteers used in the toponym resolution step. For each query, all constituent geographic entities were transitively added, e.g. for *California*, *Orange County* was added as well as *Los Angeles*.

7.4.2 Evaluation in a GEOCLEF Context

The GEOCLEF 2005 evaluation was very similar to previous TREC and CLEF evaluations: for each run, *11-Point-Average Precision* against *interpolated Recall* and *R-Precision* against retrieved documents were determined. In addition, differences from median across participants for each topic were reported. Traditionally, the relevance judgments in TREC-style evaluations are binary, i.e. a document either meets the information need expressed in a TREC topic (1) or not (0). Intrinsically fuzzy queries (e.g. '*shark attacks near Australia*') introduce the problem that a strict yes/no decision might no longer be appropriate; there is no 'crisp' cut-off point. In the same way that the ranking has to be modified to account for geographic distance, a modification of the evaluation procedure ought to be considered. However, for GEOCLEF 2005, binary relevance assessments were used.

For organizational reasons, this series of experiments did *not* contribute any documents to the GEOCLEF 2005 judgment pool for the relevance assessments, which results in a negative bias of the performance results measured compared to the true performance of the experiments and other GEOCLEF 2005 participants. This is because all relevant documents found by the methods described herein but not returned by any other participants will have been wrongly assessed as 'not relevant'. Therefore, a discussion of the relative performance compared to other participants is omitted here. On the other hand, this makes the results comparable to future experiments with GEOCLEF data outside the annual evaluation, which will of course likewise not be able to influence the pooling a posteriori.

The simplest experiment—or 'baseline run' LTITLE—that uses only the topic title and no spatial processing performs surprisingly well, with an Average Precision averaged over queries of 23.62% and a Precision at 10 documents of just 36%. Table 7.3 gives a summary of the averaged results for each run. As for the terminology, all run names start the letter L followed

Run	Avg. Precision	R-Precision	Run	Avg. Precision	R-Precision
LTITLE	**23.62** %	**26.21** %	LCONCPHRSPAT	**20.37** %	**24.53** %
LTITLEANY	**18.50** %	**21.08** %	LCONCPHRSPATANY	16.92 %	20.36 %
LTITLEMOST	12.64 %	16.77 %	LCONCPHRSPATMOST	11.09 %	15.51 %
LTITLEALL	8.48 %	11.97 %	LCONCPHRSPATALL	7.99 %	10.89 %
LCONCPHR	15.65 %	19.25 %	LCONCPHRWNMN	17.25 %	19.36 %
LCONCPHRANY	14.18 %	19.66 %	LCONCPHRWNMNANY	12.99 %	16.22 %
LCONCPHRMOST	9.56 %	14.46 %	LCONCPHRWNMNMOST	8.18 %	11.38 %
LCONCPHRALL	7.36 %	10.98 %	LCONCPHRWNMNALL	5.69 %	8.78 %

Table 7.3: Result summary: Average Precision and R-Precision.

by an indicator of how the query was formed. CONC means using the content of the <CONCEPT> tag and posing a phrasal query to the IR engine, CONCPHRSPAT means using the content of both <CONCEPT> and <SPATIAL> tags, and <TITLE> uses the title tag. PHR refers to runs using the IR engine's phrasal query mechanism in addition to pure bag-of-terms. For these runs, queries look as follows (identifying the phrases was the only manual step):

```
(("Shark Attacks"^2.0) (("shark attack"~8)^1.5) (Shark Attacks))
```

This combined way of querying takes into account the phrase *shark attacks* (as subsequent terms in the document only) with twice the weight of the 'normal' bag-of-words query (last sub-query). The middle line searches for the lemmatized words *shark* and *attack* within an 8-term window and weights this sub-query with 1.5. Runs containing ANY, MOST, or ALL as part of their name indicate that geo-filtering with the ANY-INSIDE, MOST-INSIDE or ALL-INSIDE filtering predicates, respectively, was used. Finally, WNMN as part of a run name indicates that query expansion with WordNet meronyms was applied.

Applying the 'maximum population' heuristic alone to achieve toponym resolution together with geo-filtering in general performed poorly and in none of the four series of experiments outperformed a baseline that applied no dedicated spatial processing. Interestingly, a plain vanilla Vector Space Model with TF-IDF and the obligatory run using title-only queries (LTITLE) performs better than the median across all participant entries for 19 out of 25 (or 76%) of the queries in GEOCLEF 2005. For three geo-filtering predicates tested, a consistent relative pattern could be observed across all runs: The ANY-INSIDE filter almost consistently outperformed (in one case it was en par with) the MOST-INSIDE filter, which in turn always outperformed the ALL-INSIDE filter. While it was expected that MOST-INSIDE would not perform

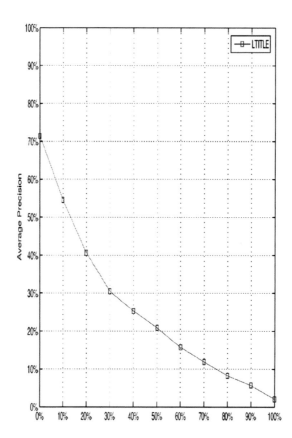

Figure 7.10: Performance of the run LTITLE (average precision).

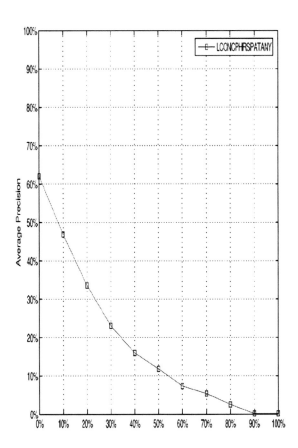

Figure 7.11: Performance of the run LCONCPHRSPATANY (average precision).

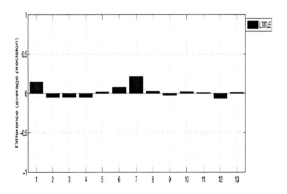

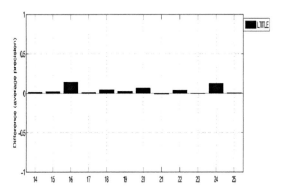

Figure 7.12: Individual topic performance (1-25) relative to the median across participants: run
LTITLE.

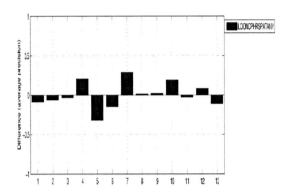

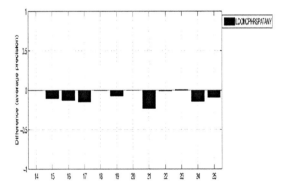

Figure 7.13: Individual topic performance (1-25) relative to the median across participants: run
LCONCPHRSPATANY.

all well as the other two filter types, it is interesting that the conservative ANY-INSIDE outperformed MOST-INSIDE on average. The evidence seems to suggest further that geographic query
expansion with WordNet meronyms is not effective as a Recall-enhancing device, independent
on whether or which geo-filter is applied afterwards. Note however, that this is true only on
average, not for all individual queries. Furthermore, two queries were actually not executed
by the Lucene engine because the query expansion caused the query to exceed implementation
limits (too many query terms).

7.4.3 Discussion

In this section, a method for geographic information retrieval was described based on named
entity tagging to identify place names (or toponym recognition, geo-parsing), toponym resolution (or geo-coding, place name disambiguation) and geographic filtering (or clipping). First
results show that a very simple method for toponym resolution based on a 'maximum population' heuristic alone is not more effective than a TF*IDF baseline when combined with
three point-in-MBR geo-filtering predicates in the setting used. I conjecture this may be due to
the lack of available population data. In addition, geographic query expansion with WordNet
meronyms appears not to improve retrieval performance.

The GEOCLEF evaluation is based on the traditional binary document judgments
[±RELEVANT], which is not optimally suited for geographic IR. I therefore propose to use *Root
Mean Squared Distance* (*RMSD*, Equation 7.6, for discussion see Chapter 6) to indicate the
(geo-) distance between a query centroid c_q and a set of location centroids $c_1, \ldots, c_N$ in a document.

$$\mathrm{RMSD}(d, q) = \sqrt{\frac{1}{N} \sum_{i=1}^{N} (d_i - q)^2} \qquad (7.6)$$

It could be used as a continuous-scale measure for geographic relevance once the assessors
annotated the test queries and the toponyms in the pooled result documents with their 'ground
truth' coordinates.

For future work, several opportunities for further study should be given consideration. The
results presented here should be compared with different, more sophisticated clipping criteria
that take the amount of spatial overlap into account. For example, instead of using MBRs
computed from sets of centroid points,

Alani et al. (2001) proposes a *Dynamic Spatial Approximation Method* (*DSAM*), which
uses Voronoi approximation to compute more precise polygons from sets of points. Once
polygons are available, spatial overlap metrics can be applied to improve retrieval (Larson and
Frontiera (2004)). It is vital to discover methods to determine a good balance when *weighting
the spatial influence* and the term influence in the query against each other in a principled way,

probably even dependent on the query type. On the query side, the specific *spatial relations* should be taken into account. However, this requires defining how users and/or CLEF assessors actually judge different relations beforehand (how near does something have to be to be considered 'near'?). On the document side, *text-local relationships* from the toponym context should be taken into account. Right now, all toponyms (LOC) are considered equal, which does not utilize knowledge from the context of their occurrence. For instance, a document collection that has one mention of *New York* in every document footer because the news agency resides in New York can pose a problem. The *impact of the particular gazetteer* used for query expansion and toponym resolution ought to be studied with respect to the dimensions size/density (e.g. UN-LOCODE/*WordNet* versus NGA GeoNames) and local/global (e.g. EDINA DIGIMAP versus NGA GeoNames). Last but perhaps most importantly, more sophisticated toponym resolution strategies (such as those described earlier in this thesis) should be compared against the simple population heuristic used in this series of experiments.

7.5 Question Answering: Knowledge-Based Approach

Since 1998, Internet search has become a pervasive technology that is widely used by a significant proportion of the population in many countries. This section suggests that toponym resolution can be useful to help answer certain types of questions more accurately than possible with state of the art methods.

Geographically related search needs constitute a significant portion of the total requests issued to publically available search engines. For instance, Jansen and Spink (2006) study query logfile samples from nine different Internet search engines and report that out of 11 content categories that the queries can be divided into, the category 'people, places and things' accounted for nearly 42%-49% of all queries in a sample from 2002. Sanderson and Kohler (2004) analyse a random 2,500 query sample taken from *Excite* in 2001 and find that 14.8% contained a toponym, while 18.6% contained a geographic term in general (such as place names, but also phone numbers postcodes/ZIP codes and trigger words like *west*).

The AOL Web query corpus, also known as the '500k User Session Collection', Pass et al. (2006) is a sequence of ≈ 20 million Web search engine queries from about 650,000 users covering the three-month period from 1 March 2006 to 31 May 2006. Unfortunately, queries are only available in a normalised form, which means that all characters are in lower case, and most punctuation was removed in a move that discarded valuable information, which renders automatic named entity tagging a much more difficult task. For instance, `in Sheffield, Jamaica` would be reduced to `in sheffield jamaica`. Nevertheless, we will be using this dataset here as it contains very recent and realistic queries.

A recent trend in search is to answer questions directly and automatically instead of returning links to documents and letting the user pick out the answer manually. In Chapter 2, we have seen that current open-domain QA systems are largely based on a retrieval paradigm, employing the notion of *answer extraction* from text. Now assume a query[11] like

```
how far is salt lake city from to denver colorado (Q-503678)
```

A Web search engine would simply find documents containing these keywords, which does not lead to the desired results (Figure 7.14), and an extractive QA system would try to find answer statements like

The distance between Salt Lake City and Denver, Colorado is X km.

However, since there millions of places, and the user may want to know the distance for any pair of them, the answer is extremely unlikely to be found explicitly on the Web, despite its large size. To solve this problem, the extractive approach can be replaced for this question type by a knowledge-based approach, i.e. instead of trying to extract the answer, we (1) resolve both toponyms in the query and (2) *compute* the geographic distance using a geometric formula (Williams (2006)):

Salt Lake City, UT, United States of America   (40 N 46, 111 W 53)

$\updownarrow$

...

Denver, AR, United States of America   (36 N 24, 93 W 19)
Denver, CO, United States of America   (39 N 44, 104 W 59)
Denver, FL, United States of America   (29 N 24, 81 W 32),

...

which yields a distance of approximately 600 km (Cleveland, 1991, p. 200) as the answer to our query.

Note that in a search scenario where a mobile device is employed (Leidner (2005b)), distance questions might be expressed in elliptical form, *How far is X?*, which is to be interpreted as *How far is X from my current position?*, where the current position can be obtained from a positioning server (Küpper (2005)). Appendix H shows further real distance queries from the AOL corpus.

---

[11]Example queries from the AOL corpus are identified using their line number.

how far is salt lake city from to denver colorado

Cover Band **Salt Lake City**, UT - **Salt Lake**, Utah Cover Bands, **Salt ...**
We travel as **far** as you need including Spokane & Seattle Washington, **Salt Lake** & Park
City Utah, Jackson Hole Wyoming, Bend & Portland Oregon . ...
www.gigmasters.com/CoverBand/CoverBand_**SaltLakeCity**_UT.asp - 60k -
Cached · Similar pages

Denver and Rio Grande Western Railroad - Wikipedia, the free ...
The D&RG then joined with the **Colorado** Midland to build a line from Glenwood Springs ...
17/18, Rio Grande Zephyr, **Denver-Salt Lake City**, 1970-1983 ...
en.wikipedia.org/wiki/**Denver**_and_Rio_Grande_Western_Railroad - 48k -
Cached - Similar pages

Denver International Airport - Wikipedia, the free encyclopedia
Denver International Airport has three midfield concourses, spaced **far** apart. ... Delta Air
Lines (Atlanta, Cincinnati/Northern Kentucky, **Salt Lake City**) ...
en.wikipedia.org/wiki/**Denver**_International_Airport - 59k - Cached - Similar pages

The **Colorado** Plateau Region—Essay References
The **far** country: A regional history of Moab and La Sal, Utah. Olympus Publishing
Company, **Salt Lake City**, UT. Utah Wilderness Coalition. 1990. ...
www.cpluhna.nau.edu/Places/coloplateau5.htm - 20k - Cached - Similar pages

Small Business Administration - **Salt Lake City**, UT
Homepage for the SBA office in **Salt Lake City**, UT ... **Far** West Bank (PLP);
www.farwestbank.com ... 1380 Lawrence; **Denver**, CO 80202-2029. (303) 595-9898 ...
www.sba.gov/ut/UT_CLPLENDERS.html - 51k - Cached - Similar pages

EJ Phillips 1830-1904 **Denver Colorado**
previous: **Salt Lake City** Sept. 1886. 1886. **Denver** Col Sept 20th [no year probably 1886].
My dear Son,. Arrived from **Colorado** Springs at 12 noon. ...
home.comcast.net/~m.chitty/**denver**.htm - 27k - Cached - Similar pages

Best Fares to **Salt Lake City**, UT
Don't see your departure **city** listed? Search here. ... Best Fares to **Salt Lake City**, UT, Sign
Up For Best Fare Alerts Track Best Fares to **Salt Lake City**, UT ...
search.travel.yahoo.com/bin/search/bfsearch?intl=us&dc=SLC - 39k -
Cached - Similar pages

ENN: Environmental News Network [[Today's News Full Story]]
Environmentally Conscious Megasuburb Planned Near **Salt Lake City** ... a Berkeley, Calif.,
consultant who designed the trendy redevelopment of **Denver's** old ...
www.enn.com/today.html?id=10219 - 24k - Cached - Similar pages

FOXNews.com - Gruesome Cat Killings Mystify Authorities in **Denver ...**
Colorado authorities are looking into possible links between the **Denver** and **Salt Lake City**
killings, but so **far** no clear connection has surfaced. ...
www.foxnews.com/story/0,2933,90954,00.html - 21k - Cached - Similar pages

New West **Salt Lake City** | News, Politics, Music, Outdoors, Arts ...
We're looking for writers to help flesh out the **Salt Lake City** node. ... **Denver** metal act,
which has in the past often been pinch-hitters, ...
www.newwest.net/index.php/**city**/main/C123/L104 - 78k - Cached - Similar pages

Figure 7.14: Google fails to answer a distance question (Q-503678).

7.6   Chapter Summary

In this chapter, we have seen several applications where toponym resolution was helpful or even vital.

The first application allows the creation of hypertext from documents in which the toponyms are resolved, which allows the linking from text to maps and satellite images. The second application uses toponyms mentioned in a story to create a polygon that functions as a visual summary of the 'spatial aboutness' of the events contained in the document. The third application allowed the automatic population of an interactive, three-dimensional terrain model of the whole globe with place marks representing news stories that happen in the places where the place marks are located. The fourth application suggested a new way of taking into account geographic notions in document retrieval to introduce a notion of geographic relevance. These three applications have been implemented in order to demonstrate the utility of toponym resolution in principle.

Last but not least, a proposal for a fifth application, which has not been implemented for this thesis, demonstrates how toponym resolution may be used to go beyond extractive question answering of distance questions.

To sum up, toponym resolution is a powerful bridging tool that allows new applications to combine text and geographic space, and therefore the development of robust methods and their principled evaluation and incremental improvement is paramount.

Chapter 8

Summary and Conclusion

A world map that does not show Utopia

is not worth looking at.

– Oscar Wilde

In this chapter, I summarise the work presented in this thesis, assess its contributions, point out some limitations, and conclude with ideas for further research.

8.1 Summary of Contributions

In Chapter 1, I have motivated research into the theme of 'bridging text and space' by outlining several potential applications. I have begun by describing the problem of *toponym resolution* in text and by contrasting it with related issues in the research area where text processing overlaps with GIS. Then I have sketched a research programme comprising seven research questions:

- *utility*: How useful are various heuristics that have been proposed for TR in the past, both in absolute terms and relative to each other?

- *type ambiguity*: How referentially ambiguous are toponyms (in a representative gazetteer), i.e. how many locations can they potentially refer to?

- *token ambiguity*: How ambiguous are toponym instances that are actually present in a corpus?

- *agreement*: How much can humans agree when marking up toponym referents in a corpus against a gazetteer with world-wide coverage?

- *geographic scalability*: Can automatic TR methods scale up to world-wide geographic scope?

- *component evaluation*: How do previously proposed TR methods compare under controlled conditions?

- *system evaluation*: How do TR methods fare in the presence of systematic toponym recognition errors, such as those introduced by typical named entity taggers compared to performance on an oracle's output?

Then the methodology was laid out and the scope of this study was defined to cover the *resolution of toponyms in contemporary open-domain news prose with global geographical scope against a present-day earth geometry using freely available sources and its evaluation.*

Chapter 2 introduced the basics from the two fields that this thesis attempts to bring closer together, namely geographic information systems and natural language processing. Systems of geographic referencing, GIS software systems and spatial databases, gazetteers were 'imported' from geography. Digital libraries, information retrieval and extraction, question answering and word sense disambiguation were imported from natural language processing. The language used to talk about geographic space then provided the theme that joins the two fields.

In Chapter 3, previous work was described and related in a systematic taxonomy based on the types of evidence used in past TR approaches. The key criticism shared by all previous work was the lack of a systematic evaluation methodology in the sense that (a) evaluations were either entirely absent, too small, done on data with idiosyncratic properties, or on data that cannot be shared, (b) the human performance on the task had never been established, (c) the geographic scope of the approaches was often limited to particular regions, and—as a consequence—(d) the performance of different approaches was not comparable.

On the basis of this, I argued that a proper evaluation methodology was due to be applied, and I offered a task definition with an associated dataset comprising a reference gazetteer and an annotated reference corpus to be used as the ground truth for the evaluation of systems in a controlled fashion.

To this end, Chapter 4 proposed TRML, a new XML-based mark-up language, and associated annotation guidelines. I designed and implemented TAME, a Web-based annotation tool and compiled a reference gazetteer from free sources in order to curate an evaluation dataset for the toponym resolution task, comprising two sub-corpora with news text, one with global (TR-CoNLL), and another with more local geographic scope (TR-MUC4). I demonstrated the feasibility of the annotation task by determining human inter-annotator agreement for the suggested TR benchmark scenario. It is hoped that this solves the problem that 'no corpus currently exists to evaluate place name disambiguation' (Pouliquen et al., 2006, p. 53).

In Chapter 5, I proposed a new heuristic algorithm for TR based on borrowing Yarowsky's bias '*one sense per discourse*' from WSD to TR ('*one referent per discourse*') and by combining it with a novel *geometric minimality heuristic* that assumes that the smallest bounding polygon can be used to assign the correct set of toponym interpretations. I have developed

TextGIS®, a software platform for the experimentation with and easy implementation of various toponym resolution algorithms. By offering a convenient C++ API and several useful command line tools, it supports the interoperability of toponym recognition, gazetteer lookup, toponym resolution, evaluation, and visualisation/navigation. Based on this infrastructure, I provided a re-implementation of a list of previously proposed heuristics, and carried out a replication study of a complete system documented in the literature (Smith and Crane (2001)), intended to serve as a non-trivial baseline for system evaluations.

Chapter 6 then presented the first empirical comparison of several individual heuristics and two complete TR systems under controlled conditions, i.e. both using the same dataset and software platform. The two available corpora allowed for the study of degradation effects comparing TR on global versus local news (component evaluation) on the one hand, and the comparison between oracle toponym recognition output versus output from a realistic state-of-the-art maximum entropy sequence tagger on the other hand (system evaluation). It was found that the extremely large number of potential labels (classes) that exceeds typical NLP sequence tagging tasks by several order of magnitudes and the extreme label bias towards the most salient toponym referent rendered a straight-forward supervised learning regime infeasible due to overfitting. To overcome this, learning heuristic weights was suggested as a robust alternative for future experiments.

Chapter 7 presented several application case studies intended to show the relevance of the toponym resolution task, and therefore, by implication, the importance of its principled evaluation to control research progress on the TR task. Implemented applications comprise the automatic generation of hypertext that links toponyms in text to maps and satellite images, automatic generation of visual story summaries and automatic news exploration using a 3-dimensional earth model, geographic information retrieval. These applications were built using the TextGIS® platform. Another application, whose implementation is left for future work, is the knowledge-based answering of distance questions.

8.2 Future Work

While this thesis has tried increase the understanding of toponym resolution as a task and its principled evaluation, there remain of course many open questions and venues for further research. Here, I list the most obvious opportunities for follow-up work:

1. *Different genres*: In this thesis, we have looked only at news prose. While this is an important text type from an application point of view, there are many other genres worth studying. For example, travel reports or encyclopedic gazetteers (e.g. Munro and Gittings (2006, to appear)) may be expected to yield interesting distributions of toponyms, distinct from news. Therefore, one line of research could investigate how TR can be

made to work robustly across different genres or how to select the best method for a genre automatically.

2. *More languages*: The emergence of the first systems capable of multilingual or language-independent TR (Pouliquen et al. (2006)) calls for TR evaluation to be extended beyond English. However, while there might be a strong practical need to do so (evaluation of non-English systems), I do not expect fundamentally different behaviour of the algorithms across languages, since the distributional properties do not depend much on the language a document is written in. Still, questions of local variants and *endonyms/exonyms* pose a challenge (to date, all large gazetteers were curated in English speaking countries).

3. *Further methods*: In this thesis, I have presented evaluations of a replication of the PERSEUS algorithm as well as a novel method based on minimality heuristics. However, it would be interesting to replicate *all* methods under similar conditions to learn about their relative performance. TextGIS® constitutes a convenient platform for further studies attempting this.

For example, a recently reported method capable of language independent TR (Pouliquen et al. (2006)) could be evaluated on the reference dataset presented in this thesis to compare results.

4. *Additional evidence*: This thesis has assessed several exemplary heuristics, but surprisingly many different heuristics are being used in published methods. It would therefore be interesting to complete the list of implemented heuristics. Furthermore, other evidence sources including URLs, phone numbers and so forth could be considered when resolving toponyms.

The evidence taken into account is by no means restricted to the text of the document collection itself: To build on-demand gazetteers for IE, Uryupina (2003) describes a method that relies on the *hit count* of an Internet search engine to classify a token according to a scheme of six feature type classes.

This idea can be extended for the task of TR: certain words (e.g. from a context window) can be correlated one by one with all alternative superordinate terms in order to find out the most salient superordinate term: (London, England) versus (London, Ontario), (Ontario, UK) versus (Ontario, Canada), (England, UK) versus (England, Canada), and so on, until we can conclude that the strongest tie indicates the referent London > England > UK. The advantage of such an approach is that default referents can be identified without seeing their corresponding toponym in training data. The disadvantage is the low speed due to network latency and the number of network accesses necessary to process a whole gazetteer (in the order of 10^7).

5. *Feature types*: This thesis has concentrated on using a geography based on the broad notion of 'populated place'. Alternatively, it would be interesting to use a much more fine-grained set of geographic feature types including man-made artefacts such as airports and monuments, physical features, geo-political entities, and so on. Before doing so, two problems need to be considered: Firstly, there has to be a commitment to using one specific hierarchy of feature types. However, currently there is no consensus in the GIS community about a standard to be used. Nevertheless, there is a tendency at the moment to use the Alexandria Digital Library Feature Type Thesaurus (Appendix I) as a common ground and basis for project-specific customisation and refinement. And secondly, changing the toponym definition implies changing the toponym tagging, which would then no longer coincide with MUC/CoNLL-style boundaries and classes. Such a deviation would necessitate the re-development or adaption of named entity taggers.

6. *Geographic phrases*: In this thesis, toponyms were the main object of the investigation. Individual toponym instances like *Frankfurt* can be assigned a straight forward *extensional semantics* such as a centroid or polygon. However, *spatial expressions* are often used as well, which combine toponyms in a compositional way with pre- or post-modifications, as in '20 km north of Phuket'. In the data covered here, these expressions have followed a simple grammar, which may not be true in general. A corpus-based study of spatial expressions could therefore complement this thesis.

7. *Outreach*: It would be highly desirable to release evaluation dataset curated as part of this thesis project through a channel such as the Linguistic Data Consortium (LDC)[1], and to establish a comparative evaluation effort in the NLP community based on it, much like the MUC contest or the CoNLL 'Shared Task' as suggested by Clough and Sanderson (2004). Possible venues for such an undertaking are CoNLL or the Cross-Language Evaluation Forum (CLEF).[2] However, this requires accommodating the objectives of a critical mass of interested parties that might potentially participate in such an endeavour.

8.3 Conclusions

One central result of this thesis is that the challenge of automatic toponym resolution is to acquire knowledge from several evidence sources (gazetteers, training corpora or the Internet) and to combine this evidence in ways that are biased, and use them in a robust way on unbiased material.

---

[1]http://www.ldc.upenn.edu/ (accessed 2006-09-13).
[2]http://www.clef-campaign.org/ (online; accessed 2006-09-13)

Appendix A

Notational Conventions

The pseudo-code notation used to describe algorithms in this thesis is exemplified in 'Algorithm' 15. All lines are numbered; statements are in normal typeface (lines 2, 5, 77 and 11), and keywords–a standard inventory of constructs from languages like C++ or Java is used–are in boldface (line 6). Logically related chunks of code are occasionally given mnemonic names (lines 1 and 9), and comments are inserted in curly braces to enhance readability (line 4).

Algorithm 15 Example: Algorithm Notation Used in this Thesis.

1: **[Step 1.]**

2: This is a statement

3: **if** condition is true **then**

4:    { This is a comment. }

5:    execute this block if condition is true

6: **else**

7:    otherwise, execute this block

8: **end if**

9: **[Step 2.]**

10: **for** as long as condition is true **do**

11:    execute this block

12: **end for**

Appendix B

Annotation Guidelines

Toponym Resolution Annotators' Instructions

Jochen L. Leidner

2004-03-25

Dear annotator,

Introduction. Your task is to mark up all occurrences of place names in a set of documents with a specification that makes it clear where the mentioned location is situated.

This corresponds to deciding the question *'Which London is it?'* for any instance of 'London' found in a text (London, UK versus London, Ontario, Canada, or any other from the set of the many Londons).

Requirements. Make sure you have been assigned a list of documents that you are supposed to work on. You will need a Web browser and a connection to the Internet.

Procedure. (I) Point your Web browser to: http://www.textgis.com/ and select a document from the list to work with. Process one document at a time, and complete each document before submitting the result.

(II) Read the text carefully. Whenever you encounter a word in boldface, you have to make several decisions: (a) verify whether the word in boldface is used to refer to a location or not, and (b) select where the place is located. In addition, you have the option of (c) marking problematic decisions for review.

(a) Every boldface word may or may not be a place name: if you think a particular boldface word is not used to refer to a location (a populated place such as a village, town, city, country or continent), select NOT A PLACENAME from the drop-down menu that follows the boldface word.

Example:

"'London calling" appealed to most of the punk generation.'

London: select NOT A PLACENAME from drop-down box.

Non-example:

'The fire in London, Ont, killed 16 people and left 42 injured.' (leave checkbox ticked, London is used to refer to a place)

(b) If the place name is used to refer to a location, choose from the drop down menu the correct description of the location referred to by the place name.

Examples:

'The fire in London, Ont, killed 16 people and left 42 injured."

London: select London > Ontario > Canada > America from the drop-down box.

'Harvard is a small village, not far from the UK's capital.'

Harvard: select Harvard > England > UK > Europe from the drop-down box.

(c) If you are unhappy or uncertain with a specific decision you have to make or the options offered, you can untick the check mark in the square box behind each drop-down menu that follows it to mark this place name for review. If, on the other hand, you think your choice is correct, then leave the box ticked (this is the default).

(III) After marking up all place names, review your results and make sure you have not left out any boldface words. Then click on the SUBMIT button on the bottom of the Web page. Now you can continue with the next document until your workpool is completed.

If several location descriptions in the drop-down menu appear to be equally suitable, pick the first one.

Thank you very much for your participation.

Appendix C

Minimal Bounding Rectangles Extracted from NGA

This appendix shows the bounding rectangles that were extracted automatically from the NGA gazetteer for the countries from each continent or sub-continent.

The MBRs for each country are computed as follows. First an initial 'rectangle' with zero area is defined by the centroid of the first location in the country concerned that is retrieved from the NGA gazetteer. Then all other places in the country are retrieved incrementally from the gazetteer, and the size of the bounding rectangle is increased if the new place lies outside the existing MBR. Far outliers are pruned to limit the impact of noisy data in the gazetteer.

Note that North America excludes the US itself as it is covered by the USGS gazetteer.

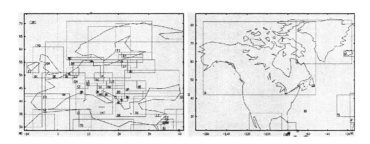

Figure C.1: Bounding Rectangles for countries in Europe (left) and North America (right).

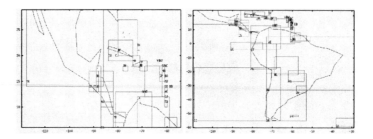

Figure C.2: Bounding Rectangles for countries in Central America (left) and South America (right).

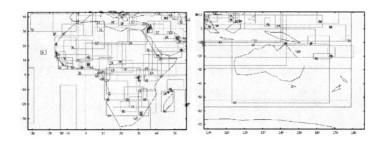

Figure C.3: Bounding Rectangles for countries in Africa (left) and Australia (right).

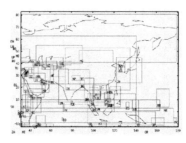

Figure C.4: Bounding Rectangles for countries in Asia.

Appendix D

TR-CoNLL Sample Used in 'Prose Only' Evaluation

To simplify replication of some experiments described in this thesis, here follows the list of documents from TR-CoNLL used in Chapter 6:

D102	D103	D104	D107	D108	D109	D10	D110	D111	D112
D113	D114	D115	D116	D117	D118	D119	D11	D120	D122
D123	D124	D126	D127	D128	D129	D12	D130	D136	D139
D13	D140	D142	D144	D147	D148	D14	D150	D151	D156
D157	D158	D159	D15	D160	D162	D163	D166	D167	D16
D170	D174	D177	D178	D179	D17	D180	D181	D182	D183
D185	D186	D188	D189	D18	D190	D191	D192	D193	D194
D195	D196	D197	D1	D200	D20	D21	D22	D237	D24
D26	D29	D2	D32	D36	D39	D3	D41	D43	D47
D4	D50	D52	D53	D54	D57	D58	D5	D61	D62
D63	D64	D65	D66	D67	D6	D70	D72	D73	D75
D76	D77	D78	D79	D81	D82	D84	D85	D86	D88
D89	D901	D90	D910	D911	D912	D913	D915	D916	D917
D918	D919	D920	D921	D922	D923	D924	D926	D928	D92
D930	D931	D934	D935	D936	D938	D93	D941	D943	D94
D95	D96	D97	D99						

The next Appendix shows that controlling for English prose (leaving out 'noisy' documents containing e.g. cricket tables) does not prose much of a problem: on the contrary, the LSW03 described earlier performs best on the full TR-CoNLL dataset.

Appendix E

TR-CoNLL Evaluation (All Documents Used)

This appendix shows the results of the TR-CoNLL evaluation. In contrast to the evaluation chapter, this appendix uses the *full* collection, whereas the evaluation chapter was restricted to the list of documents listed in the previous appendix, guaranteed to contain English prose language only. Recall that this selection was intended to avoid that results are in any way biased by noise introduced by non-prose (see the section on the thesis scope), such as sport results tables (especially cricket tables with lots of team names represented by their home cities/countries), financial indicator tables, REUTERS "press digets" clippings, and tables of contents, which do not fall into the scope of this thesis due to the focus on prose here.

Nevertheless, results restricted to any subset of a collection may not show the full picture, and in some sense represent a bias by itself. Therefore, the tables for both the 'in vitro' and 'in vivo' evaluation are included here for completeness' sake.

As we can see LSW03 is not at all negatively affected by the presence of non-prose; in contrary, it behaves robustly and significantly outperforms MAXPOP in this setting.

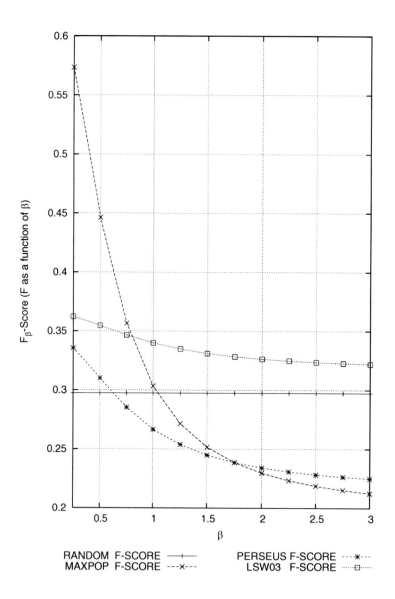

Figure E.1: Performance of the two systems against two baselines on TR-CoNLL (complete corpus) as a function of the F-score's β parameter on gold standard data. LSW03 is able to outperform MAXPOP for $\beta > 0.75$ and PERSEUS for all weightings between P and R considered. F1(MAXPOP) drops below F1(MAXPOP) in high-recall settings ($\beta > 1.75$).

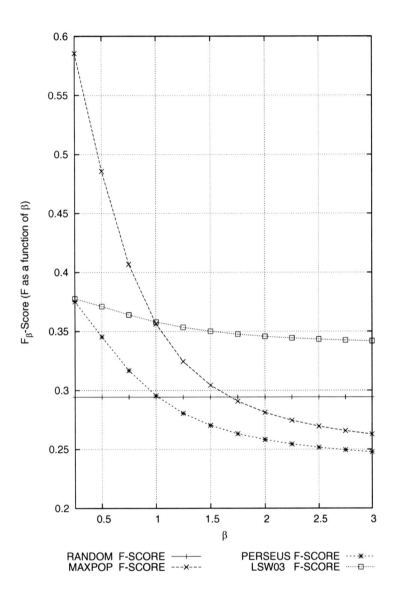

Figure E.2: Performance of the two systems against two baselines on TR-CoNLL (complete corpus) as a function of the F-score's β parameter using MaxEnt toponym tagging. Obviously, reporting F1 only conceals the fact that LSW03 as very good recall, which lets it outperform MAXPOP and all other methods reported here beyond $\beta = 1$.

TR-CoNLL $N = 5463$	(gold NERC)	P	R	$F_{\beta=1}$	significant? $\mathcal{H}_x$ v RAND	significant? $\mathcal{H}_x$ v $\mathcal{H}_{0+3}$
	RAND	0.2973	0.2973	0.2973	n/a	n/a
$\mathcal{H}_{0+3}$	MAXPOP	**0.6506**	0.1976	0.3032	−	n/a
$\mathcal{H}_0$	1REF	**1.0000**	0.1272	0.2257	▼	▼
$\mathcal{H}_{0+1}$	LOCAL	0.9256	0.1411	0.2449	▼	▼
$\mathcal{H}_{0+2}$	SUPER	0.3040	0.0767	0.1225	▼	▼
$\mathcal{H}_{0+1+5}$	YAROWSKY	0.8659	0.1442	0.2473	▼	▼
$\mathcal{H}_{0+4}$	MINIMALITY	0.5055	**0.2370**	**0.3227**	▲	▲
$\mathcal{H}_{0+1,9-12}$	PERSEUS	0.3474	0.2164	0.2667	▼	▼
$\mathcal{H}_{0+1,4+5,12}$	**LSW03**	**0.3650**	**0.3177**	**0.3397**	▲	▲

Table E.1: Micro-averaged evaluation results for TR-CoNLL collection (all documents used) for automatic toponym resolution on human oracle NERC results ('in vitro'). LSW03 is the strongest method on the whole, unfiltered dataset, outperforming both MAXPOP and PERSEUS.

TR-CoNLL $N = 2672$	(gold NERC)	P	R	$F_{\beta=1}$	significant? $\mathcal{H}_x$ v RAND	significant? $\mathcal{H}_x$ v $\mathcal{H}_{0+3}$
	RAND	0.2941	0.2941	0.2941	n/a	n/a
$\mathcal{H}_{0+3}$	**MAXPOP**	**0.6404**	0.2466	**0.3561**	▲	n/a
$\mathcal{H}_0$	1REF	**1.0000**	0.1467	0.2559	▼	▼
$\mathcal{H}_{0+1}$	LOCAL	0.9724	0.1579	0.2717	▽	▼
$\mathcal{H}_{0+2}$	SUPER	0.3489	0.0700	0.1166	▼	▼
$\mathcal{H}_{0+1+5}$	YAROWSKY	0.9594	0.1594	0.2734	▽	▼
$\mathcal{H}_{0+4}$	MINIMALITY	0.4468	**0.2907**	**0.3523**	▲	−
$\mathcal{H}_{0+1,9-12}$	PERSEUS	**0.3890**	0.2380	0.2953	−	▼
$\mathcal{H}_{0+1,4+5,12}$	**LSW03**	0.3802	**0.3379**	**0.3578**	▲	−

Table E.2: Micro-averaged evaluation results for TR-CoNLL collection (all documents used) for automatic toponym resolution on automatic (MaxEnt) NERC results ('in vivo'). LSW03 outperforms all other methods in terms of F1-score, but it is not significantly different from MAXPOP. PERSEUS performs significantly worse than LSW03 ($p < 0.001$) in this setting, which is not shown but can be inferred.

Appendix F

Performance Plots for Individual Heuristics

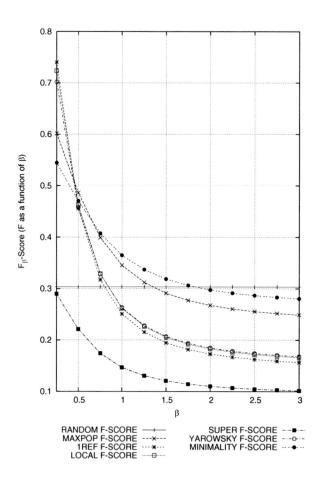

Figure F.1: Plot of the performance of the heuristics and two baselines on TR-CoNLL (subset) as a function of the F-score's β parameter on gold standard NERC. The heuristics used in isolation perform almost identically at $\beta = 0.5$. The MINIMALITY heuristic is very competitive for $\beta > 0.75$.

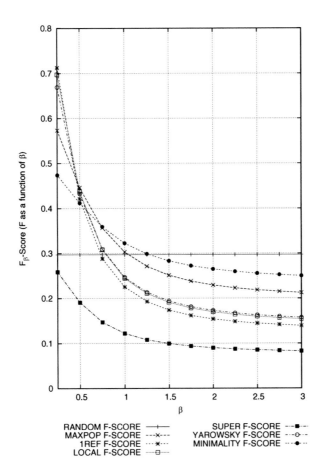

Figure F.2: Plot of the performance of the heuristics and two baselines on TR-CoNLL (all documents) as a function of the F-score's β parameter on gold standard NERC.

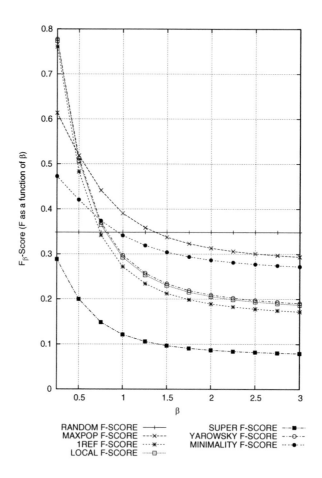

Figure F.3: Plot of the performance of the heuristics and two baselines on TR-CoNLL (subset) as a function of the F-score's β parameter on MaxEnt NERC.

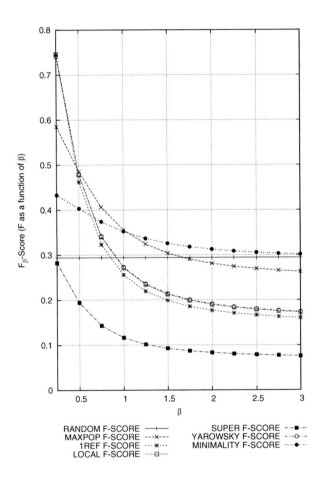

Figure F.4: Plot of the performance of the heuristics and two baselines on TR-CoNLL (all documents) as a function of the F-score's β parameter on MaxEnt NERC.

Appendix G

Stories Used in the Visualization Study

G.1 Story 'Royal Mercy Flight Baby Dies'

A baby who was flown to Scotland for specialist treatment on an aircraft normally used to carry the Royal Family has died in hospital. Baby Khola was born at St George's Hospital in Tooting, south London, last month with an undisclosed rare condition.

She was transferred to the Royal Hospital for Sick Children at Glasgow's Yorkhill Hospital on 23 January.

However, Khola - who was just over a month old - died on Monday.

"The last few days have been very sad for Khola and her parents," said a spokesman for the hospital.

Khola's parents, who wish to remain anonymous, thanked the Queen for allowing the use of the jet.

"We would like to say thank you for all the care Khola has received," they said in a statement.

"We wish to thank the hospital staff in Glasgow and London, the team who transported Khola, and the Queen for allowing the use of her plane. We also wish to thank everyone who prayed for our daughter."

Khola was taken to Yorkhill Hospital An RAF Hercules had initially been scheduled to take the baby to Glasgow last month. However, it burst a tyre as it landed at Northolt.

It was then decided to fly the baby and the medical team to Glasgow in an aircraft from the Royal Squadron.

The four-engine British Aerospace 146 was the same aircraft used for the Queen's Jubilee Tour of Britain last year.

A Royal Navy helicopter at Prestwick was mobilised and flown in bad weather to RAF Northolt where the specialist medical team on board was transferred to St George's Hospital in Tooting.

The baby was stabilised in an incubator throughout the night before the transfer to Glasgow. Doctors at Yorkhill said Khola had been in need of respiratory support.

Four hospitals in the UK can provide extracorporeal membrane oxygenation (ECMO) for breathing difficulties, but Glasgow was the only hospital able to accommodate Khola.

The process involves taking the baby's blood out of the body, through an artificial lung and pumping it back in, allowing the baby's lungs to rest. □

G.2   Story 'News Crews Wait and Watch as Police Search Home of Missing Woman'

Mercury News.   MODESTO – The search for Laci Peterson took on a carnival air

Wednesday as dozens of reporters and 18 satellite trucks staked out the missing woman's home while police completed a two-day search for evidence.

The big news of the day? Police measured Laci and Scott Peterson's driveway. They declined to explain why.

But there was so much jostling for tidbits that police strung yellow crime-scene tape around the home to keep reporters back.

The media circus was only the latest in a long line that have sprung up around high-profile criminal cases, where the news is scant but the demand for information – even the smallest morsel – soars off the charts. "People have been interested in this type of story since pre-biblical times," said Joe Saltzman, associate dean at the Annenberg School for Communications at the University of Southern California. "We live in a global village where everyone is our neighbor, and this is an interesting story about a man whose pregnant wife is kidnapped."

As Modesto police completed their second day combing through the home that missing mother-to-be Laci Peterson shared with her husband, Scott, more than a dozen news crews from Los Angeles to Sacramento camped out front. Many of the reporters huddled under a tent hastily erected by one reporter as it rained and hailed.

Detective Doug Ridenour said Wednesday that investigators had completed their work, removing about 95 bags of evidence. On Tuesday, Amy Rocha, the sister of the missing woman, accompanied detectives into the modest three-bedroom home for about two hours. But on Wednesday, investigators worked alone – completing their task about 5 p.m. They also planned to do a walk-through with Scott Peterson.

"We've been able to accomplish a lot," Ridenour told reporters at the Peterson house. "But here at this point we just don't have the significant evidence we need to find Laci or to move in another direction."

Ridenour would not reveal when detectives would analyze what they took away or when they would release a detailed description of what they found.

He also repeated a familiar refrain: Scott Peterson is not a suspect, but he has not been ruled out as one. Suspicion has hovered over Peterson since his wife vanished Dec. 24, a day he said he was fishing at the Berkeley Marina 85 miles away.

[...]

Since Laci Peterson disappeared, news that her husband was having an affair with a Fresno-area massage therapist has only deepened doubts about his credibility and led to a bitter estrangement from his wife's family. The two sides no longer communicate.

Just a few weeks ago, Laci Peterson's family expressed outrage when Scott sold his wife's Land Rover and bought himself a truck. That truck was confiscated by police Tuesday but has been returned to Peterson.

As suspicions about Scott Peterson have grown, so too has the media encampment outside his home. On Wednesday there were satellite trucks parked along the street and more than two dozen cameras were set up facing the home. Yards of electrical cables ran along the curbs and lawns of Peterson's neighbors.

Two police cruisers and four orange cones blocked access on one side of the street. When one neighbor wanted to back her sport utility vehicle out of her driveway, it was a 15-minute production, requiring the rearrangement of half a dozen cameras.

A crowd of at least 75 journalists and onlookers waited in the middle of the street with little to do for most of the day, though they snapped to attention every time a rubber-gloved police officer emerged from the Petersons' house.

"It's really, really hard to know what to think," said Michelle Brink, a bystander who said she went to high school with Laci Peterson. "At church, we're praying for everyone – Laci, her family and the police."

The story attracted national media attention almost immediately. It has been featured numerous times on Fox's "On the Record with Greta Van Susteren," CNN's "Connie Chung Tonight" and "Larry King Live," which focused on the Peterson case again Wednesday.

Lloyd LaCuesta, reporter for Oakland-based KTVU-TV, was happy to explain the media obsession: "It has everything that intrigues the public – a pregnant woman, her husband having an affair. It's the kind of thing we think our viewership or readership is interested in."

And he couldn't help but bring up Modesto's other spin in the tabloids.

"I have to say this brings back memories of being in front of Chandra Levy's house. It was a quiet little street just like this."

Juan Fernandez, reporter for KCBS-TV and KCAL-TV, two Los Angeles stations, said that Southern California media have focused on the story since Laci Peterson was reported missing, even though Modesto is far from their broadcast market. In part, that's because it was a compelling story, and, in part, because it was another story from Modesto.

"Laci was a pregnant woman who disappeared for no reason. People on the street are curious about the case. They just want to know what's going on."

On the media coverage, he added: "This is big. I compare this to a Chandra or a Robert Blake. When we were chasing the Robert Blake case, there were just as many crews."

Saltzman, who is director of the Image of the Journalist in Popular Culture Project at the University of Southern California, said the media circuses can't really be blamed on the media – or the public that allegedly pants for each new tidbit.

"It's not really the media's fault," he said. "The police are there, it's an official action. This has to do with basic human curiosity."

Such spectacles have only grown in intensity and size for more than a decade.

"It's the criminal case that feeds on itself," said New York attorney Marvyn Kornberg, who has been in the glare of television lights on high-profile criminal cases several times. "It becomes a soap opera, it becomes the proverbial 'sex, lies and videotape.' "

Kornberg, who is best known for representing a man the public loved to hate—Joey Butta-fuoco, who had a torrid affair with Long Island teenager Amy Fisher – said the only way to end such sideshows is to convert the American system of justice "to the English system, where you announce the arrest of an individual and then you announce the verdict when it's over." □

Appendix H

Distance Queries

distance and time to fly from chicago to tokyo	(Q-3586659)
distance between anaheim ca and los angeles	(Q-33165089)
distance between anaheim ca and los angells	(Q-33165088)
distance between apple valley ca and los angeles ca	(Q-23389227)
distance between asheville nc and charlotte nc	(Q-12144425)
distance between athens ohio and columbus ohio	(Q-36362084)
distance between bangkok and phuket	(Q-34485616)
distance between boston and chicago	(Q-18847449)
distance between boston and providence ri	(Q-22332854)
distance between brunswick ga and dow city tx	(Q-11888586)
distance between buffalo niagra airport and toronto canada	(Q-15785768)
distance between burlington and new york city	(Q-18847132)
distance between burlington vt and brattleboro vt	(Q-13075696)
distance between cabo san lucas and la paz mexico	(Q-28447376)
distance between calgary and vancouver	(Q-18847059)
distance between cancun and cozumel	(Q-28719077)
distance between chennai and rameshwaram	(Q-27665336)
distance between chesaning michigan and nashville tennessee	(Q-18178481)
distance between chicago and los angeles	(Q-23386337)
distance between cincinnati and lexington	(Q-33156581)
distance between cities in finland	(Q-21959029)
distance between cuba and florida	(Q-9847066)
distance between dallas and san antonio	(Q-24538767)

distance between daytona beach and sun city center   (Q-8496326)

distance between daytona beach and the villages   (Q-8496168)

distance between deadwood sd and fargo nd   (Q-33412029)

distance between denver colorado and telluride colorado   (Q-34650630)

distance between dublin ireland and dungannon ireland   (Q-19754907)

distance between eze and aeairport in argentina   (Q-30211466)

distance between florida and poland   (Q-34555995)

distance between grand canyon to flagstaff   (Q-8791180)

distance between greenland and newfoundland   (Q-21896486)

distance between hendricks and parke county indiana   (Q-16141158)

distance between hershey pa and new york city   (Q-4966691)

distance between home plate and end of in-field in softball   (Q-16754868)

distance between home plate and end of the outfield in softball   (Q-16754871)

distance between home plate and the pitcher's mound in softball   (Q-16754877)

distance between honolulu and phoenix   (Q-876704)

distance between hornell ny and michigan   (Q-8755716)

distance between indepedance mo and warrensburg mo   (Q-24776621)

distance between jerusalem and bethlehem   (Q-7245220)

distance between kitchener and toronto   (Q-4714532)

distance between l a and santa babara   (Q-13282829)

distance between lafayette and baton rouge louisiana   (Q-29745743)

distance between laguna beach and san diego   (Q-24534773)

distance between lake cumberland and mammoth caves   (Q-6096121)

distance between lansing and flint mi   (Q-27641887)

distance between las vegas and grand canyon   (Q-21964316)

distance between las vegas and laughlin   (Q-238712)

distance between las vegas and reno   (Q-5364346)

distance between las vegas casino and airport   (Q-3721309)

distance between little rock and chicago   (Q-10131788)

distance between london and gatwich   (Q-12944405)

distance between london canada and welland canada   (Q-24151386)

distance between london canada and wellend canada   (Q-24151385)

distance between los angeles and san diego   (Q-307064)

distance between lyons and cap ferrat   (Q-12398375) *distance between massachusetts and florida*   (Q-297281)

distance between michigan and maine   (Q-33837384)

distance between milan and santa margherita   (Q-29441639)

distance between minsk and kiev   (Q-19172781)

distance between myrtle beach and murrells inlet sc   (Q-16526437)

distance between mytrle beach and murrells inlet sc   (Q-16526436)

distance between nazareth and bethlehem   (Q-7245222)

distance between niagara falls ny and olean ny   (Q-11582329)

distance between north carolina and california   (Q-29363779)

distance between noth carolina and california   (Q-29363778)

distance between ny city and napanoch ny   (Q-29728023)

distance between ontario ca and los angeles   (Q-2503316)

distance between oxnard ca and san antonio tdx   (Q-17091325)

distance between palm springs ca and los angeles   (Q-33165091)

distance between paris and niece france   (Q-10026048)

distance between paris and the loire valley   (Q-34467000)

distance between philadelphia and bolivia   (Q-23860030)

distance between pocatello id and west yellowstone montana   (Q-27479338)

distance between prague and vienna   (Q-304682)

distance between puerto vallarto and zihuatanejo mexico   (Q-5143722)

distance between rock hill s.c. and statesville n.c.   (Q-32343897)

distance between rome and bologna italy   (Q-1635146)

distance between rotterdam and amsterdam   (Q-5526432)

distance between sacramento ca and reno nevada   (Q-5364350)

distance between san antonio tx and corpus christi tx   (Q-22157690)

distance between san diego and seattle   (Q-17723522)

distance between san diego and   (Q-17723520)

distance between san francisco and chicago   (Q-18847294)

distance between san jose and santa cruz   (Q-18847176)

distance between san luis obispo califonia and los angeles california   (Q-7232345)

distance between san luis obispo california and los angeles california (Q-7232346)

distance between san rafael and san jose   (Q-18847422)

distance between seatac and redmond washington   (Q-36162548)

distance between sedona and flagstaff   (Q-32082352) *distance between sedona to grand canyon*   (Q-8790627)

distance between spokane and kennewick   (Q-27905746)

distance between st louis and nashville   (Q-18847445)

distance between st louis mo and tulsa ok   (Q-2620700)

distance between stonehenge and southhampton port   (Q-26478617)

distance between sun and moon   (Q-32655069)

distance between syracuse and binghamton ny   (Q-2653693)

distance between tampa and miami   (Q-1217988)

distance between tennesse and dallas   (Q-21895313)

distance between the most western point of russia and the most eastern point of russia   (Q-8878187)

distance between turin and florence italy   (Q-16433800)

distance between vancouver and salt lake city   (Q-18847126)

distance between viero florida and melbourne florida   (Q-34917558)

distance between yuma az and spokane wa   (Q-12327516)

distance between yxu and dtw   (Q-34151989)

distance between zurich and graz   (Q-23927740)

distance in communicating between male and females   (Q-19943196)

distance in miles between africa and jerusalem   (Q-1087660)

distance in miles between africa and jerusalem   (Q-1087834)

distance mileage between africa and jerusalem   (Q-1087661)

distance mileage between africa and jerusalem   (Q-1087835)

distance of dalton georgia from florida   (Q-21688166)

distance of planet pluto from sun   (Q-4011587)

distance to kenya africa from united states   (Q-23286220)

distance to orlando fl from phoenix az   (Q-20647277)

distance to south carolina from new york   (Q-29209481)

distance to stand from dartboard   (Q-29496675)

driveing distance to las vegas from sun city west az   (Q-11264171)

driving distance between chicago and los angeles   (Q-23386338)

driving distance between hagerstown md and johnson city ny   (Q-33790306)

driving distance between kansas city and des moines   (Q-35970270)

driving distance between new orleans and baton rouge   (Q-23983588)

driving distance to grand canyon from las vegas   (Q-8790733)

find distance between little rock air port and lonoke   (Q-11752500) *find the distance between orlando and sanford florida*　　　　　(Q-10228533)

how far from augusta georgia to dallas texas　　　　　(Q-7388421)

how far from berkeley street london to oxford university england　　　　　(Q-13241777)

how far from calais to bonn　　　　　(Q-4914314)

how far from hillsboro oregon to board of california　　　　　(Q-6923734)

how far from hillsboro oregon to boarder of california　　　　　(Q-6923733)

how far from medford oregon to grand cannon　　　　　(Q-1772518)

how far from miami to port canaveral　　　　　(Q-35490877)

how far from nashville tenn. to montgomery alabama　　　　　(Q-4689931)

how far from nashville tn. to montgomery alabama　　　　　(Q-4689933)

how far from new jersey to sanannah georgia　　　　　(Q-23319583)

how far from new jersey to savannah georgia　　　　　(Q-23319584)

how far from newcastle to edenburgh　　　　　(Q-8212186)

how far from north miami beach to south beach　　　　　(Q-22405233)

how far from okinawa japan to south korea　　　　　(Q-29307639)

how far from pompano beach to orlando　　　　　(Q-34577697)

how far from poznan poland to gdansk poland　　　　　(Q-19077550)

how far from sedona to grand canyon　　　　　(Q-8790785)

how far from the arcadian house to food court　　　　　(Q-1591873)

how far from the southern coast of vietnam to singapore　　　　　(Q-7249393)

how far from the southern coast of vietnam to the equator　　　　　(Q-7249394)

how far from twenty nine palms to san deago　　　　　(Q-27080352)

how far from twentynine palms to san diego　　　　　(Q-27080353)

how far from venice florida to hernando florida　　　　　(Q-3646985)

how far from vicksburg ms to atlanta ga　　　　　(Q-22338670)

how far from virginia to las vegas　　　　　(Q-1028492)

how far from volcano copahue to santiago　　　　　(Q-7157120)

how far is drive from milan airport to como　　　　　(Q-4481905)

how far is in from ardmore to sulphur oklahoma　　　　　(Q-17909185)

how far is is from roanoke va to hurt va　　　　　(Q-5993689)

how far is it driving from penn stater hotel to the campus of penn state university　　　　　(Q-17852531)

how far is it from adrian michigan to flint michigan　　　　　(Q-14806194)

how far is it from amarillo tx. to colorado springs co.　　　　　(Q-25864967)

how far is it from anchorage to denali　　　　　(Q-25813705)

how far is it from ashland ky to myrtle beach sc   (Q-1074753)

how far is it from atlanta ga. to riverside california   (Q-4011581)

how far is it from austin tx to orlando fl   (Q-32963617)

how far is it from cairo egypt to petra   (Q-22236909)

how far is it from corpus christi to san antonio tx   (Q-25814081)

how far is it from corpus christi tx to san antonio   (Q-25814077)

how far is it from el paso texas to midland odessa texas   (Q-7434259)

how far is it from here to yonder   (Q-30691750)

how far is it from howard kansas to colorado springs colorado   (Q-27338861)

how far is it from iowa city iowa to cedar rapids iowa   (Q-16584202)

how far is it from lamesa tx to saint lawernce   (Q-34686546)

how far is it from lansing mi to ypsalanti mi   (Q-16725567)

how far is it from lansing mi to y   (Q-16725566)

how far is it from lawton oklahoma to wausau wisconsin   (Q-11966666)

how far is it from new york to the bahamas   (Q-15799899)

how far is it from nkoxville to nashvill   (Q-20923148)

how far is it from ocala to crystal river   (Q-18795454)

how far is it from otay mesa to tiajuana mexico   (Q-33073692)

how far is it from pascagoula ms to merrititt la   (Q-29426825)

how far is it from quarryville . to philiidelephia pa.   (Q-4228065)

how far is it from san diego to tiajuana mexico   (Q-33073693)

how far is it from seattle to north bend   (Q-23362423)

how far is it from seattle to noth bend   (Q-23362422)

how far is it from the university of virginia to the red lobster restaruant   (Q-8031597)

how far is it from uarryville . to philiidelephia pa.   (Q-4228064)

how far is it from uarryville . to philiidelephia pa.   (Q-4228066)

how far is it in finland from town to town   (Q-21959265)

how far is it to meadville pa from annapolis md   (Q-35745005)

how far is russia from the east to the west   (Q-6740073)

how far is the drive from anchorage to denali   (Q-25813708)

how far is the driving distance from lawton oklahoma to wausau wisconsin   (Q-11966667)

how far of a drive from ft. lauderdale to miami   (Q-18891204)

how far of a flight is it from miami to rio de janiero   (Q-14682755)

how to dial long distance calls to philippines from usa   (Q-13801396)

how to get from florida to illinois how far	(Q-9027023)
how to solve if the distance between the points 4 3 and x 6 is 5 find the value of x	(Q-12789904)
if the distance between the points 4 3 and x 6 is 5 find the value of x formula for finding x	(Q-12789905)
if the distance between the points 4 3 and x 6 is 5 find the value of x	(Q-12789903)
list of mobile home movers for distance between ashboro nc and hamlet nc	(Q-30803907)
little league distance between home plate and pitchers mound	(Q-35576513)
map distance between gangtok and pemako	(Q-36215874)
map distance between tucson az and new york ny	(Q-15878909)
mile distance between san diego and los angelos	(Q-2200625)
mileage distance between sedona and grand canyon	(Q-8790632)
observed angular distance in the sky between the sun and the moon	(Q-31378647)
on map of africa how far from ivory coast to kenya	(Q-34515685)
show me distance to new zealand from nc	(Q-3132900)
the distance between hollywood cal and sandiego cal.	(Q-6358237)
the distance between moncton and edmundston	(Q-6706552)
the distance between washington dc and virginia	(Q-5533954)
what is the distance between baltimore and silver spring	(Q-18472473)
what is the distance between cincinnati ohio and knoxville tennessee	(Q-3634920)
what is the distance between claremont n.c. and marion va.	(Q-5377141)
what is the distance between coconut creek fl and coral springs fl	(Q-12681338)
what is the distance between coconut creek fl and pompano beach fl	(Q-12681339)
what is the distance between gatwick and trafalgar square	(Q-13241781)
what is the distance between lafayette louisiana and shreveport louisiana	(Q-29745714)
what is the distance between lava hot springs and pocatello idaho	(Q-31411837)
what is the distance between pompano beach fl and coral springs fl	(Q-12681334)
what is the distance between pompano beach fl. and coconut creek fl.	(Q-12681340)
what's the distance between hoboken nj and new york ny	(Q-6630864)

Appendix I

ADL Feature Type Thesaurus

This appendix contains the hierarchical listing of preferred terms of the feature thesaurus of the Alexandria Digital Library (ADL)[1] as of 2002-07-03.

```
administrative areas
. cadastral areas
. military areas
. political areas
. . countries
. . countries, 1st order divisions
. . countries, 2nd order divisions
. . countries, 3rd order divisions
. . countries, 4th order divisions
. . multinational entities
. populated places
. . cities
. . . capitals
. postal areas
. school districts
. statistical areas
. . census areas
. . Metropolitan Statistical Areas
. territorial waters
. tribal areas

hydrographic features
. aquifers
```

---

[1]http://www.alexandria.ucsb.edu/gazetteer/FeatureTypes (accessed 2006-09-14).

. bays
. . fjords
. channels
. drainage basins
. estuaries
. floodplains
. gulfs
. guts
. ice masses
. . glacier features
. lakes
. seas
. . oceans
. . . ocean currents
. . . ocean regions
. streams
. . rivers
. . . bends (river)
. . . rapids
. . . waterfalls
. . springs (hydrographic)
. thermal features

land parcels

manmade features
. agricultural sites
. buildings
. . capitol buildings
. . commercial sites
. . . industrial sites
. . . . power generation sites
. . court houses
. . institutional sites
. . . correctional facilities
. . . educational facilities
. . . medical facilities
. . . religious facilities

. . library buildings
. . museum buildings
. . post office buildings
. . research facilities
. . . data collection facilities
. . residential sites
. . . housing areas
. . . mobile home parks
. cemeteries
. disposal sites
. firebreaks
. fisheries
. fortifications
. historical sites
. . archaeological sites
. hydrographic structures
. . breakwaters
. . canals
. . dam sites
. . gaging stations
. . harbors
. . . marinas
. . levees
. . offshore platforms
. . piers
. . reservoirs
. . waterworks
. launch facilities
. mine sites
. monuments
. oil fields
. parks
. . viewing locations
. recreational facilities
. . amusement parks
. . camps
. . performance sites
. . sports facilities

. reference locations
. research areas
. . ecological research sites
. . paleontological sites
. reserves
. storage structures
. telecommunication features
. towers
. transportation features
. . airport features
. . . heliports
. . . seaplane bases
. . aqueducts
. . bridges
. . cableways
. . locks
. . parking sites
. . pipelines
. . railroad features
. . roadways
. . trails
. . tunnels
. wells
. windmills

physiographic features
. alluvial fans
. arroyos
. badlands
. banks (hydrographic)
. bars (physiographic)
. basins
. . storage basins
. beaches
. bights
. capes
. caves
. cirques

. cliffs

. craters

. deltas

. dunes

. flats

. gaps

. isthmuses

. karst areas

. ledges

. massifs

. mesas

. mineral deposit areas

. moraines

. mountains

. . continental divides

. . mountain ranges

. . mountain summits

. . ridges

. . . drumlins

. natural rock formations

. . arches (natural formation)

. plains

. plateaus

. playas

. reefs

. . coral reefs

. seafloor features

. . abyssal features

. . continental margins

. . fracture zones

. . hydrothermal vents

. . ocean trenches

. . seamounts

. . submarine canyons

. tectonic features

. . earthquake features

. . faults

. . . fault zones

```
. . . rift zones
. . folds (geologic)
. . . anticlines
. . . synclines
. valleys
. . canyons
. volcanic features
. . lava fields
. . volcanoes


regions
. agricultural regions
. biogeographic regions
. . barren lands
. . deserts
. . forests
. . . petrified forests
. . . rain forests
. . . woods
. . grasslands
. . habitats
. . jungles
. . oases
. . shrublands
. . snow regions
. . tundras
. . wetlands
. climatic regions
. coastal zones
. economic regions
. land regions
. . continents
. . islands
. . . archipelagos
. . subcontinents
. linguistic regions
. map regions
. . chart regions
```

. . map quadrangle regions
. . UTM zones

Zusammenfassung in deutscher Sprache

Hintergrund. Auf dem Gebiet der geographischen Informationssysteme (GIS), einer Fachrichtung, die zwischen Informatik und Geographie angesiedelt ist, bezeichnet der Begriff *Geoparsing* den Vorgang der Erkennung von Ortsnamen (Toponymen) in Texten, welcher in der Computerlinguistik auch als Eigennamenerkennung und -klassifikation (engl. *named entity tagging and classification*, NERC) bekannt ist. Der Begriff *Geokodierung* wird gebraucht, um die Abbildung von implizit geo-referenzierten Datenbeständen (wie struktuierten postalischen Addressdatensätzen) auf explizit georeferenzierte Datstellungen (z.B. Längen- und Breitengrad) zu bezeichnen. Der Stand der Technik der GIS-Systeme erlaubte bisher keine automatische Geokodierungsfunktionalität für *unstrukturierten Text*.

Auf dem Gebiet der Informationsextraktion (IE) wird die Verarbeitung von Eigennamen in Text traditionell als zweistufiger Vorgang verstanden bestehend aus der Teilaufgabe der Erkennung flacher Textabschnitte sowie einer atomaren Klassifikationsteilaufgabe. Das Verknüpfen des Textabschnitts mit einem Weltmodell wird bisher bei Evaluierungskampagnen wie MUC oder ACE hingegen nicht beachtet (Chinchor (1998); U.S. NIST (2003)).

Allerdings beziehen sich Raum- und Zeitausdrücke auf Ereignisse, die in der physikalischen Raumzeit stattfinden, und die "Erdung" (Resolution) von Ereignissen ist eine Voraussetzung für das genaue Schließen und Folgern. Daher kann die automatische Resolution viele Anwendungen verbessern, wie automatisches Zeichnen geographischer Karten (z.B. durch automatische Fokuswahl) und Fragebeantwortung (z.B. bei Fragen wie *Wie weit ist Saarbrücken von Karlsruhe entfernt?*, gegeben eine Nachrichtenmeldung in der beide Toponyme auftreten und aufgelöst werden können). Während temporale Resolution in der jüngeren Vergangenheit bereits beachtliche Aufmerksamkeit erfahren hat (Mani and Wilson (2000); Setzer (2001)) wurde die robuste räumliche Resolution lange vernachlässigt.

In dieser Dissertation wird ausgehend von einem Fokus auf geographische Namen für bewohnte Orte die Aufgabenstellung der automatischen *Toponymresolution* (TR) definiert und als Berechnung der Abbildung von Vorkommnissen von Eigennamen für Orte aufgefaßt, wie sie in Texten vorgefunden werden, un zwar auf eine Darstellung der extensionalen Semantik des Ortes, auf den der Name verweist (der *Referent* des Toponyms), wie beispielsweise ein geographisches Modellkorrelat, das als Längen- und Breitengrad des Mittelpunkts (Zentroiden) des Ortes gegeben ist.

Die Aufgabe der Abbildung von Namen auf Orte ist schwierig aufgrund unvollständiger und fehlerhafter Datenbanken sowie einem großen Grad von Mehrdeutigkeit: gemeine Wörter müssen von Eigennamen unterschieden werden (Geo-/nicht-geo-Ambiguität), und die Beziehung zwischen and the Namen und Orten ist mehrdeutig (*London* kann sich auf die Hauptstadt Großbritanniens beziehen, auf London, Ontario, Kanada oder auf eines von etwa vierzig weiteren Londons auf Erden). Hinzu kommt, daß sich Ortsnamen und die Grenzen der Gebilde, auf die sie verweisen, im Laufe der Zeit verändern und alle Dankenbanken unvollständig sind.

Zielsetzung. Es wird untersucht, wie referentiell mehrdeutige räumliche Eigennamen in nichtrestringierten Nachrichtentexten robust aufgelöst werden können in Bezug auf ein extensionales Koordinatenmodell. Ausgehend von einem Vergleich publizierter Verfahren und der Erstellung (re-)konstruierter semi-formaler Beschreibungen derselben wird ein gemeinsames Repertoir linguistischer Heuristiken (e.g. Regeln, Muster) und außer-linguistischer Wissensquellen (e.g. Einwohnerzahl) entwickelt. Dann wird untersucht, wie diese Evidenzquellen kombiniert werden können, um zu einer überlegenen Methode zu gelangen.

Desweiteren werden Degradierungseffekte untersucht, die sich durch den Einsatz eines automatischen Eigennamenannotationsschritts einstellen, die Toponymresolutionsmethoden im Rahmen einer sequellen Systempipelinearchitektur voraussetzen.

Skopus. In dieser Dissertation wird ein gegenwäriger Schnappschuß der irdischen Geography betrachtet, wie er durch den die verwendete Gazetteer-Datenbank gegeben ist, sowie ein Nachrichtentextkorpus, ebenfalls aus der Gegenwart. Diese Untersuchung ist beschränkt auf bewohnte Orte: Geokodierung von Artefaktnamen (wie z.B. Flughäfen oder Brücken), kompositionelle geographische Beschreibungen (wie *40 miles SW of London*, *near Berlin*) werden ausgeklammert. Historische Veränderungen sind ein wichtiger Faktor, der Gazetteer-Konstruktion bestimmt und damit letzlich auch die Toponymresolution, ist aber ebenfalls außerhalb des Rahmens dieser Arbeit.

Methode. Während es eine kleine Anzahl von existierenden Versuchen gibt das Toponymresolutionsproblem zu lösen, so wurde diese Ansätze doch entweder nicht evaluiert, oder die Evaluierung erfolgte durch manuelle Inspektion der Systemausgabe, anstatt apriori ein wiederverwendbares Referenzkorpus zu schaffen. Da die relevante Literatur über mehrere Disziplinen (GIS, Digitale Bibliotheken, Informationswiedergewinnung, natürliche Sprachverarbeitung) verstreut ist und die Beschreibung der Algorithmen meist in informeller Prosa gehalten sind, wird hier der Versuch einer systematischen Beschreibung gemacht in Form einer *Rekonstruktion in einer uniformen, semi-formalen Pseudokode-Notation* zwecks Erleichterung einer Reimplementierung. Ein systematischer Vergleich führt dann zu einem *Inventar von*

Heuristiken und anderen Evidenzquellen.

Um eine vergleichende Evaluierung durchzuführen, wird eine Evaluierungsressource benötigt. Leider wurde bisher in der Forschergemeinde kein Goldstandard geschaffen. Daher wurde im Rahmen dieser Dissertation ein Referenzgazetteer und ein zugehöriges, neues Referenzkorpus mit Referentenannotation durch Menschenhand entwickelt. Diese werden anschließend verwendet, um eine Auswahl der rekonstruierten Algorithmmen und neuer Rekombinationen der Heuristiken des eruierten Inventars erstmalig auszuwerten.

Die Performanz der gleichen TR-Algorithmmen unter drei Bedingungen verglichen, nämlich (i) unter Verwendung der manuellen Eigennamenannotation, (ii) unter Verwendung automatischer Annotation, gewonnen durch ein existierendes Sequenzannotierungsmodell nach dem Entropiemaximierungsprinzip, und (iii) einem naivem Gazetteer-Nachschlagmechanismus zur Toponymerkennung.

Evaluierung. Die Verfahren, die im Rahmen dieser Dissertation implementiert wurden, werden einer intrinsischen Evaluierung (*Komponentenevaluierung*) unterzogen. Dazu wird ein aufgabenspezifisches Abpassungskriterium definiert, das mit traditionellen Metriken wie Präzision (*precision P*) und Ausbeute (*recall R*) verwendet werden kann. Dieses Kriterium ist tolerant bezüglich numerischer Ungenauigkeiten im Gazetteer in Situationen, in denen eine Toponyminstanz im Goldstandard-Korpus und im Test-Korpus mit verschiedenen Referenten ausgezeichnet wurde, wobei diese aber intuitiv auf den selben Kandidatenreferenten verweisen, was durch mehrere Nahezu-Duplikateinträge im Referenzgazetteer auftreten kann.

Wesentliche Beiträge. Die hauptsächlichen Beiträge dieser Dissertation sind:

- Ein *neues Referenzkorpus*, in dem due Instanzen von Eigennamen für bewohnte Orte manuell mit Resolutionsinformation annotiert wurden, sowie ein zugehöriger *Referenz-Gazetteer*, von dessen Kandidatenvorrat die zugewiesenen Referenten ausgewählt wurden. Dieser Referenzgazetteer bietet numerische Längen- und Breitengradinformation (wie z.B. 51° 32′ nord, 0° 5′ west) und hierarchische Pfadbeschreibungen (wie z.B. London > UK) bezüglich einer geographischen Taxonomie mit weltweiter Abdeckung, die durch Kombination mehrerer großer, aber nicht fehlerfreier Gazetteerquellen konstruiert wurde. Dieses Korpus beinhaltet Nachrichtenmeldungen und besteht aus zwei Subkorpora: Das erste Teilkorpus ist eine Teilmenge des REUTERS-RCV1 Nachrichtenkorpus, welches bereits für die sog. CoNLL "shared task ("gemeinsame Aufgabe", Tjong Kim Sang and De Meulder (2003)) verwendet wurde. Das zweite Teilkorpus ist eine Teilmenge der *Fourth Message Understanding Contest* (MUC4; Chinchor (1995)). Beide Teile sind bereits vor-annotiert mit Eigennamen in Gold-Standard-Qualität. Gazetteer und Korpus werden als Referenzdaten für die Evaluierung zur Verfügung gestellt.

- Eine *neue Methode und ein diese implementierendes System zur Toponymres-*

olution, welche in der Lage ist, unbesehenen Text (Online-Nachrichten ohne Domänenbeschränkung) zu verarbeiten und die darin enthaltenen Toponyminstanzen bezüglich eines extensionalen Modells aufzulösen, das Zentroidkoordinaten in Längen- und Breitengradform sowie hierarchische Pfadbeschreibungen verwendet und auf text-interne und externe Evidenz (aus dem Gazetteer) aufbaut.

- Eine *empirische Analyse der relativen Nützlichkeit verschiedener Heuristiken und anderen Evidenzquellen* bezüglich der Toponymresolutionsaufgabe bei der Analyse nichtrestringierter Texte aus dem Nachrichtengenre.

- Ein *Vergleich zwischen einer replizierten Methode* aus der Literatur, die als Grundlinie dient, *und einem neuen Algorithmus basierend auf Minimalitätsheuristiken*.

- Einige exemplarische *prototypische Anwendungen*, die die Bedeutung der Toponymres-olution aufzeigen sollen: Toponymresolution kann unter anderem verwendet werden,

  - um visuelle Surrogate für Nachrichtentexten zu generieren
  - um einen geographischen Nachrichten-Browser zu entwickeln
  - geographische Relevanz in die Dokumentenwiedergewinnung einzuarbeiten und
  - die Beantwortung räumlicher Fragen (*How far...?*) in einem Fragebeantwor-tungssystem ohne Domänenbeschränkung zu verbessern.

Diese Anwendungen haben nur beispielhaften Charakter, denn eine ausführliche quan-titative aufgabenbasierte (extrinsische) Evaluierung des Nutzens automatischer To-ponymresolution liegt außerhalb des Skopus dieser Dissertation und bleibt daher zukünftigen Arbeiten vorbehalten.

Bibliography

Natalia Adrienko and Gennady Adrienko. 2005. *Exploratory Analysis of Spatial and Temporal Data. A Systematic Approach.* Springer, Berlin, Germany.

Harith Alani, Christopher B. Jones, and Douglas Tudhope. 2001. Voronoi-based region approximation for geographical information retrieval with gazetteers. *International Journal of Geographical Information Science*, 15(4):287–306.

James Allan, editor. 2002. *Topic Detection and Tracking. Event-based Information Organization.* Number 12 in Kluwer International Series on Information Retrieval (INRE). Kluwer, Dordrecht, The Netherlands.

Einat Amitay, Nadav Har'El, Ron Sivan, and Aya Soffer. 2004. Web-a-Where: Geotagging Web content. In Mark Sanderson, Kalervo Järvelin, James Allan, and Peter Bruza, editors, *SIGIR 2004: Proceedings of the 27th Annual International ACM SIGIR Conference on Research and Development in Information Retrieval, Sheffield, UK, July 25-29, 2004*, pages 273–280. ACM.

Douglas E. Appelt, Jerry R. Hobbs, John Bear, David J. Israel, and Mabry Tyson. 1993. FASTUS: A finite-state processor for information extraction from real-world text. In *Proceedings of the International Joint Conference on Artificial Intelligence (IJCAI-93)*, pages 1172–1178. Chambery, France.

Ricardo Baeza-Yates and Berthier Ribeiro-Neto. 1999. *Modern Information Retrieval.* Addison-Wesley, Harlow, England, UK.

Amit Bagga and Breck Baldwin. 1999. Cross-document event coreference: annotations, experiments and observations. In *Proceedings of the ACL'99 Workshop on Coreference and Its Applications*, pages 1–8.

Reed S. Beaman and Barry J. Conn. 2003. Automated geoparsing and georeferencing of Malesian collection locality data. *Telopea*, 10(1):43–52.

Richard K. Belew. 2000. *Finding Out About. A Cognitive Perspective on Search Engine Technology and the WWW.* Cambridge University Press, Cambridge, England, UK.

Frédérik Bilhaut, Thierry Charnois, Patrice Enjalbert, and Yann Mathet. 2003. Geographic reference analysis for geographic document querying. In *HLT-NAACL 2003 Workshop: Analysis of Geographic References*, pages 55–62. Association for Computational Linguistics, Edmonton, Alberta, Canada.

Esra Black. 1988. An experiment in computational discrimination of English word senses. *IBM Journal of Research and Development*, 32(2):185–194.

Andrew Borthwick, John Sterling, Eugene Agichtein, and Ralph Grishman. 1998. NYU: Description of the MENE named entity system as used in MUC-7. In *Proceedings of the Seventh Message Understanding Contest (MUC-7)*.

Frederick Bull. 2004. *Aberdeens around the World: Strandloopers, Turpentine and Little Green Ants. Recollections of a Global Journey.* Scottish Cultural Press, Dalkeith, Scotland, UK.

J. Carletta, S. Evert, U. Heid, J. Kilgour, J. Robertson, and H. Voormann. 2003. The NITE XML Toolkit: flexible annotation for multi-modal language data. *Behavior Research Methods, Instruments, and Computers*, 35(3). Special issue on Measuring Behavior.

Nancy A. Chinchor. 1995. Overview of MUC-4. In Beth Sundheim, editor, *Proceedings of the Fourth Message Understanding Conference (MUC-4)*. U.S. Defense Advanced Research Projects Agency (DARPA), Fairfax, VA, USA.

Nancy A. Chinchor. 1998. Overview of MUC-7/MET-2. In Beth Sundheim, editor, *Proceedings of the Seventh Message Understanding Conference (MUC-7)*. SAIC, Morgan Kaufmann, San Mateo, CA, USA. [online; cited 2006-09-22] http://www.itl.nist.gov/iaui/894.02/related_projects/muc/proceedings/muc_7_proceedings/overview.html.

James Clark. 1999. XSL Transformations (XSLT) Version 1.0. W3C Recommendation 16 November 1999 [online; cited 2006-09-15] http://www.w3.org/TR/xslt.

Stephen Clark and James R. Curran. 2004. Parsing the WSJ using CCG and log-linear models. In *Proceedings of the 42nd Annual Meeting of the Association for Computational Linguistics (ACL)*, pages 103–110. ACL.

William A. Cleveland, editor. 1991. *Britannica Atlas*. Encyclopaedia Britannica Inc., Chicago, IL, USA, 14th edition. Atlas to accompany the Encyclopaedia Britannica in 32 volumes.

Paul Clough. 2005. Extracting metadata for spatially-aware information retrieval on the Internet. In Chris Jones and Ross Purves, editors, *Proceedings of the ACM Workshop on Geographic Information Retrieval (GIR) held at the Conference on Information and Knowledge Management (CIKM)*, pages 25–30. ACM Press.

Paul Clough and Mark Sanderson. 2004. A proposal for comparative evaluation of automatic annotation for geo-referenced documents. In *Workshop on Geographic Information Retrieval held at the Twenty-Seventh Annual International ACM SIGIR Conference on Research and Development in Information Retrieval*. Association for Computing Machinery, Sheffield, England, UK. (pages unnumbered).

Paul Clough, Mark Sanderson, and Hideo Joho. 2004. Extraction of semantic annotations from textual web pages. Technical Report Deliverable D15 6201, University of Sheffield, Sheffield, England, UK. SPIRIT Project (EU IST-2001-35047).

Ken A. L. Coar and David R. T. Robinson. 1999. The WWW Common Gateway Interface Version 1.1. W3C Recommendation [online; cited 2006-09-15] http://cgi-spec.golux.com/draft-coar-cgi-v11-03-clean.html.

Anthony G. Cohn, Brandon Bennett, John Gooday, and Nicholas Mark Gotts. 1997. Qualitative spatial representation and reasoning with the region connection calculus. *GeoInformatica*, 1(3):275–316.

Jim Cowie and Wendy Lehnert. 1996. Information extraction. *Communications of the ACM*, 39(1):80–91.

Scott Crosier. 2004. *Geocoding in ArcGIS 9*. ESRI Press, Redlands, CA, USA.

Hamish Cunningham. 2000. *Software Architecture for Language Engineering*. Ph.D. thesis, Department of Computer Science, University of Sheffield, Sheffield, England, UK.

James R. Curran and Stephen Clark. 2003a. Investigating GIS and smoothing for maximum entropy taggers. In *Proceedings of the 11th Annual Meeting of the European Chapter of the Association for Computational Linguistics (EACL 2003)*, pages 91–98. Budapest, Hungary.

James R. Curran and Stephen Clark. 2003b. Language independent NER using a maximum entropy tagger. In *Proceedings of the Seventh Conference on Natural Language Learning (CoNLL-03)*, pages 164–167. Edmonton, Alberta, Canada.

M. R. Curry. 1999. Rethinking privacy in a geocoded world. In Paul A. Longley, Michael F. Goodchild, David J. Maguire, and David W. Rhind, editors, *Geographical Information Systems*, volume 2, chapter 55, pages 757–766. Wiley, Hoboken, NJ, USA, second edition.

Doug Cutting. 2006. Lucene. [online; cited 2006-06-16] http://lucene.apache.org/.

Peter Dalgaard. 2002. *Introductory Statistics with R*. Statistics and Computing. Springer, New York, NY, USA.

Tiphaine Dalmas and Bonnie Webber. 2004. Answer comparison: Analysis of relationships between answers to 'where'-questions. In *Proceedings of the Seventh Annual CLUK Research Colloquium (CLUK-7)*. Computational Linguistics Research Colloquium in the UK, Birmingham, United Kingdom. (pages unnumbered).

Morris H. DeGroot and Mark J. Schervish. 2001. *Probability and Statistics*. Addison-Wesley, Reading, MA, USA, third edition.

Gerald F. DeJong. 1982. An overview of the FRUMP system. In W. G. Lehnert and M. H. Ringle, editors, *Strategies for Natural Language Processing*, chapter 5, pages 149–176. Lawrence Erlbaum, Hillsdale, NJ, USA.

Ian Densham and James Reid. 2003. A geo-coding service encompassing a geo-parsing tool and integrated digital gazetteer service. In *Proceedings of the HLT-NAACL 2003 Workshop on Analysis of Geographic References*, pages 79–80. Association for Computational Linguistics, Morristown, NJ, USA.

Richard O. Duda, Peter E. Hart, and David G. Stork. 2000. *Pattern Classification*. Wiley, New York, NY, USA, second edition.

Schuyler Erle, Rich Gibson, and Jo Walsh. 2005. *Mapping Hacks: Tips & Tools for Electronic Cartography*. O'Reilly, Sebastopol, CA, USA.

Christiane Fellbaum, editor. 2001. *WordNet: An Electronic Lexical Database*. MIT Press, Cambridge, MA, USA.

R. Fielding, J. Gettys, J. Mogul, H. Frystyk, L. Masinter, P. Leach, and T. Berners-Lee. 1999. Hypertext Transfer Protocol – HTTP/1.1. Network Working Group 2616 [online; cited 2006-09-15] http://www.ietf.org/rfc/rfc2616.txt.

Michael Fleischman and Eduard Hovy. 2002. Fine grained classification of named entities. In *Proceedings of the 19th International Conference on Computational Linguistics (COLING)*, pages 1–7. Association for Computational Linguistics, Morristown, NJ, USA.

John R. Frank. 2004. Desktop client interaction with a geographical text search system. United States Patent #20040078750, MetaCarta, Inc., filed 2003-08-04, granted 2004-04-22.

W. Gale, K. Church, and D. Yarowsky. 1992. One sense per discourse. In *Proceedings of the Fourth DARPA Speech and Natural Language Workshop*, pages 233–237. Defense Advanced Research Projects Agency, Morgan Kaufmann, San Mateo, CA.

William A. Gale, Kenneth W. Church, and David Yarowsky. 1993. A method for disambiguating word senses in a large corpus. *Computers and the Humanities*, 26(5/6):415–439.

Aliasgar Gangardiwala and Robi Polikar. 2005. Dynamically weighted majority voting for incremental learning and comparison of three boosting based approaches. In *Proceedings of the 2005 IEEE International Joint Conference on Neural Networks*, pages 1131–1138. IEEE, IEEE.

Klaus Peter Gapp and Wolfgang Maass. 1994. Spatial layout identification and incremental descriptions. In *AAAI-94 Workshop on Integration of Natural Language and Vision Processing*. Amercian Association for Artificial Intelligence. Also published as: Bericht Nr. 102, Sonderforschungsbereich 314, Universität des Saarlandes.

Claire Gardent and Bonnie Webber. 2001. Towards the use of automated reasoning in discourse disambiguation. *Journal of Logic, Language and Information*, 10(4):487–509.

Fredric Gey, Ray Larson, Mark Sanderson, Hideo Joho, Paul Clough, and Vivien Petras. 2006. GeoCLEF: The CLEF 2005 cross-language geographic information retrieval track overview. In *Proceedings of the Cross Language Evaluation Forum 2005*, volume 4002 of *Lecture Notes in Computer Science*. CLEF, Springer, Berlin, Germany.

Google, Inc. 2006a. Google Earth. [online; cited 2006-06-16] http://earth.google.com.

Google, Inc. 2006b. Google Earth KML tutorial. [online; cited 2006-06-16] http://earth.google.com/kml.

Otis Gospodnetić and Erik Hatcher. 2005. *Lucene in Action*. Manning, Greenwich, CT, USA.

B. F. Green, A. K. Wolf, C. Chomsky, and K. Laughery. 1961. Baseball: An automatic question answerer. In *Proceedings of the Nineteenth Western Joint Computer Conference*, pages 219–224.

R. W. Greene. 2004. *Confronting Catastrophe. A GIS Handbook*. ESRI Press, Redlands, CA, USA.

H. Grice. 1975. Logic and conversation. In P. Cole and J. Morgan, editors, *Syntax and Semantics*, volume 3, pages 41–58. Academic Press, New York, NY, USA.

Claire Grover, Harry Halpin, Ewan Klein, Jochen L. Leidner, Stephen Potter, Sebastian Riedel, Sally Scrutchin, and Richard Tobin. 2004. A framework for text mining services. In Simon J. Cox, editor, *Proceedings of the UK e-Science Programme All Hands Meeting 2004 (AHM 2004)*, pages 878–885. Nottingham, England, UK.

Claire Grover, Colin Matheson, Andrei Mikheev, and Marc Moens. 2000. LT TTT–A flexible tokenisation tool. In *Proceedings of Second International Conference on Language Resources and Evaluation (LREC 2000)*. ELRA, Paris, France.

D. Gruhl, L. Chavet, D. Gibson, J. Meyer, P. Pattanayak, A. Tomkins, and J. Zien. 2004. How to build a WebFountain: an architecture for very large-scale text analytics. *IBM Systems Journal*, 43(1):64–77.

Trevor Hastie, Robert Tibshirami, and Jerome Friedman. 2001. *The Elements of Statistical Learning*. Springer, New York.

Alexander G. Hauptmann and Andreas M. Olligschlaeger. 1999. Using location information from speech recognition of television news broadcasts. In Tony Robinson and Steve Renals, editors, *Proceedings of the ESCA ETRW Workshop on Accessing Information in Spoken Audio*, pages 102–106. University of Cambridge, Cambridge, England. [online; cited 2004-10-20] http://svr-www.eng.cam.ac.uk/~ajr/esca99/.

Linda L. Hill. 2000. Core elements of digital gazetteers: placenames, categories, and footprints. In José Luis Borbinha and Thomas Baker, editors, *Proceedings of the 4th European Conference on Research and Advanced Technology for Digital Libraries (ECDL)*, volume 1923 of *Lecture Notes In Computer Science*, pages 280–290. Springer, London, UK.

Linda Ladd Hill. 1990. *Access to Geographic Concepts in Online Bibliographic Files: Effectiveness of Current Practices and the Potential of a Graphic Interface*. Ph.D. thesis, University of Pittsburgh, Pittsburgh, PA, USA.

Linda Ladd Hill. 2006. *Georeferencing. The Geographic Associations of Information*. MIT Press, Cambridge, MA, USA.

Lynette Hirshman and Robert Gaizauskas. 2001. Natural language question answering: The view from here. *Natural Language Engineering*, 7(4):275–300.

Jerry R. Hobbs. 1986. Overview of the TACITUS project. *Computational Linguistics*, 12(3):220–222.

Jerry R. Hobbs. 1992. FASTUS: A system for extracting information from natural-language text. Technical Report 519, AI Center, SRI International, Menlo Park, CA, USA.

Nancy Ide and Jean Véronis. 1998. Word sense disambiguation: The state of the art. *Computational Linguistics*, 24(1):1–40.

ISO, editor. 1998. *ISO/IEC 14882:1998: Programming languages — C++*. International Organization for Standardization, Geneva, Switzerland.

Ivar Jacobson, Grady Booch, and James Rumbaugh. 1999. *The Unified Software Development Process*. Addison Wesley Longman, Reading, MA, USA, first edition.

Bernard J. Jansen and Amanda Spink. 2006. How are we searching the World Wide Web? A comparison of nine search engine transaction logs. *Information Processing & Management*, 42(1):248–263.

Jardine and van Rijsbergen. 1971. The use of hierarchic clustering in information retrieval. *Information Storage & Retrieval*, 7:217–240.

Marilyn Eileen Jessen. 1975. *A Semantic Study of Spatial and Temporal Expressions in English*. Ph.D. thesis, University of Edinburgh, Edinburgh, Scotland, UK. 2 volumes.

Changhao Jiang and Peter Steenkiste. 2002. A hybrid location model with a computable location identifier for ubiquitous computing. In *Proceedings of UbiComp 2002: Ubiquitous Computing: 4th International Conference*, pages 246–263. Springer, Göteborg, Sweden.

A. Kent, M. Berry, F. U. Leuhrs, and J. W. Perry. 1955. Machine literature searching VIII: Operational criteria for designing information retrieval systems. *American Documentation*, 6(2):93–101.

Adam Kilgarriff and Joseph Rosenzweig. 2000. Framework and results for English SENSE-VAL. *Computers and the Humanities*, 34(1):15–48. Special Issue on SENSEVAL.

R. E. Korf. 1985. Depth-first iterative-deepening: An optimal admissible tree search. *Artificial Intelligence*, 27(3):97–109.

Marcus Kracht. 2004. Language and space. Unpublished course reader, Department of Linguistics, University of California at Los Angeles, Los Angeles, CA, USA.

Hans-Ulrich Krieger. 2003. SDL—a description language for building nlp systems. In *Proceedings of the Workshop on Software Engineering and Architecture of Language Technology Systems (SEALTS) held at the Joint Conference for Human Language Technology and the Annual Meeting of the North American Chapter of the Association for Computational Linguistics 2003 (HLT/NAACL 2003)*, pages 84–91. ACL, Association for Computational Linguistics.

Klaus Krippendorf. 1980. *Content Analysis: An Introduction to its Methodology*. Sage Publications, Beverly Hills, CA, USA.

J. B. Kruskal. 1956. On the shortest spanning subtree of a graph and the traveling salesman problem. *Proceedings of the American Mathematical Society*, 7:48–50.

Axel Küpper. 2005. *Location-Based Services: Fundamentals and Operation*. Wiley, Hoboken, NJ, USA.

George Lakoff. 1993. *Women, Fire and Dangerous Things*. Chicago University Press, Chicago, IL, USA.

J. Larkin and H. Simon. 1987. Why a diagram is (sometimes) worth ten thousand words. *Cognitive Science*, 11:65–99.

Ray R. Larson. 2003. Geographic information retrieval and spatial browsing. [online; cited 2003-12-27] http://sherlock.berkeley.edu/geoir/PART1.html.

Ray R. Larson and Patricia Frontiera. 2004. Spatial ranking methods for geographic information retrieval (GIR) in digital libraries. In *Proceedings of the Eight European Conference on Research and Advanced Technology for Digital Libraries (ECDL)*, volume 3232 of *Lecture Notes in Computer Science*, pages 45–56. Springer.

Ray R. Larson, Christian Plaunt, Allison G. Woodruff, and Marti Hearst. 1995. The Sequoia 2000 electronic repository. *Digital Technical Journal of Digital Equipment Corporation*, 7(3):50–65.

Geoffrey N. Leech. 1981. *Semantics. The Study of Meaning*. Penguin, London, England, UK, second edition.

Jochen L. Leidner. 2003a. Current issues in software engineering for natural language processing. In *Proceedings of the Workshop on Software Engineering and Architecture of Language Technology Systems (SEALTS) held at the Joint Conference for Human Language Technology and the Annual Meeting of the North American Chapter of the Association for Computational Linguistics 2003 (HLT/NAACL 2003)*, pages 45–50. Edmonton, Alberta, Canada.

Jochen L. Leidner. 2003b. Grounding spatial named entities and generating visual document surrogates. Poster presented at the University of Edinburgh Informatics Jamboree 2003.

Jochen L. Leidner. 2004a. Toponym resolution in text: "Which Sheffield is it?". In *Proceedings of the the 27th Annual International ACM SIGIR Conference (SIGIR 2004)*, page 602. Sheffield, England, UK.

Jochen L. Leidner. 2004b. Towards a reference corpus for automatic toponym resolution evaluation. In *Proceedings of the Workshop on Geographic Information Retrieval held at the 27th Annual International ACM SIGIR Conference (SIGIR)*. Sheffield, England, UK. (pages unnumbered).

Jochen L. Leidner. 2005a. Experiments with geo-filtering predicates for information retrieval. In *Working Notes, Cross Language Evaluation Forum (CLEF 2005)*. Vienna, Austria. (pages unnumbered) Published electronically in the DELOS Digital Library.

Jochen L. Leidner. 2005b. A wireless natural language search engine. In *Proceedings of the 28th Annual International ACM SIGIR Conference on Research and Development in Information Retrieval (SIGIR 2005)*, pages 677–677. ACM Press, New York, NY, USA. Demonstration.

Jochen L. Leidner. 2006a. An evaluation dataset for the toponym resolution task. *Computers, Environment and Urban Systems*, 30(4):400–417. Special Issue on Geographic Information Retrieval.

Jochen L. Leidner. 2006b. Experiments with geo-filtering predicates for information retrieval. In Carol Peters, editor, *Multilingual Information Repositories: 6th Workshop of the Cross-Language Evaluation Forum, CLEF 2005, Vienna Austria, Revised Selected Papers*, volume 4002 of *Lecture Notes in Computer Science*, pages 987–996. Springer, Berlin, Germany.

Jochen L. Leidner. 2006c. Review of: Adrienko & Adrienko, Exploratory Analysis of Spatial and Temporal Data. *ACM Computing Reviews*. CR133101. [online; cited 2006-07-24] http://www.reviews.com/.

Jochen L. Leidner. 2006d. *TextGIS® API Reference Manual*. Linguit GmbH, Bad Bergzabern, Germany, first edition. Unpublished handbook. 319 pp.

Jochen L. Leidner. 2006e. Toponym resolution: A first large-scale comparative evaluation. Research Report EDI–INF–RR–0839, School of Informatics, University of Edinburgh, Edinburgh, Scotland, UK.

Jochen L. Leidner, Johan Bos, Tiphaine Dalmas, James R. Curran, Stephen Clark, Colin J. Bannard, Mark Steedman, and Bonnie Webber. 2004. The QED open-domain answer retrieval system for TREC 2003. In *Proceedings of the Twelfth Text Retrieval Conference (TREC 2003)*, pages 595–599. Gaithersburg, MD. NIST Special Publication 500–255.

Jochen L. Leidner, Gail Sinclair, and Bonnie Webber. 2003. Grounding spatial named entities for information extraction and question answering. In *Proceedings of the Workshop on the Analysis of Geographic References held at the Joint Conference for Human Language Technology and the Annual Meeting of the North American Chapter of the Association for Computational Linguistics 2003 (HLT/NAACL 2003)*, pages 31–38. Edmonton, Alberta, Canada.

Michael Lesk. 1986. Automatic sense disambiguation using machine readable dictionaries: how to tell a pine cone from an ice cream cone. In *Proceedings of the Fifth Annual International Conference on Systems Documentation (SIGDOC 1986)*, pages 24–26. ACM Press, New York, NY, USA.

David D. Lewis, Yiming Yang, Tony G. Rose, and Fan Li. 2004. RCV1: A new benchmark collection for text categorization research. *Journal of Machine Learning Research*, 5:361–397.

Huifeng Li, Rohini K. Srihari, Cheng Niu, and Wei Li. 2002. Location normalization for information extraction. In *Nineteenth International Conference on Computational Linguistics (COLING 2002)*, pages 549–555. Taipei, Taiwan.

Huifeng Li, Rohini K. Srihari, Cheng Niu, and Wei Li. 2003. InfoXtract location normalization: a hybrid approach to geographic references in information extraction. In András Kornai and Beth Sundheim, editors, *HLT-NAACL 2003 Workshop: Analysis of Geographic References*, pages 39–44. Association for Computational Linguistics, Edmonton, Alberta, Canada.

Nick Littlestone and Manfred K. Warmuth. 1994. The weighted majority algorithm. *Information and Computation*, 108(2):212–261.

Paul A. Longley, Michael F. Goodchild, David J. Maguire, and David W. Rhind, editors. 1999. *Geographical Information Systems*, volume 1. Wiley, Hoboken, NJ, USA, second edition.

Paul A. Longley, Michael F. Goodchild, David J. Maguire, and David W. Rhind. 2005. *Geographic Information Systems and Science*. Wiley, Chichester, England, UK, second edition.

Alexander Mädche. 2002. *Ontology Learning for the Semantic Web*. Number 665 in Kluwer International Series in Engineering and Computer Science. Kluwer, Dordrecht, The Netherlands.

Inderjeet Mani, James Pustejovsky, and Rob Gaizauskas, editors. 2005. *The Language of Time: A Reader*. Oxford University Press, Oxford, England, UK.

Inderjeet Mani and George Wilson. 2000. Robust temporal processing of news. In *Proceedings of the 38th Annual Meeting of the Association for Computational Linguistics*, pages 69–76. Hong Kong.

Christopher D. Manning and Hinrich Schütze. 1999. *Foundations of Statistical Natural Language Processing*. MIT Press, Cambridge, MA, USA.

Katja Markert and Malvina Nissim. 2002. Towards a corpus annotated for metonymies: the case of location names. In *Proceedings of the Third International Conference on Language Resources and Evaluation (LREC 2002)*, pages 1385–1392. ELRA, Paris, France.

David Masterson and Nicholas Kushmerick. 2003. Information extraction from multi-document threads. In *Proceedings of the International Workshop on Adaptive Text Extraction and Mining held in conjunction with the 14th European Conference on Machine Learning and the 7th European Conference on Principles and Practice of Knowledge Discovery in Databases*, pages 34–41. Catvat, Dubrovnik, Croatia.

Colin Matheson. 2003. Geoparser evaluation. Internal Memo. Language Technology Group (LTG), University of Edinburgh.

Mark T. Maybury, editor. 2004. *New Directions in Question Answering*. AAAI Press / MIT Press, Menlo Park, CA, USA / Cambridge, MA, USA.

David Medyckyj-Scott, Cressida Chappell, Tom Waugh, Any Corbett, and Nat Evans. 2001. Geo-crosswalk project overview and recommendations. Geo-crosswalk project deliverable, EDINA & Edinburgh University Data Library (EUDL), University of Edinburgh, Edinburgh, Scotland, UK.

Andrei Mikheev, Marc Moens, and Claire Grover. 1999. Named entity recognition without gazetteers. In *Proceedings of the Ninth Conference of the European Chapter of the Association for Computational Linguistics (EACL)*, pages 1–8. Association for Computational Linguistics.

David Munro and Bruce Gittings, editors. 2006, to appear. *Scotland: An Encyclopedia of Places & Landscape*. Harper Collins.

Mor Naaman, Yee Jiun Song, Andreas Paepcke, and Hector Garcia-Molina. 2006. Assigning textual names to sets of geographic coordinates. *Computer, Environment and Urban Systems*, 30(4):418–435. Special Issue on Geographic Information Retrieval.

Markus Neteler. 2004. *Open Source GIS: A Grass GIS Approach*. International Series in Engineering and Computer Science. Kluwer, Dordrecht, The Netherlands, second edition.

Chris Newman. 2005. *SQLite – A Practical Guide to Using, Administering, and Programming the Database Bundled with PHP 5*. SAMS Publishing, Indianapolis, IN, USA.

A.-M. Nivala and L. T. Sarjakoski. 2003. An approach to intelligent maps: Context awareness. In B. Schmidt-Belz and K. Cheverst, editors, *Proceedings of the workshop HCI in Mobile Guides held at the Fifth International Symposium on Human Computer Interaction with Mobile Devices and Services (Mobile HCI)*, pages 45–50.

Douglas W. Oard, David Doermann, Bonnie Dorr, Daqing He, Philip Resnik, Amy Weinberg, William Byrne, Sanjeev Khudanpur, David Yarowsky, Anton Leuski, Philipp Koehn, and Kevin Knight. 2003. Desparately seeking Cebuano. In Marti Hearst and Mari Ostendorf, editors, *HLT-NAACL 2003: Short Papers*, pages 76–78. Association for Computational Linguistics, Edmonton, Alberta, Canada.

Donough O'Brien. 2003. *Fame by Chance. An A-Z of places that became famous (or infamous) by a twist of fate.* Bene Factum Publishing, Honiton, England, UK.

Patrich Olivier and Klaus-Peter Gapp, editors. 1998. *Representation and Processing of Spatial Expression.* Lawrence Erlbaum Associates, Mahwah, NJ, USA.

Andreas M. Olligschlaeger and Alexander G. Hauptmann. 1999. Multimodal information systems and GIS: The Informedia digital video library. In *1999 ESRI User Conference.* Environmental Systems Research Institute (ESRI) Inc., San Diego, CA, USA.

Joseph O'Rourke. 1998. *Computational Geometry in C.* Cambridge University Press, Cambridge, England, UK, second edition.

Simon E. Overell and Stefan Rüger. 2006. Identifying and grounding descriptions of places. In Ross Purves and Chris Jones, editors, *Third Workshop on Geographic Information Retrieval held at SIGIR 2006.* ACM Press.

Sharon L. Oviatt. 1997. Multimodal interactive maps: Designing for human performance, human-computer interaction. *Human-Computer Interaction,* 12:93–129.

Greg Pass, Abdur Chowdhury, and Cayley Torgeson. 2006. A picture of search. In *Proceedings of the First International Conference on Scalable Information Systems (InfoScale 2006),* page 1. ACM Press, New York, NY, USA.

Steven Pemberton. 2002. XHTML 1.0 The Extensible HyperText Markup Language. W3C Recommendation, 26 Januar 2000, Revised 1 August 2002 [online; cited 2006-09-15]. URL `http://www.w3.org/XML/`.

Zgon-Ren Peng and Ming-Hsiang Tsou. 2003. *Internet GIS: Distributed Geographic Information Services for the Internet and Wireless Networks.* Wiley, Hoboken, NJ, USA.

A. V. Philips. 1960. A question-answering routine. Memo 16, Massachusetts Institute of Technology, Cambridge, MA, USA.

S. M. Pollack. 1968. Measures for the comparison of information retrieval systems. *American Documentation,* 19(4):387–397.

Bruno Pouliquen, Marco Kimler, Ralf Steinberger, Camelia Ignat, Tamara Oellinger, Ken Blackler, Flavio Fluart, Wajdi Zaghouani, Anna Widiger, Ann-Charlotte Forslund, and Clive Best. 2006. Geocoding multilingual texts: Recognition, disambiguation and visualisation. In *Proceedings of The Fifth International Conference on Language Resources and Evaluation (LREC),* pages 53–58. ELRA.

Bruno Pouliquen, Ralf Steinberger, Camelia Ignat, and Tom De Groeve. 2004. Geographical information recognition and visualization in texts written in various languages. In *Proceedings of the 2004 ACM Symposium on Applied Computing*, pages 1051–1058. ACM Press.

Robert Clay Prim. 1957. Shortest connection networks and some generalizations. *Bell System Technical Journal*, 36:1389–1401.

James Pustejovsky and Inderjeet Mani. 2003. Annotation of temporal and event expressions. In James Allan, Jason Eisner, and Wayne Ward, editors, *HLT-NAACL 2003 Tutorials*, pages 6–6. Association for Computational Linguistics, Edmonton, Alberta, Canada.

David A. Randell, Zhan Cui, and Anthony Cohn. 1992. A spatial logic based on regions and connection. In Bernhard Nebel, Charles Rich, and William Swartout, editors, *Principles of Knowledge Representation and Reasoning: Proceedings of the Third International Conference (KR 1992)*, pages 165–176. Morgan Kaufmann, San Mateo, CA, USA.

Erik Rauch, Michael Bukatin, and Kenneth Baker. 2003. A confidence-based framework for disambiguating geographic terms. In András Kornai and Beth Sundheim, editors, *HLT-NAACL 2003 Workshop: Analysis of Geographic References*, pages 50–54. Association for Computational Linguistics, Edmonton, Alberta, Canada.

Philippe Rigaux, Michel Scholl, and Agnès Voisard. 2002. *Spatial Databases With Applications to GIS*. Morgan Kaufmann, San Francisco, CA, USA.

Ellen Riloff and Rosie Jones. 1999. Learning dictionaries for information extraction by multilevel bootstrapping. In *Proceedings of the 6th National Conference on Artificial Intelligence (AAAI-99); Proceedings of the 11th Conference on Innovative Applications of Artificial Intelligence*, pages 474–479. AAAI/MIT Press, Menlo Park, CA, USA.

Ronald L. Rivest. 1987. Learning decision lists. *Machine Learning*, 2(3):229–246.

S. E. Robertson and K. Spärck Jones. 1997. Simple, proven approaches to text retrieval. Technical Report 356, Computer Laboratory, University of Cambridge, Cambridge, England, UK.

Tony G. Rose, Mark Stevenson, and Miles Whitehead. 2002. The Reuters Corpus Volume 1 – from yesterday's news to tomorrow's language resources. In *Proceedings of the Third International Conference on Language Resources and Evaluation (LREC)*, volume 3, pages 827–833. Las Palmas de Gran Canaria, Spain.

Naomi Sager. 1981. *Natural Language Information Processing: A Computer Grammar of English and Its Applications*. Addison-Wesley, Reading, MA, USA.

Kenneth B. Sall. 2002. *XML Family of Specifications: A Practical Guide*. Addison-Wesley, Boston, MA, USA.

H. Samet. 1984. The quadtree and related hierarchical data structures. *ACM Computing Surveys*, 16(2):187–260.

H. Samet. 1989. *The Design and Analysis of Spatial Data Structures*. Addison-Wesley, Reading, MA, USA.

Mark Sanderson. 1994. Word sense disambiguation and information retrieval. In *Proceedings of the 17th Annual International ACM SIGIR Conference on Research and Development in Information Retrieval (SIGIR 1994)*, pages 142–151. Springer, New York, NY, USA.

Mark Sanderson and Janet Kohler. 2004. Analyzing geographic queries. In *Workshop on Geographic Information Retrieval held at the Twenty-Seventh Annual International ACM SIGIR Conference on Research and Development in Information Retrieval*. Association for Computing Machinery, Sheffield, England, UK. (pages unnumbered).

Frank Schilder, Yannick Versley, and Christopher Habel. 2004. Extracting spatial information: grounding, classifying and linking spatial expressions. In *Workshop on Geographic Information Retrieval held at the Twenty-Seventh Annual International ACM SIGIR Conference on Research and Development in Information Retrieval*. Association for Computing Machinery, Sheffield, England, UK. (pages unnumbered).

H. Seeger. 1999. Spatial referencing and coordinate systems. In Paul A. Longley, Michael F. Goodchild, David J. Maguire, and David W. Rhind, editors, *Geographical Information Systems*, volume 1, chapter 30, pages 757–766. Wiley, Hoboken, NJ, USA, second edition.

Satoshi Sekine, Kiyoshi Sudo, and Chikashi Nobata. 2002. Extended named entity hierarchy. In *Proceedings of the Third International Conference on Language Resources and Evaluation (LREC-2002)*, volume V, pages 1818–1821. ELRA, Paris, France.

Andrea Setzer. 2001. *Temporal Information in Newswire Articles: an Annotation Scheme and Corpus Study*. Ph.D. thesis, University of Sheffield, Sheffield, England, UK.

Andy Shaw. 2003. New media approaches to mapping humanitarian response. In ESRI Inc., editor, *Proceedings of the 2003 ESRI User Conference*, pages 1205–1212. ESRI Inc., San Diego, CA, USA.

S. Siegel and N. J. Castellan Jr. 1988. *Nonparametric Statistics for the Behavioral Sciences*. McGraw-Hill, London, England, UK, second edition.

Robert. F. Simmons. 1973. Semantic networks: computation and use for understanding English sentences. In R. C. Schank and K. M. Colby, editors, *Computer Models of Thought and Language*, pages 63–113. W. H. Freeman and Co., San Francisco, CA, USA.

R. W. Sinnott. 1984. Virtues of the haversine. *Sky and Telescope*, 68(2):159.

David A. Smith and Gregory Crane. 2001. Disambiguating geographic names in a historical digital library. In *Research and Advanced Technology for Digital Libraries: Fifth European Conference (ECDL 2001)*, pages 127–136.

David A. Smith and Gideon S. Mann. 2003. Bootstrapping toponym classifiers. In András Kornai and Beth Sundheim, editors, *HLT-NAACL 2003 Workshop: Analysis of Geographic References*, pages 45–49. Association for Computational Linguistics, Edmonton, Alberta, Canada.

Benjamin Snyder and Martha Palmer. 2004. The English all-words task. In Rada Mihalcea and Phil Edmonds, editors, *Senseval-3: Third International Workshop on the Evaluation of Systems for the Semantic Analysis of Text*, pages 41–43. Association for Computational Linguistics.

Rohini K. Srihari, Cheng Niu, and Wei Li. 2000. Hybrid approach for named entity and sub-type tagging. In *Proceedings of the Sixth Conference on Applied Natural Language Processing (ANLP 2000)*, pages 247–254. Morgan Kaufmann, San Francisco, CA, USA.

Beth Sundheim, editor. 1992. *MUC-4 — Proceedings of the Fourth Message Understanding Conference*. U.S. Defense Advanced Research Projects Agency (DARPA), Fairfax, VA, USA.

Soteria Svorou. 1994. *The Grammar of Space*. Number 25 in Typological Studies in Language. Benjamins, Amsterdam, The Netherlands.

Erik F. Tjong Kim Sang and Fien De Meulder. 2003. Introduction to the CoNLL-2003 shared task: language-independent named entity recognition. In Walter Daelemans and Miles Osborne, editors, *Seventh Conference on Natural Language Learning (CoNLL 2003)*, pages 142–147. Association for Computational Linguistics, Edmonton, Alberta, Canada. In association with HLT-NAACL 2003.

Roland Tretau, David Chiang, Daniel Greisokh, Scotland Leman, and Roman Shekhtmeyster. 2003. *WebFountain Application Development Guide*. International Business Machines Corporation, IBM Research Almaden Laboratory, first edition.

Yi-Fu Tuan. 1977. *Space and Place: the Perspective of Experience*. Edward Arnold, London, England, UK.

Olga Uryupina. 2003. Semi-supervised learning of geographical gazetteer from the internet. In András Kornai and Beth Sundheim, editors, *HLT-NAACL 2003 Workshop: Analysis of Geographic References*, pages 18–25. Association for Computational Linguistics, Edmonton, Alberta, Canada.

U.S. NIST. 2003. *The ACE 2003 Evaluation Plan*. U.S. National Institute for Standards and Technology (NIST), Gaithersburg, MD. [online; cited 2003-08-20] http://www-nlpir.nist.gov/related_projects/tipster/.

C. J. van Rijsbergen. 1979. *Information Retrieval*. Butterworths, London, second edition.

Jean Véronis. 2003. Sense tagging: does it make sense? In Paul Rayson, Andrew Wilson, Tony McEnery, Andrew Hardie, and Shereen Khoja, editors, *Corpus Linguistics by the Lune: a festschrift for Geoffrey Leech*. Lang, Frankfurt, Germany.

E. Voorhees. 2004. Overview of trec 2004. In Ellen M. Voorhees and Lori P. Buckland, editors, *The Thirteenth Text REtrieval Conference Proceedings (TREC 2004)*, TREC Working Notes, pages 1–12. National Institute of Standards and Technology.

E. Voorhees and Dawn M. Tice. 1999. The TREC-8 question answering track evaluation. In E. M. Voorhees and D. K. Harman, editors, *The Eighth Text REtrieval Conference (TREC 8)*, NIST Special Publication 500–246, pages 1–24. National Institute of Standards and Technology, Gaithersburg, Maryland.

Ellen M. Voorhees and Donna K. Harman, editors. 2005. *TREC: Experiment and Evaluation in Information Retrieval*. MIT Press, Cambridge, MA, USA.

Howard D. Wactlar, Alexander G. Hauptmann, Michael G. Christel, Ricky A. Houghton, and Andreas M. Olligschlaeger. 2000. Complementary video and audio analysis for broadcast news archives. *Communications of the ACM*, 43(2):42–47.

Richard Waldinger, Douglas E. Appelt, Jennifer L. Dungan, John Fry, Jerry Hobbs, David J. Israel, Peter Jarvis, David Martin, Susanne Riehemann, Mark E. Stickel, and Mabry Tyson. 2004. Deductive question answering from multiple sources. In Maybury (2004), chapter 19, pages 253–262.

Richard Waldinger, Peter Jarvis, and Jennifer Dungan. 2003. Pointing to places in a deductive geospatial theory. In András Kornai and Beth Sundheim, editors, *HLT-NAACL 2003 Workshop: Analysis of Geographic References*, pages 10–17. Association for Computational Linguistics, Edmonton, Alberta, Canada.

P. Wessel and W. H. F. Smith. 2004. *The Generic Mapping Tools (GMT) version 4.0 Technical Reference & Cookbook*. Laboratory for Satellite Altimetry (NOAA/NESDIS/NODC),

School of Ocean and Earth Science and Technology, University of Hawaii at Manoa, Manoa, Hawaii, USA.

Ed Williams. 2006.   Aviation formulary v1.42.   [online; cited 2006-09-12] http://williams.best.vwh.net/avform.htm.

Ian H. Witten and David Bainbridge. 2003. *How to Build a Digital Library*. Morgan Kaufmann, San Francisco, CA, USA.

Ian H. Witten and Eibe Frank. 2005. *Data Mining: Practical Machine Learning Tools and Techniques*. The Morgan Kaufmann Series in Data Management Systems. Morgan Kaufmann, San Francisco, CA, USA, second edition.

Allison Woodruff and Christian Plaunt. 1994. GIPSY: Automated geographic indexing of text documents. *Journal of the American Society of Information Science*, 45(9):645–655.

Hui Yang, Tat-Seng Chua, Shuguang Wang, and Chun-Keat Koh. 2003. Structured use of external knowledge for event-based open domain question answering. In *Proceedings of the 26th Annual International ACM SIGIR Conference on Research and Development in Information Retrieval*, pages 33–40. ACM Press.

David Yarowsky. 1995. Unsupervised word sense disambiguation rivaling supervised methods. In *Proceedings of the 33rd Annual Meeting of the Association for Computational Linguistics*, pages 189–196. Association for Computational Linguistics, Morristown, NJ, USA.

François Yergeau, John Cowan, Tim Bray, Jean Paoli, C. M. Sperberg-McQueen, and Eve Maler. 2004. XML 1.1: Extensible Markup Language (XML) 1.1. W3C Recommendation, 4th February 2004 [online; cited 2006-09-15] http://www.w3.org/TR/xml11.

GuoDong Zheng and Jian Su. 2002. Named entity tagging using an HMM-based chunk tagger. In *Proceedings of the 40th Annual Meeting of the Association for Computational Linguistics*, pages 209–219. Philadelphia, PA.

Wenbo Zong, Dan Wu, Aixin Sun, Ee-Peng Lim, and Dion Hoe-Lian Goh. 2005. On assigning place names to geography related web pages. In Tamara Sumner, Frank Shipman, and Mary Marlino, editors, *Proceedings of the 5th ACM/IEEE-CS Joint Conference on Digital Libraries (JCDL)*, pages 354–362. ACM Press, New York, NY, USA.

Index